The Great Eastern Railway

FRONT

24 The GER installed water troughs near Tivetshall in 1896 and at Halifax Junction just south of Ipswich in 1897. Class D56 4-4-0 No 1823 is seen taking water on the water troughs at Halifax Junction on the 1pm Liverpool Street to Cromer on 10 September 1910. (Ken Nunn).

REAR MAIN

17 The GER's London suburban service was the heaviest in Britain with many routes worked by 0-6-0 side tank locomotives. Class C72 0-6-0 side tank No 50 is seen passing Bethnal Green on 2pm Liverpool Street to Enfield Town on 11 June 1915. (Ken Nunn)

REAR TOP LEFT

18 A world away from the express services and the busy suburban services were the branch lines where No 1 Class 2-4-0 No 0104 is seen on the 10.01am Wells to Norwich near Wymondham on 6 April 1910. (Ken Nunn)

REAR TOP RIGHT

21 The GER's largest goods locomotives were 0-6-0s. Coals train over the Company's line came either via the Joint Line or from the GNR at Peterborough. Class G58 No 1224 on a Peterborough to Aldersbrook train near Ingrave signal box on 26 May 1915. (Ken Nunn).

The Great Eastern Railway

The Late Nineteenth and Early Twentieth Century, 1862–1924

Charles Phillips

AN IMPRINT OF PEN & SWORD BOOKS LTD.
YORKSHIRE – PHILADELPHIA

First published in Great Britain in 2024 by
Pen and Sword Transport
An imprint of
Pen & Sword Books Ltd.
Yorkshire - Philadelphia

Copyright © Charles Phillips, 2024

ISBN 9781399024655

The right of Charles Phillips to be identified as author of this work has been asserted by him in accordance with the Copyright, Designs and Patents Act 1988.

A CIP catalogue record for this book is available from the British Library.

All rights reserved. No part of this book may be reproduced or transmitted in any form or by any means, electronic or mechanical including photocopying, recording or by any information storage and retrieval system, without permission from the Publisher in writing.

Typeset in INDIA by IMPEC eSolutions
Printed and bound in the UK on paper from a sustainable source by
CPI Group (UK) Ltd., Croydon. CR0 4YY.

Pen & Sword Books Ltd. incorporates the imprints of Pen & Sword Books: After the Battle, Archaeology, Atlas, Aviation, Battleground, Discovery, Family History, History, Maritime, Military, Politics, Select, Transport, True Crime, Fiction, Frontline Books, Leo Cooper, Praetorian Press, Seaforth Publishing, Wharncliffe and White Owl.

For a complete list of Pen & Sword titles please contact

PEN & SWORD BOOKS LIMITED
George House, Beevor Street, Off Pontefract Road,
Hoyle Mill, Barnsley, South Yorkshire, England, S71 1HN
E-mail: enquiries@pen-and-sword.co.uk
Website: www.pen-and-sword.co.uk

or

PEN AND SWORD BOOKS
1950 Lawrence Rd, Havertown, PA 19083, USA
E-mail: Uspen-and-sword@casematepublishers.com
Website: www.penandswordbooks.com

Contents

Introduction		7
Section 1	The Great Eastern Railway From its Formation in 1862 to the End of 1895	11
	Beginnings	11
	Finances	12
	Ships	15
	Manningtree to Harwich Line	17
	Lines in Hertfordshire	19
	Lines in Essex	22
	Lines in Suffolk	39
	Lines in Cambridgeshire	46
	Lines in Norfolk	50
	Lines in Metropolitan Essex	54
	Changes to the GER	103
	Carriage Lighting	104
	Record breaking construction!	105
	Braking	106
	Signalling	107
	Industrial relations	109
	Natural hazards	110
Section 2	The Great Eastern Railway 1896 to 1922	111
	GER New Lines	112
	Light Railways	114
	Unbuilt Lines	118
	N&SJR New Lines	119
	The Lancashire, Derbyshire and East Coast Railway	122

Widening and doubling of lines	127
New and Branch Lines	130
Trams and Light Railways	136
The Southwold Railway	140
Mid-Suffolk Light Railway	141
Southend	144
The Midland Railway London, Tilbury and Southend Railway takeover Act	154
Attempted Amalgamation	155
Electrification	162
Signalling	169
Water troughs	170
Named trains	172
Pullman Cars	173
Changes to Services	177
Road Services	181
Ships	184
Hotels	185
National Events	186
The Flood of 1912	189
Accidents	191
The Great War	195
Peace	219
Miners' Strike	221
The Grouping begins	222
Appendix: Locomotives, Rolling Stock, Ships and Motor Buses 1862 to 1924	226
Bibliography and Sources	259
Index	262

Introduction

This is the second volume of a short history of the Great Eastern Railway (GER) and its constituents and its successors. By its nature it is a short history as, given the amount of material available, to write a fully detailed history would take a very long time. I have written this book because I live in the territory of the former GER and I like the Railway and the Eastern Counties of England. I am old enough to just remember the last days of steam on the former GER and travelled on it behind steam.

This volume covers the history of the GER from its formation in 1862 until the absorption of the last minor standard gauge railway in the Eastern Counties by the London and North Eastern Railway (LNER) in 1924 – the MSLR. Within the book will be found details of the railway, its trains, ships and motor buses as well as the building of Liverpool Street station in London. The GER was one of the pioneers of the use of oil as a locomotive fuel and the Company looked into electrification though it did not take place. The rivalry between the GER and the LT&SR is fascinating, as is the failure of the former to acquire the latter and the latter's acquisition by the Midland Railway (MR) in 1912. The proposed working union between the Great Central, the Great Northern and the Great Eastern railways, the GER's involvement in the First World War and finally the GER's absorption into the newly created LNER in 1923 under the Railways' Act 1921 all comes under the remit of this book.

I have tried within this book to include illustrations relevant to the subjects covered in it. In this and any other material that might be deemed copyright I have made all efforts to trace the copyright holders. Where it has not been possible the author and the publishers apologise for the omission.

I am a member of the GER Society to whose members I apologise for asking awkward questions on the internet group. The GER Society is the premier railway historical society of England and has produced CDs of a number of magazines which I have used in the writing of this book. These are the *Great*

Eastern Railway Magazine, *Railway and Travel Monthly* and *The Locomotive Magazine* for the period 1896 to 1923. The Society also inspired the North Eastern Railway Association to produce a CD of the *North Eastern Railway Magazine* which was also used in the writing of this history. The Great Eastern Railway Society has for the record also produced CDs of the *LNER Magazine*, the *British Railways Eastern Region Magazine* and the Directors' Report to Shareholders of the Eastern Counties, Great Eastern and London and North Eastern railways.

Charles Phillips

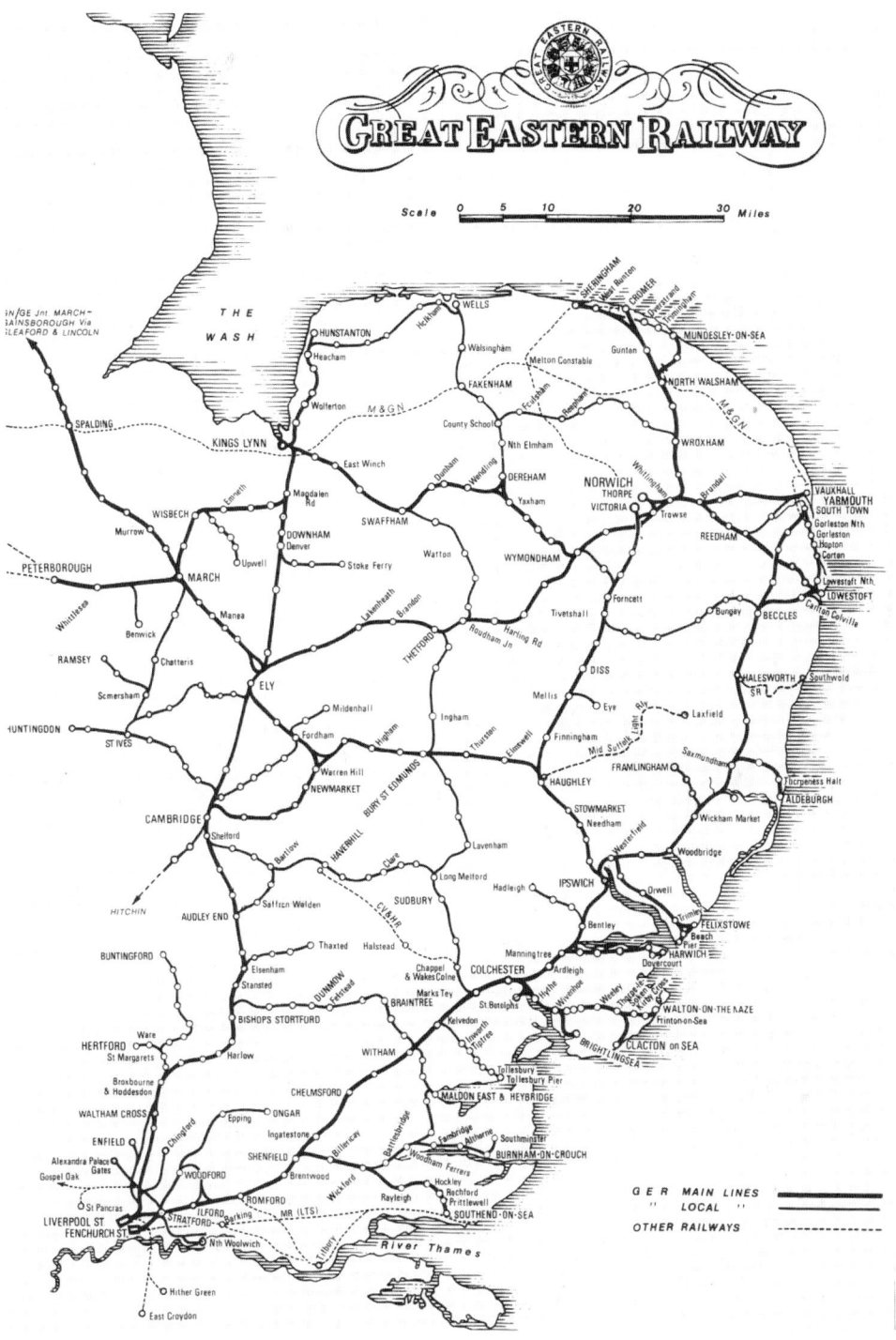

A Map of the GER showing the complete system and connecting and competing railways. (Author's collection)

Section 1

The Great Eastern Railway From its Formation in 1862 to the End of 1895

The years 1862 to 1895 saw continued expansion in and outside the London area. As well as the construction of Liverpool Street station in London and its subsequent enlargement, the GER took over the working of the London and Blackwall Railway (L&BR), whilst the London, Tilbury and Southend Railway (LT&SR) acquired its own rolling stock and motive power and took over its own working. There was competition with the Great Northern Railway (GNR) and the subsequent formation of the Great Northern and Great Eastern Joint Railway and the GER's involvement in the East London Railway (ELR). There was the continued rise of what became the Midland and Great Northern Joint Railway (M&GNJR). Shortly after the start of this period, the GER obtained powers to operate steam ships.

Beginnings

The GER came into existence on 7 August 1862 under its Act of incorporation of that date. The formation of the Company was backdated to 1 July. The coat of arms of the new Company had on the outside the crests of Essex, Maldon, Ipswich, Norwich, Huntingdonshire, Cambridgeshire, Hertfordshire and Northamptonshire. In the middle was the crest of the City of London. As to why the crest of Maldon instead of that of Colchester was on the coat of arms is not known. Chelmsford, the county town of Essex, did not become a borough until 1888.

In the earliest days of the Company, it did not have a good reputation. R.C. Riley in *Great Eastern Album* (Ian Allan 1968) said that there was a joke of a ticket collector remonstrating with a youth of 16 for travelling at half fare and the youth replying that he had only been 12 when the train started. It may have been on the GER, but another joke relates to a ticket collector commenting on a woman's advanced stage of pregnancy and being told by her that she was not pregnant when the train started!

Finances

The Company's financial position on its formation was not healthy! The Company was dependent for its income on the agricultural and rather limited passenger traffic of the Eastern Counties which produced rather low revenue in return for high operational costs. The GER was at this time attempting to gain a share of the heavy coal traffic from the coal mines of South Yorkshire to London.

The rolling stock was in a poor shape and this was partially attributable to the deaths of five passengers in an accident at North Wotton on 3 August 1863 involving the collision of a train with a cow.

At a meeting of the Company's Board in February 1865, it was reported that passenger receipts were outstripping goods receipts, when goods traffic was the principal traffic of the railway.

The international financial crisis was caused by the failure of the banking company of Overend, Gurney and Company in London and the suspension of Italy's monetary standard – *corso forzoso*. The crisis saw loan interest rates rise to 10 per cent on 12 May. On 8 June, the Board approached parliament for the right to borrow more money and raise additional money through new shares to fund the expansion programme under its GER (Metropolitan Station and Railways) Act which authorised not only the construction of a new line from the old Eastern Counties Railway (ECR) viaduct at Tapp Street (just west of Bethnal Green station) to a new terminus at Liverpool Street, but also the lines from Bethnal Green to Lower Edmonton and Hackney Downs to Copper Mill Junction on the N&ER line (the detour avoiding Stratford). Other features of this scheme were the doubling of the Enfield branch outwards from Lower Edmonton, links with the then proposed T&HJR (both of these being completed) and a link with the NLR at Hackney. Another Act passed that year authorised the GER to build a line from Hall Farm Junction to High Beech and a connection to the line from Hackney Downs to Copper Mill Junction at Clapton Junction. In 1865 under the GER (Additional Powers) Act of 19 June that year the GER obtained powers for a branch line from Tottenham to Winchmore Hill and a loop line from Lower Edmonton to Ordnance Factory (Enfield Lock). The Board's request to Parliament was confirmed on 4 July.

Unfortunately, by this time there was not much money available for dividends and the Company had to look very carefully firstly at their expansion programme and more especially at their unprofitable branch lines. By December 1866 it was clear that no investors were really interested in the new shares, so the Board went, unsuccessfully, to the Bank of England and to the Union Bank for further loans.

Things were not helped by the cattle plague which began in 1865 and devastated cattle in this country. In the nineteenth century, the usual term was 'cattle plague' and it is never clear precisely which of the many cattle diseases it was. The plague of 1865 was designated rinderpest, which is still wide-ranging but a little more specific – and with close to 80,000 cattle dead and only two counties unaffected in England, prayers were said in churches and many farmers went bankrupt.

Things got so bad financially that by 1867 the GER was in Chancery. Not the most healthy thing and the Company's prospects were looking rather gloomy. At this point, Samuel Laing MP, who was a man of considerable financial repute and had been a former Finance Minister for India, was asked to join the Company's Board. Laing consented on the understanding that his responsibility would be limited to the Company's financial affairs and he was duly elected to the board on 17 February 1867.

Under the GER Additional Powers Act 1866, the Company had been authorized to raise £80,000 in 5 per cent convertible debenture shares payable in 62 years. Laing's scheme was to provide a half per cent sinking fund for the redemption of the debentures at the end of the period. But only a part of the debenture capital was subscribed and the Directors went to the largest holders of the preference and ordinary stock to confer with them as to the best course of action to pursue. A committee of shareholders was then formed and met with the Directors frequently. At the same time, the preference shareholders proposed to accept debenture stock in lieu of dividends for the following four years; this scheme would in effect have raised £1.5million. The Company then made an application to parliament to raise that amount in debenture stock, to rank after the existing debentures, but the House of Commons rejected the

Bill on the grounds that the amount was not enough to get the Company out of its difficulties. The rejection of the Bill made matters worse for the Company and increased the hesitation of the investing public to take up the Company's debentures and when on 1 July 1867 £80,000 of the ordinary debentures became due, the holders of them refused to renew them. The Company had no available capital with which to take them up and one of the debenture holders made an application to the Court of Chancery for a Receiver of the tolls of the line. The Court granted the application on 2 July 1867.

The Receiver, however, was authorized to pay the interest on the Company's debentures as it became due. The Company's Directors then called a meeting of all of the preference shareholders and the upshot of this was that a further application was made to parliament for authority to raise £3million of debenture stock on terms which would give those shareholders a considerably greater control of the Company's affairs. The Bill was passed by both Houses of Parliament and received its Royal Assent on 26 August 1867. This was a turning point for the better for the GER from which it never looked back. Just under 50 years later, on 3 July 1917, all of 'Laing's Mortgages' as they were known had been redeemed. January the following year saw an event that was unique in British railway history when Lord Cranborne, who was later to succeed to the title of the Marquis of Salisbury and who was Prime Minister from 1895 to 1902, became Chairman of the GER. His tenure as Chairman lasted from January 1868 to the end of 1871 and his place on the directorate of the Company after he left was taken by Lord Claud John Hamilton, the second son of the first Duke of Abercorn and who was destined to succeed to the Chairmanship of the Company in 1893 and was the most famous of the Company's Chairmen. 1868 also saw the GER apply for extension of time for the completion of the works authorized under the Acts of 1864. Although Lord Cranborne's tenure as Chairman of the GER was short, he did succeed in getting the Company out of Chancery to the point of being able to pay a small dividend on its ordinary shares.

The first Half Yearly Meeting of the new Company was held on 27 February 1863, at the Company's Offices at Bishopsgate station in London. Amongst things that were discussed were the provision of a new London terminus, as Bishopsgate had become rather inconvenient for travellers. The Company was at the same time looking at the provision in the London area of a new line for Cambridge traffic to avoid having to share it with Colchester traffic between

London and Stratford. The Company was also looking at acquiring powers to operate steam ships.

Ships

At the Half Yearly Meeting of the GER on Friday 27 February 1863 the Chairman reported under the heading 'STEAM BOATS':

> The Shareholders are aware that the Amalgamation Bill, as originally proposed, contained Clauses authorizing this Company to establish Steam Boats, but the Company were unsuccessful. Your Directors feel that they should fail in their duty to the Proprietors if they did not seek to obtain powers similar to those which Parliament has granted to almost every Railway Company which has appropriate harbours.
>
> The South Eastern, the London, Chatham, and Dover, the London and Brighton, the London and South Western, the Great Western, the London and North Western, the Lancashire and Yorkshire, and other Companies have all acquired and exercise Steam Boat powers; and seeing that Harwich is unquestionably the best Port for Trade with Ostend, Rotterdam, and the Scheldt; that Lowestoft is the most convenient Port for Tonning and Hamburgh; and that Lynn and Wisbeach are largely engaged in Trade with Hull, &c., your Directors feel that this Company should at least possess powers for the establishment of a traffic which might not only be productive in itself, but by indirectly increasing the Trade, and promoting the activity and enterprise of the population of the district, might contribute even still more largely to the revenues of the Company. The importance of obtaining such powers is increased by the fact that the Dutch are at the present time engaged in constructing a Railway to Flushing, which will open up a direct trade between that Port and the interior of Germany, and which will also shorten and facilitate our communications with Holland and Belgium. It is also to be borne in mind that whilst the River Navigation of Holland is frequently closed by ice, and interrupted by fogs and other causes, Flushing is a non-tidal harbour accessible at all times, whilst on the East Coast, Harwich is the only

Harbour which enjoys the same advantage. In the event of such powers being acquired it does not necessarily follow that in all cases Steam Boats should be provided at the cost of this Company. In the first instance your Directors only desire to obtain the powers which they think it would be advantageous to possess. Were they to embark any Capital in Steam Boat enterprise they would well consider the necessity of such a proceeding, and would apply to the Shareholders for their direct sanction.

There had been opposition to the Railway's plans to run steam boats; principally from the General Steam Navigation Company, which ran services between London and Antwerp, London and Hamburg and London and Rotterdam. The Netherlands Steam Boat Navigation Company also ran a service between London and Rotterdam, twice a week.

At the Half Yearly Meeting of the GER on Thursday 13 August 1863, the chairman reported under the heading 'STEAM BOATS':

After a very strenuous opposition on the part of the General Steam Navigation Company and other parties, interested in Steam Navigation, the Bill promoted by this Company for authorizing the running of Steam Boats between the ports of Harwich and those of Antwerp, Rotterdam, and Flushing, was passed by the Committees of both Houses. Your Directors anticipate a great accession of traffic between those ports.

Cecil J. Allen, in *The Great Eastern Railway* (Ian Allan 1967), tells us that the Act authorising the GER to run steam boats was passed on 28 July 1863.

Ambrose Greenway, in *A Century of North Sea Passenger Steamers* (Ian Allan 1986), says that whilst new ships were under construction, chartered cargo and cattle steamers were placed in service between Harwich and Rotterdam.

According to Allen, three steamers, *Blenheim*, *Norfolk* and *Prince of Wales*, were chartered forthwith and a once weekly service was begun to Rotterdam in October 1863, followed the following year by a similar service to Antwerp.

At the Half Yearly Meeting of the Company on 18 February 1864, the Directors' Report said that the most friendly relations exist between your Board and that of the Dutch Rhenish Railway Company, and there are now being organised the most perfect arrangements for the through booking of all traffic between England, Holland, and Germany'. The Dutch Rhenish Railway ran from Rotterdam and Amsterdam via Utrecht and Arnhem to Emmerich on the border with Germany.

The GER's first passenger ships were the paddle steamers *Avalon* and *Zealous* which opened the Rotterdam and Antwerp passenger services on 13 June and 1 August 1864 respectively. *Cook's Continental Timetable* for March 1873 shows each service operating three times a week. *Bradshaw's Railway Guide* for August 1887 has the service to both places as running daily except Sundays.

A port was created in the Hook of Holland and a railway was opened to it in 1893, in which year steam boat services from Harwich started calling. *Bradshaw's Railway Guide* for December 1895 shows the service from Harwich to the Hook of Holland, Rotterdam and Antwerp as running daily. Other shipping lines that started using Harwich were the United Steam Ship Company of Copenhagen which started a Harwich to Esjberg in Denmark service in 1880, and the General Steam Navigation Company which started a service from Harwich to Hamburg in 1888 or rather took over such a service, as *Bradshaw* for August 1887 shows the service run by the Hamburg-Harwich Line.

Prior to 1883, all of the GER's ships were paddle steamers, the last one being the *Adelaide* built by the Barrow Shipbuilding Company and launched on 8 May 1880. In 1883, the Company took delivery of two screw steamers from Earle's Shipbuilding and Engineering Company of Hull. These were *Norwich*, launched on 6 March 1883, and *Ipswich*, launched on 21 May 1883.

Manningtree to Harwich Line

The Manningtree to Harwich line, when it was opened in 1854, was originally single track throughout with intermediate stations at Mistley, Wrabness and Dovercourt. The line was equipped with the electric telegraph and was worked in accordance with special regulations contained in the ECR Rule Book. Early in 1856 a new station was opened at Bradfield between Mistley and Wrabness and about the same time the line between Manningtree and Mistley was doubled.

At Harwich, a hotel, the Great Eastern Hotel, sometimes called the Harwich Hotel in contemporary documents, was opened in 1865 and, despite being well-equipped and furnished, it struggled to make a profit (especially after Parkeston Quay opened).

18   The Great Eastern Railway

By 1872, the shipping trade at Harwich had increased so that more capacity was required at the port and the GER obtained permission to reclaim land at Ray Farm, a mile to the west of Harwich, and build a new quay. This new quay was opened on Thursday, 15 March 1883, by Charles H. Parkes, the Chairman of the GER Company, appropriately enough as it was named after him: Parkeston Quay. The port had its own railway station and a hotel, the Great Eastern Hotel, sometimes called the Parkeston Hotel in contemporary documents, with twenty-six bedrooms built between the northern platform and the quay. The steamers *Adelaide* and *Pacific* could now dock there direct from the Continent.

The rest of the track on the branch line was doubled in 1882 and the Manningtree North Curve which allows direct running between Ipswich and Harwich was also added at that time.

On 1 September 1882, the GER started a through service from Parkeston Quay to Doncaster, by way of Ely and March, in connection with their Hook of Holland service. In 1891 the service was improved by the addition of a Restaurant Car Train. This was the first train in the country to offer third class passengers dining facilities. Prior to that, since the introduction of the first dining car in this

Other than Liverpool Street, the GER's most important station was Parkeston Quay. From here the GER's trains ran in connection with the Company's steam ships sailing to Belgium and to the Netherlands. (Author's collection).

country on the GNR in 1879, the facility had only been available to first class passengers. This train, splendidly equipped with restaurant cars, and carrying its own conductor-interpreter, ran in conjunction with the GER steamers. It was the first train on the GER to have a Restaurant Car and the only one to have one until 1896. The Restaurant Car set was vestibule within the set and there was no connection to the rest of the train. Within the set, a compartment for women only had only a connection to a toilet and not to the rest of the set. In 1892 the service was extended to York after the GER gained running powers over the NER between Shaftholme Junction and York.

Lines in Hertfordshire

The branch line from St Margaret's on the Hertford branch line to Buntingford was the only other GER branch line in Hertfordshire.

The origin of the Buntingford branch went back to a meeting held in the George Hotel in Buntingford on 1 August 1856 to discuss building a branch line to the town. *The Hertford Mercury and Reformer* of Saturday, 26 July 1856 carried an article about the proposed railway. George Mickley, a local promoter, estimated that it would cost £70,000 to construct ten miles of single track railway plus £30,000 for land and stations, making a grand total of £100,000. Annual receipts were forecast to be £10,083, and a 5 per cent profit on the railway was expected. A second meeting was held on 28 August, and it was reported that there was no opposition locally when people were circulated by letter about the proposed railway. It was then decided to proceed and the Bill was submitted to parliament in November 1857. The Bill passed through parliament and the Royal Assent was granted for the Ware, Hadham and Buntingford Railway on 12 July 1858 with authorised share capital of £50,000.

The *Herts Guardian, Agricultural Journal and General Advertiser* and the *Hertford Mercury and Reformer* of 23 July 1859 carried reports of the start of construction of the Railway with the turning of the first sod taking place at Westmill, near Buntingford, on 20 July.

Whilst land for the Railway was being acquired, opposition was encountered from a landowner near Ware, and the decision was taken to alter the route of the Railway to join the Hertford branch at St Margaret's instead of Ware. Many other difficulties were encountered in acquiring land. In 1860, a deviation Bill was submitted to parliament to improve the gradients and shorten the line. This received its Royal Assent on 22 July 1861. The line needed an unusual number of bridges, increasing the cost per mile of construction.

Because of a shortfall in subscribed capital and the borrowing powers in the Company's Act of Incorporation being conditional on a proportion of the capital having been raised, the Directors of the Railway considered mortgaging it, but attempts to find a financial house willing to take debenture shares proved impossible and the company lacked funds.

The GNR had built a branch line from Welwyn to Hertford and there was a possibility that the Ware, Hadham and Buntingford Railway might be sold to that Company. Obviously not something the ECR wanted. At the 52nd Half Yearly Meeting of the Company on 27 August 1862, the Chairman reported:

> At the extraordinary meeting in November, 1861, authority was given to the Directors to contribute £22,000 towards the Ware, Hadham, and Buntingford Railway. This railway is now approaching completion, and your Directors have entered into an agreement, subject, to your approval, for working it on terms mutually advantageous, which will be submitted at the extraordinary meeting of the Proprietors after the conclusion of the half-yearly meeting.

What the ECR agreed was to provide financial assistance to the extent of £22,000. Two ECR board members joined the Ware, Hadham and Buntingford Railway board, and the ECR agreed to work the Railway for 50 per cent of receipts. The GER took on these commitments on its formation.

By the beginning of February 1863, the Railway was complete and on 10 February 1863 a special train ran from London to Buntingford for shareholders to attend the Shareholders' Meeting in Buntingford. All that was needed now for the Railway to be opened was the approval of the Board of Trade. On 18 April 1863, Captain J.H. Rich of the Board inspected the Railway. Rich was critical. He found that the permanent way was below the required standard and the underbridges were badly constructed; one at Bog Ford Bridge was reported to have sunk three inches under the inspection train. There were no facing point indicators, no turntable at St Margaret's, and several stations had no distant signals. There was inadequate fencing, and overbridges were not properly fenced on the road approach wing walls. This was a serious blow to the Company. It had assumed that early opening was within its grasp. Bog Ford Bridge was reconstructed, a 91-feet depth of piling driven to get a proper foundation. The work committed the Company to considerable unforeseen expenditure and a further Act of 22 June 1863 obtained authorisation to take an additional £40,000 share capital.

The inspection on 30 June 1863 by Col Yolland of the Board of Trade did not bring perfect results, but he reluctantly gave approval for it to open and the first trains ran on 3 July. There were four trains each way daily, two on Sundays. The journey time of fifty minutes was reduced by ten minutes by 1 August 1863. On opening there were only minimal goods facilities. Income for the first quarter year (to 30 September 1863) was £1,221, of which £862 came from passenger traffic and £359 was from goods. Both the *Herts Guardian, Agricultural Journal and General Advertiser* and the *Hertford Mercury and Reformer* of 4 July 1863 carried accounts of the opening of the Railway. The same newspapers of 25 July 1863 carried a report of a dinner held in the George Hotel, Buntingford, to which the Directors of the Railway invited several gentlemen connected with the GER and other friends.

It seems that by early 1865, goods trains on the single line were causing congestion and it was decided by the Board that a passing loop at Hadham was required. The Board authorised the expenditure for this on 24 May 1865. The work was to be done by the GER at the Buntingford Company's expense.

Due to poor usage, Widford station was closed after 31 December 1868, but a petition was raised locally and it reopened on 1 April 1869, just three months later.

The Railway had been expensive to construct and it was only with finance from both the ECR and its successor company, the GER, that it was completed. The capital subscribed to the Company, including the GER's subscription, was £106,871 and there were outstanding liabilities of £50,000 and a debenture debt of £29,403. This state of affairs could hardly continue long, and on 21 June 1865 the Company wrote to the GER asking them to take over the Railway. The Board admitted that they were 'not yet in a state to pay a dividend'.

Walter Bentinck had debenture bonds due on 10 February 1866. The Company was unable to pay him, and Bentinck took them to the Court of Chancery where he obtained judgment in his favour for £3,039, 'payable in land if not in cash'. The Company had no cash and no spare land, so the matter escalated, and in the end the GER paid Bentinck in order to settle the matter in November 1866. On 7 March 1867, the GER, realising that the initiative rested with it, wrote to the company suggesting absorption. Its motivation was that the GNR might get control of the Buntingford Company and use it to gain entry into GER territory.

On 26 March 1867, the shareholders of the Buntingford Company met and voted in favour of selling to the GER; the deed of transfer was ratified on 30 July 1868 and became effective on 1 September 1868.

The other development in Hertfordshire was when on 27 February 1888 a new station was opened at Hertford replacing the existing station further to the east. The original station was a simple affair on the eastern edge of the town and by the 1880s the GER decided that the town deserved a more salubrious station. The elegant station was designed by W.N. Ashbee and was some 400 yards nearer to the centre of the town. The old terminus was relegated to a goods depot. The *Herts Advertiser* of Saturday, 3 March 1888 reported that 'the new station at Hertford on the GER was opened for passenger and general traffic on Monday morning. The structure is convenient, being nearly 400 yards nearer the centre of the town than the old station'.

Lines in Essex

Beyond Loughton on the branch line from Stratford was the market town of Epping and five miles east beyond that was the small market town of Chipping Ongar. Both tempting places to which to build a railway.

An early scheme for a railway to Epping from the L&BR at Stepney, and another scheme from the ECR at Ilford, came to nothing. In 1858, a Company was promoted to build a railway from Loughton to Epping and Chipping Ongar. The name of the Company was the Epping Railways. The Company received its Royal Assent on 13 August 1859. To avoid passing through higher ground, the railway left the existing Loughton station about a quarter of a mile south of the station and swerved east through a new two platform Loughton station that was very close to the junction. The old station was closed and its approaches used to extend the goods yard and carriage sidings. Later an 'excursion platform' was erected on the site to cater for holiday traffic to Epping Forest, which lay not too far away. Prior to the opening of the Railway it had been taken over by the ECR in 1862 under the The ECR (Epping Lines) Act, 1862. The Act received its Royal Assent on 29 July 1862, just prior to the formation of the GER.

At the 52nd yearly meeting of the ECR on 27 August, 1862, the Directors' Report said 'Power was obtained to transfer the Epping and Ongar Lines to this Company'.

In the Report to 2nd Yearly Meeting of the GER held on 13 August 1863, the Company's Engineer, Robert Sinclair, wrote:

> On the New Lines considerable progress has been made, especially on the lines from Cambridge to Sudbury, and from Loughton to Epping. The Works have been somewhat interrupted by the harvest, a number of labourers having left for employment in gathering it in, but in a short time I expect that the Contractors will proceed with renewed vigour, and not slacken until the works are completed.

The new railway was opened as a single line from Loughton through Epping to Chipping Ongar on 24 April 1865. The *Chelmsford Chronicle* of 28 April 1865 recorded that the first train on the new line on its arrival at Chipping Ongar station was greeted with a salute from the Cadet Corps of Dr Clark's Grammar School and that the first person to buy a ticket at the station was Mr Low of Stanford Rivers. When the train was ready to make its return journey, the Cadets fired another salute and yet another as the train started on its way. The opening day was somewhat marred when the engine of the last train of the day to Ongar (Chipping Ongar) derailed at North Weald without causing death or injury to anyone, but causing a lot of inconvenience. Problems arose because the telegraph was hardly in working order and a messenger had to be sent to Loughton. The *Essex Herald* of 2 May in its report of the incident does not say how. From Loughton, a telegram was sent to Stratford. It was 5am before the engine could be rerailed and the train finally reached Ongar. The line from Loughton to Epping was later doubled tracked with the work being completed in January 1893.

The Epping Railways was an ambitious company and even before it had opened was planning extensions. One was from Ongar to Dunmow for which a Bill was put to parliament under the title Epping Railways Dunmow Extension Bill. The other was from Woodford Station, on the Loughton Branch of this Company, to join the London, Tilbury and Southend Railway near Barking. The ECR was not in favour of either and whilst the Directors' report to the half Yearly Meeting of the Company held on the 23 February 1860 noted that powers had been sought for the lines, that of the Half Yearly Meeting held on 23 August 1860 noted that 'EPPING RAILWAYS.—Extension to Dunmow: passed and 'EPPING RAILWAYS—Access to London by Tilbury Line: withdrawn in consequence of the opposition of this Company'. The Report also said:

> Your Directors consider the Epping Railway, and the Bedford and Cambridge Railway, as lines directly opposed to the interests of the Eastern Counties Railway, and not required for the reasonable convenience of the public. They have, therefore, done their best to point out to the Parliamentary Committees, before which these projects were brought, the unfairness towards the Eastern Counties Company, of sanctioning them. It is to be regretted that the efforts of the Directors have not been successful, and as it cannot be doubted that the object of the promoters of these hostile schemes will not be fully served without further extensions, tending to the establishment of another system of lines in the Eastern Counties District, and to the consequent injury of your property, it has become absolutely necessary, as anticipated in the remarks made in the Report of your Directors of August 1859, to take measures for preventing the spread of this aggressive system, by promoting the formation of such lines as may appear to be really required for the reasonable convenience of the district, in directions which shall be advantageous instead of inimical to your property. For this purpose it will be necessary somewhat to increase the capital expenditure of the Company, the particulars of which will be duly laid before you. Meantime, for obvious reasons, it is not desirable to give any further indications of the policy of the Directors.

Although the extension from Ongar to Dunmow had received its Act it was not built.

Great Dunmow, to give Dunmow its correct name, was a small market town of just under 3,000 people in 1861. It had one daily connection to London by a coach in the morning from Great Bardfield via Dunmow to Bishop's Stortford where it connected with the ECR. There was also a return working in the evening.

In 1858 there was a proposal for a London, Dunmow, Clare and Bury St Edmunds Railway. This line was to run from Barking on the LT&SR and could be seen as a threat to the ECR as it could mean that the LT&SR could be running trains to Bury St Edmunds.

Meanwhile, on Tuesday 3 July 1860 in consequence of an earlier printed announcement, a meeting was held in the Town Hall in Dunmow informing the inhabitants of the intention of a proposed railway from Bishop's Stortford through Dunmow to Braintree.

The *Chelmsford Chronicle* of 9 November 1860 reported that the Bishop's Stortford, Dunmow and Braintree Railway intended depositing with parliament a Bill for the proposed Railway. It would have included a junction with the proposed extension of the Epping Railway to Dunmow and for the ECR to subscribe to and enter into arrangements for the working and maintenance of the Railway.

According to the *Essex Standard* of 16 November 1860, the ECR was in favour of this Railway as a matter of self-defence.

Meanwhile, according to the *Essex Standard* of 21 November, what was now known as the London and Bury St Edmunds Railway announced its intention to deposit a Bill with parliament for its construction and maintenance of its Railway.

The *Essex Standard* of 5 December 1860 reported that the plans for both Railways had been deposited with the Clerk of the Peace for Essex. The Epping Railway's extension from Ongar to Dunmow had been passed earlier that year. To maintain a reasonable say in the Bishop's Stortford, Dunmow and Braintree Railway, the Epping Railway had resolved to subscribe a third of the £100,000 capital required to build the Railway.

The Bills for the two Railways were deposited with Parliament. The *Essex Standard* of 23 January 1861 said that the Directors of the Eastern Union and Norfolk railways thought it proper and necessary to lay before their shareholders a list of various proposed railways which included the London and Bury St Edmunds and Bishop's Stortford, Dunmow and Braintree railways.

According to the *Essex Standard* of 8 March, the London and Bury St Edmunds Railway was rejected by parliament for noncompliance with Standing Orders.

The Bishop's Stortford, Dunmow and Braintree Railway received its Act on 22 July 1861. The authorised capital had now risen to £120,000, with the ECR taking over the agreement to subscribe a third of the capital.

Whilst the inhabitants of Dunmow may have been understandably enthusiastic about the Railway, those of Bishop's Stortford and Braintree were rather less so, regarding the Railway as just an expensive way of travelling faster between those two towns, and of course getting to and from Dunmow. At a meeting of the shareholders held on 22 January 1862, it was announced that shares in the Company had only been taken up to the amount of £6,000, but the contactors for building the Railway, Messrs Brassey, Ogilvie and Harrison, had said that they were willing to accept a third of their contract in shares. During 1862, negotiations with the contractor were rather protracted: quite understandably given the Company's financial position.

In 1863, the GER put a Bill before parliament which included a clause that gave it the power to lease or purchase the Bishop's Stortford, Dunmow and Braintree Railway.

The 1st Half-Yearly Meeting of the GER held on 27 February 1863 had the following notice included in the papers of the meeting:

NOTICE is HEREBY FURTHER GIVEN, That immediately after the conclusion of the business of the above General Meeting, the meeting will be made Special for the purpose of authorising the Company to guarantee such amount of interest not exceeding the rate of £5 per centum per annum on any mortgages or debentures that may be created by the Bishop's Stortford, Dunmow, and Braintree Railway Company, or by the Ware, Hadham, and Buntingford Railway Company. The Transfer Books of the Company will close on the evening of Friday, the 6th day of February, and will not be opened until Saturday, the 28th day of February, 1863.

The 2nd Half-Yearly Meeting of the GER held on 13 August 1863 carried the following report on the Bishop's Stortford, Dunmow and Braintree Railway. 'BISHOP'S STORTFORD AND DUNMOW. The contract for these works has now been taken by an eminent Contractor, and the construction of the line will be proceeded with as soon as the necessary forms have been complied with.'

Things dragged on and it was not until 23 February 1864 that digging the first sod to commence the building of the Railway took place. This was performed amidst much celebration at Dunmow by Lady Justina Henniker, the wife of Sir Brydges Henniker of Newton Hall.

Given that the Railway was entirely dependent on what was now the GER for support and finance, it was inevitable that the Company should want to vest itself in the larger company and a motion authorising this was passed at a meeting of the Bishop's Stortford, Dunmow and Braintree Railway's shareholders on 2 May 1865. Following this, a Bill was put to parliament which subsequently became the second Bishop's Stortford, Dunmow and Braintree Railway Act and was passed on 28 June 1865, vesting the Railway in the GER immediately on the completion of the works and the opening of the Railway.

By early 1866, it had become clear that the cost of building the Railway was exceeding all forecasts and Brassey, the contractor, was constantly requesting additional finance to purchase land adjacent to the Railway because of serious underestimation by the surveyors. In many places, the formation was too narrow for basic earthworks and with the works nearing completion it was imperative that the money was quickly found. On 22 March 1866, the GER's Directors asked their agents to secure parliamentary authority to allow a subscription to the local company. On the same day, three GER directors were appointed as that Company's representatives on the Bishop's Stortford, Dunmow and Braintree Railway Board.

By the autumn of 1866, all the major earthworks on the Railway were complete and an application was made to the Board of Trade for an inspection of the Railway. This was done by Colonel Yolland on 20 November. Any hope that the Colonel would allow the line to open were dashed. He found that whilst the line was in fair order, it wanted lifting in some places. At Dunmow there was no signal box, and one should be provided. There were no clocks at stations or, if there were, they were not visible from the train. At Bishop's Stortford there was a sharp curve which needed a check rail. Worse, heavy and recent rains had caused many of the embankments to subside. They required carefully looking after and he said that traffic should be worked at a moderate pace. The line could not be opened without danger to the public.

Meanwhile, the first consignment of coal had arrived at Dunmow by rail. The *Essex Standard* of Wednesday 28 November 1866 reported that the previous Wednesday, the contractors had allowed one of their engines to bring twelve trucks of coal from Bishop's Stortford to Dunmow as the first instalment of winter fuel and that it was hoped that the line would be open for general traffic at an early date.

Brassey had problems with obtaining money to pay for the construction of the Railway and several times asked for payment of outstanding money due to him and his company. When this happened in January 1867, the matter was placed in the hands of the GER's Solicitor. The amount owed to Brassey was, according to him, £132,665 in respect of completion of the works to the end of 1866. The GER's Solicitor advised his Company's Board that the Company had already paid £30,000 in excess of the £40,000 initially budgeted for land purchase. Unfortunately, the GER had only raised £80,000 share capital to pay the contractor and it was the original intention that the local Company should make up any deficiency and this money the latter having no shareholding, did not have. The GER was also having financial problems of its own at that time and accepted that the authorised capital had been exceeded, but was loath to expend any further capital on the line to settle outstanding debts. It requested an independent inquiry to investigate the outstanding debts and liabilities owed to the contractor. The inquiry established that the GER had subscribed £40,000, raised shares to the value of £80,000, but the arbitration committee ruled that the excess £70,000 to £80,000 would also have to be guaranteed by the GER. The GER was not happy with this and tried to find an alternative solution. It is quite clear that because of what was happening, Brassey had stopped all work on the Railway. However, with the promise of financial returns he had somewhat relented and his men returned to work.

The coach that connected Dunmow to the outside world had ceased running and the town was left dependent on the carriers' carts for communication. The *Essex Herald* of 28 May 1867 reported:

Dunmow: Having had a railway completed for some months between this place and Bishop's Stortford and Braintree, but having no trains running and also no omnibuses or other regular conveyances to the neighbouring railway stations during the whole of the past winter, the inhabitants of Dunmow ever since the last autumn been greatly inconvenienced respecting any means of transit to the metropolis. It was therefore with much pleasure many read an announcement last week that we were to have a new omnibus to Ongar three times a week to communicate with London by means of the Epping line, and our spirited young townsman Mr F. Cates Jun started on Monday night with ... a respectable load. He has the hearty wishes of his neighbours that the undertaking will be remunerative.

Work was carried out to bring the line up to standard and on Thursday, 18 February 1869 Colonel Yolland of the Board of Trade made another inspection of the line and this time pronounced it fit for public service. As reported by the *Essex Standard* of Wednesday, 24 February 1869, following that the railway opened on Monday morning. There were fewer passengers than might have been expected. The only notice given of the opening was a few train lists distributed at inns. The weather was rough – snow and rain. The initial passenger service was two Up and two Down trains a day on Mondays to Saturdays except on Thursdays when there were three trains in each direction. There was no Sunday service. The GER then absorbed the Bishop's Stortford, Dunmow & Braintree Railway.

The line was single track with intermediate stations at Takeley, Dunmow, Felsted and Rayne. That at Dunmow had the facility to pass two passenger trains having two platforms, unlike the others which had only one platform.

At Braintree a new station was opened replacing the original station, which was then given over to goods traffic.

In 1895 a station was opened to serve Easton Lodge; the Earl and Countess of Warwick, who lived there, provided £140 plus £52 annually for 10 years for upkeep and they kindly also allowed it to be used by the general public. The line was not a financial success and it was reported in the papers of the 19th Half Yearly Meeting of the GER on 16 February 1872 that 'The Dunmow Railway traffic barely pays the working expenses, and is never likely to yield any appreciable portion of the £7,500 which has to be paid annually as interest for the capital laid out upon it'.

The origins of the Tendring Hundred Railway go back to 1858 when some time in that year it was decided by a group of interested people to apply to parliament to build a railway from Hythe to Wivenhoe. The earliest reference is in Norfolk News for 20 November 1858. The Railway was to be called the Tendring Hundred Railway. According to the Essex Standard of 29 December 1858 the bill for the Railway had been deposited in the Private Bill Office of the House of Commons at 8 o'clock in the evening of 23 December for the ensuing 1859 session of parliament. On 13 August 1860 the Company obtained its Act. The working of the Railway was to be in the hands of the Eastern Counties Railway and following its formation the Great Eastern Railway. The Tendring Hundred Railway was opened to passenger and goods traffic on 8 May 1863. I have not found an account of the opening of the Railway, but the working timetable of the GER for June 1863 shows the service running on Mondays to Saturdays only. There were six passenger trains a day in each direction. There was a daily goods train to and from

Wivenhoe. All of these started or finished at Colchester, but there was also a daily goods train in each direction to and from London to Hythe. On Saturdays only there was a cattle train from Hythe to Stratford.

Things started to get a bit complicated. At the mouth of the Colne lay the town of Brightlingsea, a small port, whose industries were fishing and shipbuilding. It was a member of the Cinque Ports and was the only such port outside of Kent and Sussex. It was actually a limb of the port of Sandwich. To the Directors of the Tendring Hundred Railway, Brightlingsea seemed a good place for development and to build a railway to the town. Unfortunately for the Tendring Hundred Railway, a certain George Bradley and two acquaintances were also interested in building a railway to Brightlingsea. Bradley and his acquaintants were not local men. None of them came from the eastern counties. Bradley came from Yorkshire, although he had been born in Lincolnshire. He was a speculator and his main speculations were buying up Manorial rights, but in the case of Brightlingsea he decided to build a railway as well.

The earliest mention of a railway from Wivenhoe to Brightlingsea is in the *Chelmsford Chronicle* of 19 October 1860 when a notice appeared giving the intention to apply to parliament in the next session for powers to build and maintain a railway from Wivenhoe to Brightlingsea. In the *Essex Standard* of 16 November, it was reported that the Railway was to make arrangements with the contemplated Tendring Hundred Railway. The *Essex Standard* of 7 December 1860 reported that the plans of the projected railway had been deposited with the Clerk of the Peace for Essex. Following an announcement in various local newspapers, a meeting about the railway was held in the Duke of Wellington in Brightlingsea on 14 December 1860. The meeting supported the promotion of the railway, and it was decided that petitions should be sent to both Houses of Parliament in favour of the railway. Although the Tendring Hundred Railway's Directors objected to the Wivenhoe and Brightlingsea Railway, it got its Act passed on 11 July 1861.

The cutting of the first sod of the Railway took place on 21 September 1863 at Wivenhoe and was performed by Mrs Waters, the wife of the Rev E.T. Waters, the Rector of Wivenhoe.

Whilst all this was going on, the Tendring Hundred Railway had obtained powers for two extensions. The first in 1862 was to build a railway consisting of two sides of a triangle off the existing line from Colchester to Hythe to a terminus in Colchester near the remains of St Botolph's Priory. The new station was nearer to the centre of Colchester than the existing station, although it could only be used by trains on the Tendring Hundred line or trains from London. The distance of Colchester's main station from the centre of the town would result in powers in 1883/4 being obtained to construct a steam tramway from the main railway station to the High Street. Construction had started and track had been laid from the main station as far as Middleborough, when financial difficulties caused the tramway company to collapse and the scheme fell through. The track, along with other material, was forfeited to Colchester Corporation, who removed the track. The Tendring Hundred Railway's line, which received its Royal Assent on 3 June 1862, included powers to construct a tramway from the terminus in Colchester to the military camp which was then under construction. There is no evidence that the tramway was ever built. The line opened on 1 March 1866.

The other extension was to Walton-on-the-Naze. The proposal for the extension to Walton-on-the-Naze was first mentioned at the Half Year Meeting of the shareholders of the Tendring Hundred Railway on 27 September 1862. In their report to the shareholders, the Directors said that they did not feel that the Wivenhoe and Brightlingsea Railway would afford provisions for the main population and produce of the district. They felt that that would be accommodated by a line nearer to the centre of the district – Walton-on-the-Naze. The Directors said that Walton was a town annually visited by thousands coming from London, Cambridgeshire, Suffolk and Essex. Experience had shown that the establishment of railway communication would increase the number of visitors to, and also the number of residents of, Walton.

The *Suffolk Chronicle* of 1 November reported that an application would be made to parliament for an Act to extend the Tendring Hundred Railway to Walton.

Just to make matters more interesting there was now another railway proposed for the Tendring Hundred. This was the Mistley, Thorpe and Walton Railway, which was originally proposed to run from Mistley on the Harwich branch via Tendring to Walton. Support for the Tendring Hundred Railway's extension to Walton came from Colchester and from Weeley. The extension received its Royal Assent on 13 July 1863.

There was a slight problem for the Tendring Hundred Railway. The Wivenhoe and Brightlingsea Railway's line to the latter town started with an end on junction with the Tendring Hundred Railway's line from Hythe and trains from Walton would have to use a small part of the former Company's line to get to the Tendring Hundred Railway's extension to Walton.

When the Wivenhoe and Brightlingsea Railway had got its Act 1861 the Tendring Hundred Railway, which was still interested in Brightlingsea, considered building a line from Thorington to Brightlingsea and in 1861 at a shareholders' meeting the Company stated that it would build the line if the rival company did not meet with success. The Company even tried to get permission to build the section of line from Wivenhoe to Great Bentley without an Act so that the Brightlingsea section could get under way as soon as possible. In November 1864, whilst the Wivenhoe and Brightlingsea Railway was still under construction, it proposed an extension from Brightlingsea to St Osyth. Nothing came of this.

Reverting back to the Mistley, Thorpe and Walton Railway, according to the *Essex Standard* of 14 November 1862, there was an intention to make an application to parliament to construct and maintain a railway from Mistley to Walton. The same newspaper of 5 December 1862 says that a meeting of the provisional committee of the Railway was held at the Thorn Inn in Mistley on 28 November. The meeting had said that the GER had given the undertaking its fullest support and had agreed to take an important share in it.

By agreement with the GER, both the Tendring Hundred Railway and the Mistley, Thorpe and Walton Railway agreed not to oppose each other's Bill and on 21 July 1863 the Mistley, Thorpe and Walton Railway received its Act.

The GER knew what it was doing. It was going to work both lines. As both lines were going to serve Walton at a single station, a further agreement was reached in 1864 whereby the Tendring Hundred Railway slightly altered its course between Kirby Cross and Walton and the Mistley, Thorpe and Walton Railway agreed to join the Tendring Hundred Railway at Thorpe-le-Soken. These proposals were sanctioned by the Tendring Hundred Railway Act of 23 June 1864 and the Mistley, Thorpe and Walton Railway Act of 30 June 1864.

At this point things started to go a bit wrong. Under the Tendring Hundred Railway's Act of 1864, the Wivenhoe and Brightlingsea Railway was supposed to complete the first quarter of a mile from Wivenhoe to the junction with the Tendring Hundred Railway by 1 November 1864. If it failed to do this, the Tendring Hundred Railway could complete the section of line at the Wivenhoe and Brightlingsea Railway's expense. Unfortunately, William Munro, who was the contractor for the Wivenhoe and Brightlingsea, the Tendring Hundred and the Mistley, Thorpe and Walton railways, went broke at this point and Peter Bruff, who was the engineer for the Tendring Hundred Railway, had to step in and take charge of the building of both the Tendring Hundred and the Wivenhoe and Brightlingsea railways. According to the *Bury and Norwich Post* of 27 December 1864, work was proceeding satisfactorily on the extension of the Tendring Hundred Railway to Weeley and Walton. Work on the Tendring Hundred Railway was sufficiently advanced that the line was opened to Weeley on 8 January 1866. On 17 April 1866, the Wivenhoe and Brightlingsea Railway officially opened to Brightlingsea. A special train conveyed the Chairman and Directors of the Company and the Chairman and several Directors and officials of the GER to Brightlingsea where they had an oyster lunch and went on a tour of Brightlingsea. Services started the following day. On 28 July 1866, the Tendring Hundred Railway was further extended to Kirby Cross. On Friday, 17 May 1867, the Tendring Hundred Railway was opened to Walton. The following Monday, by invitation of the Tendring Hundred Railway Board, several Directors of the GER Board paid a visit to Walton, where they were treated to an excellent lunch. Both the Tendring Hundred and the Wivenhoe and Brightlingsea railways were worked by the GER. The lines were of single track. Whilst the Wivenhoe and Brightlingsea Railway had train staff stations at Wivenhoe and Brightlingsea, the Tendring Hundred Railway had them at Hythe, Wivenhoe, Weeley and Walton. No train could travel between one of these stations without a train staff or train ticket. They were a token that authorised a train to be on a particular section of line. Without them, a train could not travel on the particular section of line that they covered. The section from Colchester, St Botolph's and Hythe was worked under Electric Train Signal Regulations.

Things were not going so well on the Mistley, Thorpe and Walton Railway either. The first sod had been cut on 6 April 1864 at Mistley by the wife of the Chairman, Captain H.J.W. Jervis. On this railway, the contractor, William Munro, had not given up but was making very slow progress. Following a pitched battle between fifty of his men and sixty Harwich longshoremen hired by the Company on 11 April 1865, he was evicted and the work given to Frederick Furness to whom Munro had assigned the completion of the contract by November 1865; the railway was far from complete, but an application was made to parliament to build an extension from Manningtree to Bures. Nothing came of this.

Before the end of 1866, the Mistley, Thorpe and Walton Company's debt to Furness had amounted to nearly £12,000, and in consequence work ceased completely. By that time four bridges had been completed, carrying public roads over the line along the first 3¼ miles, and two further south had been partially constructed. Neither of the two stations at Bradfield and Tendring and Weeley had been built. A quantity of sleepers however had been deposited along the track, and for these and other material, Furness obtained judgment. The financial position of the undertaking had by then become hopeless, and the period allowed for completion of the works had expired the previous year. At a private meeting of the shareholders held on 8 July 1869, it was resolved to make application to the Board of Trade for the abandonment of the railway. This the Company did the following month, and sanction was given under the provisions of the Abandonment of Railways Act 1850 and the Railway Companies Act of 1867. As to whether any rails had been laid is not certain.

While this had been going on, Furness had been arranging for the disposal of the Company's goods upon which execution had been levied. This took place at the Thorn Inn at Mistley on 11 and 13 August 1869. The disposal of the land acquired took a bit longer. In November 1873 there was an attempt to revive the project with a proposed East Essex Railway to run from Mistley to Thorpe-le-Soken but nothing came of this.

It was during this time that we first hear of the mention of Clacton. In October 1865, Peter Bruff acquired a small estate in the village of Great Clacton for the purpose of founding a new seaside resort – Clacton-on-Sea – and promptly set about acquiring an Act for a railway – The Thorpe and Clacton Railway – from Thorpe-le-Soken and a pier. The Act was obtained on 16 July 1866 and stipulated that the work was to be completed within five years. Unfortunately, owing to financial difficulties Bruff was not able to build the railway and so the powers lapsed. He did however manage to find the money to build the pier which opened on 18 July 1871 with the arrival of the paddle steamer *Queen of the Orwell*. And so began the growth of Clacton-on-Sea.

In 1872, with the backing of the GER, the Tendring Hundred Railway proposed a line from west of Weeley station to St Osyth and thence on to Clacton. Even though plans were deposited with Parliament and approved by it in November of that year, nothing came of it.

The Tendring Hundred and the Wivenhoe and Brightlingsea railways were not exactly on the best of terms during the 1860s and 1870s, particularly after the former had completed the latter's line into Wivenhoe. The row over liability for payment went on until 1875 when the Wivenhoe and Brightlingsea Railway finally agreed to pay £7,000 to the Tendring Hundred Railway.

In 1876, the Wivenhoe and Brightlingsea Railway had a quarrel with the GER over the working of the Railway and bought an engine and two carriages so as to work the Railway itself. As the Tendring Hundred Railway was not in dispute with the GER, it would not let the smaller company use its station at Wivenhoe and so the Wivenhoe and Brightlingsea Railway built its own station there. In 1879, the dispute with the GER was settled and that Company again took over the working of the Wivenhoe and Brightlinsea Railway including the engine and carriages, whilst the latter's station at Wivenhoe then closed.

Whilst Walton was expanding, Clacton was expanding even faster. In 1876, a railway was promoted to connect Clacton to Thorpe-le-Soken – the Clacton-on-Sea Railway. This was after the original proposal of that year for a line from Thorrington via St Osyth had met strong opposition from landowners along the proposed route. The company obtained its Act on 2 August 1877. Under the Act there was to be a spur at Thorpe-le-Soken to permit direct running from Clacton to Walton but this was never built. The Railway was supported by the GER.

Construction of the Railway commenced on 1 August 1878, with the first sod being turned at the site of the Clacton terminus by Miss Law, the daughter of the Vicar Designate of Clacton.

Owing to difficulties in providing adequate drainage for the Railway it was not until 4 July 1882 that it was opened. An inspection of the Railway by Major-General Hutchinson of the Board of Trade took place on 24 June. The event was celebrated in Clacton with great celebrations. These included a special train conveying dignitaries from Colchester, a procession and a lunch.

The GER did not merely like working the railways in the Tendring Hundred – it liked to own them. At the end of 1882, negotiations were begun with the Tendring Hundred and Clacton-on-Sea Railways and following successful negotiations under an Act of 29 June 1883 they became part of the GER. The Wivenhoe and Brightlingsea Railway held out for its independence and was not taken over by the GER until 9 June 1893. As traffic on the lines was growing, the section between

Colchester and Wivenhoe was doubled between 1884 and 1886, thus displacing working by Electric Train Signal Regulations on that section of line.

On 1 July 1888, a station was opened at Frinton-on-Sea between Kirby Cross and Walton. In 1890, the GER doubled the section of line from Great Bentley to Thorpe-le-Soken, but because a small section of the line between Wivenhoe and Great Bentley was owned by the still independent Wivenhoe and Brightlingsea Railway, this remained single track.

An unfortunate railway was the South Essex Railway which was promoted in 1864 to build a railway from Great Warley on the GER to Southminster with a branch from Rettendon to Heybridge. In 1866, it obtained powers to build a line from Rettendon to Pitsea on the LT&SR. Despite having obtained powers to build the lines, the Railway was never built.

In Essex, away from the Metropolitan area and the line to Southend, the principal developments were the closure in 1877 of Sir John Tyssen Tyrell's private station at Boreham House, 3½ miles north-east of Chelmsford, following his death and the opening on 1 March 1878 of a station at Hatfield Peverel on the site of what had been Hatfield station which had existed between 1844 and its destruction by fire in February 1849.

The Colne Valley and Halstead Railway unsuccessfully promoted a bill to construct lines from Haverhill to Cambridge and from Chapel to Colchester and had made a deal with the London and North Western Railway (L&NWR), which was the prospective lessee of the Bedford and Cambridge Railway which received its Act on 6 August 1860. The deal was for the Colne Valley and Halstead Railway to extend to join the Bedford and Cambridge Railway south of Cambridge and to build a separate line to Colchester nearer the town.

At the same time, the ECR promoted bills for the construction of lines from Sudbury to Long Melford, Long Melford to Clare, Clare to Shelford, Long Melford to Bury St Edmunds and a connecting line at Haverhill between the Colne Valley and Halstead Railway and the ECR and the Act for these lines was passed on 22 July 1861.

In 1863, the Colne Valley and Halstead Railway promoted a bill for a line at Haverhill from the junction with the now GER to link up with the GER's Clare and Shelford line in the adjoining parish of Withersfield and a branch from Birdbrook to a junction with the Clare and Shelford line in the parish of Wixhoe. It also proposed to compel the abandonment of the GER lines between the points mentioned and also their Haverhill branch. In this the Colne Valley and Halstead Railway was successful and was granted powers to build the new lines. There were drawbacks for the Colne Valley and Halstead Railway as it was now dependent on the GER for access to Cambridge and Colchester. The latter omission was of great importance as it meant that the L&NWR was no longer interested and that its financial support was withdrawn. With this powerful aid lost, the Colne Valley and Halstead Railway found it impossible to fund its new venture and because of this it was allowed to lapse.

Construction of the GER's lines began at the Shelford end. Progress was somewhat slow. The *Bury Free Press* of 19 March 1864 reported under the heading GREAT EASTERN RAILWAY that the Parliamentary Committee had decided not to grant the application by the Company for an extension of time to complete the lines under construction. In constructing the lines, the GER had to cut through an ancient barrow or tumuli at Bartlow, something which is unthinkable today and would undoubtedly result in serious delays in the work.

On 1 June 1865, the GER opened the section of line from Shelford to Haverhill and on 9 August 1865 the line was extended from Haverhill to Sudbury via Long Melford. On the same day, the connecting line between the GER station at Haverhill and the Colne Valley and Halstead Railway was opened as was the line from Long Melford to Bury St Edmunds. When the connection from the Colne Valley and Halstead Railway to Haverhill Great Eastern was opened, only trains which did not connect with the Great Eastern used the Colne Valley and Halstead Railway's station at Haverhill.

Although not able to have their own line to Cambridge, the Colne Valley and Halstead Railway was anxious to get the anticipated Cambridge traffic as soon as possible and advertised in various local newspapers in May 1864 for tenders from postmasters, coach proprietors and others to run a daily omnibus from Haverhill to Cambridge (Sundays excepted). As far as is known, there were no takers. When the Colne Valley and Halstead Railway was open to the GER station at Haverhill, a through daily goods service was run to Cambridge via the Colne Valley and Halstead Railway by the GER and worked throughout by that Company's locomotives. This ceased in 1867. In addition to this goods train, there were mixed trains over the sections of line north and west of Sudbury, Sudbury having a normal goods service.

1865 also saw the opening of the first stage of the Saffron Walden Railway. Saffron Walden is a market town just under two miles north-east of the Cambridge main line at Audley End station and had been missed by that line when it was built. Because of the lack of a railway, both the town's trade and its population had started to decline. The Gibsons, who were a rich Quaker family involved in banking, had unsuccessfully tried to get the ECR to build a branch line to the town and were behind the promotion in 1861 of the Saffron Walden Railway from Audley End to Saffron Walden. The Company received its Act on 22 July 1861. On 22 June 1863, another Act was obtained for the Railway to extend its line to Bartlow. The Railway was opened from Audley End to Saffron Walden on 23 November 1865 and to Bartlow on 22 October 1866. At Bartlow, the junction faced in the direction of Cambridge rather than Suffolk and the GER – which had subscribed to the Railway and worked it from the start – refused to divert through traffic for Suffolk over the Railway. At Audley End, the junction for the line was immediately south of the main station, with the branch platform at a right angle to the main line platforms. This meant either any through carriage for or from Saffron Walden would have involved a complicated manoeuvre at Audley End or the detaching or joining taking place at the next station south – Newport; not exactly the best use of resources. The Saffron Walden Railway was not in the best of financial health and was only kept going by loans from Gibson's bank. The issued capital of the company by 1869 was £150,000, which was far too much for the meagre local patronage of the Railway to support. At one point, the Company, in order to save itself from its creditors, was obliged to have the Company Secretary, to whom it owed money for land, file a petition of bankruptcy against it in order to gain the protection of the Official Receiver. Finally, on 1 January 1877 the GER purchased the Company for £70,750.

On 1 August 1862 the L&NWR began working into Cambridge over the Bedford and Cambridge Railway, which had been promoted locally in 1860 and took over the route of the Sandy and Potton Railway between Sandy and Potton which was a private railway owned by Captain Sir William Peel and opened for goods on 23 June 1857 and passengers in November of that year. The L&NWR absorbed the Bedford and Cambridge Railway in 1865.

In 1888, the threat of the L&NWR reaching Colchester raised its head again. According to the late Dr R.F. Youell, writing in *Stour Valley Steam* in the late 1970s, in that year there was a bill before Parliament for the Cambridge, Colchester and Colnemouth Railway. According to Dr Youell, the Railway, although nominally independent, would have been an L&NWR protégé. The proposed railway would have left the L&NWR line to Cambridge via a triangular junction and would have run considerably north of the GER line via Balsham, crossing the latter near Withersfield Siding and making a head on junction with the Colne Valley and Halstead Railway. Leaving the latter railway as far west as Earls Colne and following the River Colne without a steep climb, a new line was planned to Colchester with an extension to a deepwater port at Colnemouth facing Brightlingsea. The Railway failed to get its Royal Assent and any chance of the L&NWR attempting to reach Colchester faded. Interestingly, the livery of the locomotives of the Colne Valley and Halstead Railway was black – like that of the L&NWR.

Lines in Suffolk

The final section of the Waveney Valley Railway was opened from Bungay to Beccles on 2 March 1863. On the same day, the Waveney Valley Railway was taken over by the GER. Three of the stations on the line, which were clearly not making money, closed – Starston and Redenhall were closed on 1 August 1866, whilst Wortwell was closed on 1 January 1878.

The market town of Eye, which is situated between Ipswich and Norwich, had missed out on being served by the railway when it was being constructed from Haughley to Norwich and in 1864 promoted a railway from Eye to connect with the main line at Mellis, the Mellis and Eye Railway. On 30 November, a bill was deposited with parliament for the construction of the Railway, which became law on 5 July 1865, with construction starting soon afterwards.

It was not until 8 February 1867 that the Board of Trade inspected the line, the delay being as a result of bad weather. Regular passenger services did not begin until 2 April, the delay this time being caused by the time needed for the independent company to negotiate with the GER who agreed to work the line. Eventually a deal was struck in which the GER took 50 per cent of the gross receipts in return for operating the line for ten years.

The GER exploited the fact that the small company could not afford its own locomotives and rolling stock and in fact increased its stake to 60 per cent of gross receipts in order to cover the costs of operating the line. By 1883, relations between the owning company and the GER improved and a dividend was paid. In 1898 the GER absorbed the Mellis and Eye Railway.

The Bury St Edmunds and Thetford Railway was incorporated in 1865 to build a railway between the two mentioned places. Unfortunately, it had difficulty in raising capital. Meanwhile, in 1866 the Thetford and Watton Railway had been formed to build a line from Roundham Junction on the Norwich to Ely line to the small Norfolk village of Watton. Construction proceeded quite quickly, and goods services started 26 January 1869 worked by the contractor. On 22 July, the Company, which had acquired its own motive power and rolling stock, took over the working of the goods services and on 18 October 1869 passenger services commenced. In the same year, the Watton and Swaffham Railway was incorporated and authorised to raise £62,000 and to construct a line to Swaffham on the Dereham to Lynn line. Both the Bury St Edmunds and Thetford Railway and Watton and Swaffham Railway were empowered to enter into an agreement with the GER for it to work their Railway. The Watton and Swaffham Railway – like the Bury St Edmunds and Thetford Railway – ran into financial difficulties and so in 1872 further powers were obtained to extend the time of construction to 1875. In 1873, the Thetford and Watton Railway obtained powers to work the Bury St Edmunds and Thetford Railway, which was to be reached by running powers over the GER at Thetford and to construct a spur to it at Thetford Bridge. It was also authorised to raise £21,000 and subscribe £10,000 to the Watton and Swaffham Railway which was then nearing completion. The spur and the station were opened on 15 November 1875. The Bury St Edmunds and Thetford Railway opened on 1 March 1876, worked by the Thetford and Watton as indicated. On 20 September 1875, the Watton and Swaffham Railway had been opened for goods traffic, followed on 15 November for passenger traffic. According to D.I. Gordon in *A Regional History of the Railways of Great Britain – The Eastern Counties*, all was set for a railway independent of the GER from the Ely to Norwich line to Marks Tey on the Colchester line, reaching Marks Tey over the Sudbury line. In 1878, parliament rejected a bill for the amalgamation of the three Companies. By that year all three Companies were not in a good financial state – particularly the Bury St Edmunds and Thetford Railway which sold out to the GER on 22 July 1878. On 1 August 1879, the other two companies handed over their workings to the GER, following this on 1 January 1880 with a formal lease. In 1898 the GER totally absorbed both companies.

At the mouth of the River Orwell lies the town and seaside resort of Felixstowe. The first proposal for a railway to the town was the Ipswich and Felixstowe Railway of 1865 to run from Westerfield on the East Suffolk line to Hog Lane in Felixstowe, followed in 1873 by a proposal for a tramway to run from Ipswich station to Landguard Common (near the mouth of the River Orwell) and Fagborough Cliff where it would connect with the ferry to Harwich. Neither plan actually happened so Colonel George Tomline, who had been one of the tramway's promoters, suggested that a proper railway should be built instead, to run from Westerfield to a pier to be constructed at Landguard Common. An Act of Parliament was granted for this scheme on 19 July 1875 under the name of the Felixstowe Railway and Pier Company. Two years later, the name was changed to the Felixstowe Railway and Dock Company when a new Act authorised the construction of a dock at Languard Common close to the pier with an access channel and railway lines.

Construction proceeded fairly quickly and the railway was opened on 1 May 1877 from Westerfield to a station at Felixstowe Beach, which was some distance from the more established part of Felixstowe. Tomline was a land developer and so he had made sure it was near some of his proposed future building plans. There was a rumour that it was also positioned to be away from the Ordnance Hotel, owned by his rival John Chevalier Cobbold.

When the Railway opened it possessed its own locomotives and rolling stock. There were intermediate stations at Derby Road (Ipswich), Orwell – and again Colonel Tomline's convenience was paramount as it was near his home in Nacton. The initial service was three trains a day in each direction. At Westerfield the Company's station adjoined that of the GER, which assumed the working of the Railway on 1 September 1879 and diverted trains to the main station at Westerfield with some extended through to Ipswich. In 1886, the GER acquired the railway part of the Felixstowe Railway and Dock Company from that Company.

In May 1887, an Act of Parliament was granted for a line from Felixstowe to Felixstowe Ferry but this was never built and the scheme was abandoned in 1892 due to lack of capital.

In 1891, another station was opened at Trimley.

In June 1893, the GER obtained an Act for a short deviation to the line. A terminus station was to be built on what is now Hamilton Road.

The Southwold Railway, although it never became part of the GER, almost did join it at various times. Southwold was a small port on the Suffolk coast between Lowestoft and Aldeburgh. During the nineteenth century, its importance started to decline, so in an attempt to reverse its fortunes, the Corporation of the town started to promote it as a seaside resort. When the East Suffolk Railway was being promoted, the town expected it to pass through Southwold, but instead it took an inland route because of the underlying geology of the area.

Although Southwold was served by a bus service which ran once a day to and from Darsham, in 1855 the East Suffolk Railway was asked to build a branch line from Halesworth to Southwold, but they declined. Over the following twenty years several similar schemes were proposed but none were ever begun. In 1872 the Southwold and Halesworth Tramway obtained an Act of Parliament, with the intention of building a steam tramway between the two towns, using the provisions of the Tramways Act 1870, but the project foundered.

In October 1875, two public meetings were held, chaired by local landowners, one at Halesworth chaired by Mr Charles Easton of Easton Hall and the other at Southwold chaired by the Earl of Stradbroke, who lived at Henham Hall. They invited Arthur C. Pain, a civil engineer, to speak, together with Richard C. Rapier, who was part of the engineering firm of Ransomes and Rapier. The two speakers both suggested that a 2ft 6in gauge railway would be considerably cheaper to build than a standard gauge one of 4ft 8½ in. The meetings resulted in the formation of the Southwold Railway Company. Colonel Heneage Bagot-Chester was appointed as Chairman, the two speakers became the Company's Engineers, and the Secretary was a local solicitor, H. R. Allen.

The Company obtained an Act of Parliament on 24 July 1876, to allow the Railway to be constructed. The main line was 8 miles 63½ chains long and ran from Southwold to Halesworth with two branches authorised. A branch of just under a half a mile at Halesworth linked up with the Blyth Navigation, and there was a link to Blackshore Quay, between Southwold and Walberswick, which was to be a quarter of a mile long.

The Company had powers to raise £40,000 in working capital by issuing £10 shares, and it could also borrow a further £13,000 by issuing debentures. The gauge of the railway had to be at least 2ft 6in and because the line was covered by the Regulation of Railways Act 1868, it could use a simple signalling system and light earthworks, providing loads were limited and speeds did not exceed

25mph. In practice, this meant that journey times between the two termini would be about 30 minutes, and trains were limited to 100 passengers.

Following a report by C.J. Wall, a former manager of the Bristol and Exeter Railway, the gauge of 3ft was chosen. This would make the line somewhat more expensive to build, but it was thought that the increased carrying capacity would offset this. Construction began on 3 May 1878 with sleepers bought from Norway, arriving conveniently by ship at Southwold harbour. The completed works were inspected by the Board of Trade on 19 September 1879 and passed with flying colours, so a celebration lunch was held at the Swan Hotel on 23 September. Torrential rain during that night caused significant flooding in Suffolk, and the line near Wenhaston Mill was submerged, but the official opening still took place on 24 September and the first train completed a return journey despite the water. Subsequent trains ran between Southwold and Wenhaston even as the flooding worsened. The intermediate stations at Walberswick and Blythburgh were not completed until later. Blythburgh opened by December 1879, but Walberswick was not opened until 1 July 1882. Meanwhile, on 29 January 1879, Bagot-Chester resigned from the Company, leaving a board that had no real commitment to the service of the community.

Neither of the two branches specified by the original Act were built, due to a lack of funds, and the powers were allowed to lapse. At Halesworth, the single platform had a shelter for the passengers, and was connected to the Great Eastern station by a footbridge. There was a raised timber platform between one of the sidings and a standard gauge siding, where goods were transhipped. In constructing the Railway to a narrow gauge, the Company had made a serious error as it was not possible to run goods wagons off the GER though to Southwold, nor was it possible for through carriages to run to Southwold from the GER.

During the first ten years of its operation, passenger traffic on the Railway was fairly static, at around 76,000 journeys per year, but goods traffic doubled to reach 9,144 tons. This was followed by a steady increase.

The GER took an interest in the Southwold Railway, assisting with an extension of the main line footbridge towards the Southwold Railway platform and a rearrangement of the former company's sidings to facilitate transhipment between standard and narrow gauge vehicles. According to *The Southwold Railway 1879-1929* by David Lee, Alan Taylor and Rob Shorland-Ball (Pen and Sword 2019), the GER derived £11,000 a year from traffic exchanged with the Southwold Railway.

In 1893 there was a proposal for a railway from Cambridge to Southwold. The railway would have running powers over the GER to Newmarket and then a new line to Mellis, with running powers over the branch line to Eye and then a new line from there via Stradbroke to Halesworth and the purchase and re-gauging of the Southwold Railway. Although there was a proposal for an application to parliament for the railway it never reached that point. It is uncertain which Railway Company would have worked the railway or even whether it would have had its own motive power and rolling stock.

At a meeting of the GER Board's Traffic Committee on 1 August 1893, it was noted that Richard Rapier, the Chairman of the Southwold Railway, had approached the GER's General Manager in November 1892 suggesting either that the GER should purchase the Southwold Railway or alternatively assist the smaller Company by giving it a rebate on rates for the conveyance of its traffic. The GER's General Manager had responded that 'he was unable to see his way into the matter' and suggesting that a submission be made in the summer of 1893. The Southwold Railway's Chairman's submission was discussed at the meeting of the GER's Traffic Committee on 15 May 1894 which proposed a 5 per cent discount on rates and an option to purchase the Southwold Railway within 21 years, the GER being aware of the proposed Cambridge to Southwold Railway being worked by another company out of those running into Cambridge, so a takeover of the Southwold Railway seemed a good option. The Chairman of the Southwold Railway felt that a 21-year option was too long and suggested instead a 10-year option and 5 per cent discount on traffic rates. The GER responded by proposing that the revised offer should be subject to a survey, report and valuation by the GER's Engineer and Locomotive Superintendent. The GER's valuation was based on a survey done in 1892 and updated (in pencil) in 1894. As far as is known, nothing further came of this at that time.

In 1874 parliament received plans for two rival schemes to connect the Cambridge to Bury St Edmunds line to Ely, the Ely and Newmarket Railway, backed by the GER and to run via Fordham and Soham; and the Ely and Bury Light Railway which was to run via Soham and Mildenhall. Parliament approved the Ely and Newmarket Railway and granted running powers to the Ely and Bury Light Railway from Ely to Soham which was covered by the Ely and Newmarket Railway proposal and the Ely and Bury Railway route could then be constructed from there to Bury St Edmunds. In the event nothing more came of this second scheme.

Following the passing of the Ely and Newmarket Railway Act in 1875, construction began soon afterwards. Whilst a train carrying various officers of the GER ran over the line on 6 June 1879, the line initially failed to pass inspection by the Board of Trade, and it was not until 1 September 1879 that the line opened. The Ely and Newmarket Railway was worked by the GER from its opening. Later it was leased by the GER. Some sources say 4 January 1887, whilst others say 4 January 1888, with the agreement being agreed to on 10 April that year but backdated to the date in January. In 1898 the GER absorbed the Ely and Newmarket Railway.

When the line opened, because there was not a curve off the line facing in the direction of Bury St Edmunds, trains from that direction had to reverse in the Newmarket area. On 1 September 1880, a curve was opened to enable direct running from Bury St Edmunds to Ely.

The line proved very useful as it enabled through working from the north to Ipswich and Harwich without having to either reverse at Cambridge and travel via Newmarket and Bury St Edmunds and Haughley or travel via Haverhill, Sudbury and Colchester.

The market town of Mildenhall lay to the east of Fordham on the Ely and Newmarket Railway. Not having a railway was proving something of a disadvantage to the town. In September 1867 Charles Peter Allix of Swaffham Prior submitted plans to the GER in the hope that the Company would build a railway to Mildenhall and thus open up the area in which he was interested. The GER declined, no doubt believing that the money spent on serving a remote and thinly populated area would be wasted. Allix tried to interest the L&NWR, which had reached Cambridge from Bedford, but they also said no.

The GER suffered from exceptional flooding near Lakenheath in November 1878, which blocked its main line between Ely and Norwich. During the time that the line was out of action, traffic from London to Norwich via Cambridge and Ely using the Cambridge line had to go via Bury St Edmunds with a reversal at Haughley onto the Colchester and Ipswich line.

Allix had remained in contact with the GER concerning his scheme for a railway to Mildenhall and it now occurred to him that a line from Cambridge through Mildenhall might be advantageous. If it was extended east to Thetford, it would provide a shortened route between Cambridge and Norwich, avoiding the northward sweep through Ely. The GER was persuaded of the benefits of building the line to Mildenhall and the line was included (with other plans) in the Parliamentary Bill which became the GER Act, 1881, receiving the Royal Assent on 18 July 1881. The line was to run north-eastwards from a junction at Barnwell, two miles north of Cambridge station, on to Fordham and make a junction there with the now-completed Ely-Newmarket line. From the northern end of Fordham, the line was to run eastwards to Mildenhall. The station there was to be laid out to facilitate the intended eastward extension to Thetford. However the extension to Thetford wasn't built because proper repairs to the flood-prone section proved effective. The first sod of the branch was cut on 3 January 1883.

In mid to late May 1884, the line was nearly complete between Barnwell and Fordham and on either 26 or 27 May officers of the GER conducted a tour of their line; traversing the line by special inspection train. On 28 May, Major General C.S. Hutchinson, an Inspecting Officer of the Board of Trade, carried out an inspection of the line and although certain signal interlocking changes were required, he approved the line for opening, and it did so on 2 June 1884 for all traffic. During the luncheon provided after Hutchinson's inspection, Henry Lovatt was heard to say that the line would soon be extended to Mildenhall and on to Thetford, which of course did not happen.

On 28 March 1885, Major General Hutchinson again visited the line to inspect the Mildenhall extension from Fordham. He found that the line was satisfactory, and it opened to traffic on 1 April 1885.

At Ipswich the island platform was opened (today's Platform 3 and Platform 4) in 1883 to improve operations at the station. Many of the original platform buildings exist today and close inspection reveals the heads of what are believed to be Greek Gods incorporated into the design.

Lines in Cambridgeshire

On the line from Hitchin to Cambridge under an Act of 1864 the GER conceded to the GNR full running powers to Cambridge station where a separate platform and full facilities would be provided, double track capable of carrying express services was promised between Shepreth and Shelford by 31 March 1866, the last day of the GER's lease of the Royston and Hitchin Railway on the expiration of which that railway would be returned to the GNR. This took place as agreed.

The Great Eastern Railway From its Formation in 1862 to the End of 1895

During the construction of the MR line south toward London, commercially valuable ironstone deposits were discovered in the area around Kettering. In 1860 a definite proposal was formulated to reach them and to continue to Huntingdon on the Great Northern line. The first part was authorised as the Kettering and Thrapstone Railway, which received its Act of authorisation on 29 July 1862. The line was to terminate at Thrapston adjacent to the L&NWR station on the western edge of the town. According to the *Leicester Mercury* of 9 August 1862:

> Kettering and Thrapston Railway Bill: This bill has just received the Royal assent, and we understand the works are to be commenced immediately. There are extensive quarries of iron stone of a fine quality, and also beds of white clay, which will be worked in the vicinity, and for which there is a great and increasing demand. A bill will be brought in in the next session of Parliament to extend the powers of the act to Huntingdon, so as to connect the Eastern Counties with the Midland line.

As the *Leicester Mercury* indicated, plans were afoot for the extension to Huntingdon. The Kettering, Thrapstone and Huntingdon Railway was authorised on 28 July 1863. The MR was authorised to work the line for 40 per cent of the gross receipts for the first seven years, and at 50 per cent thereafter.

The Board of Trade inspector approved the line between Kettering and Huntingdon on 15 February 1866 and the first goods train ran on 21 February 1866, with passenger trains from 1 March 1866. It was worked by the MR from the outset, and there were running powers over the GER from Huntingdon to Cambridge via St Ives. The line had sharp curves and difficult gradients and, running through sparsely populated terrain, many of the stations were not well situated for the communities they were intended to serve.

The GER in Cambridgeshire had reached Godmanchester by 1863 and two landowners, Oliver Pell and Frederick Camps, wanted to extend that line to include their estates. The more southerly route they selected had the advantage of gentle gradients. Accordingly, the Ely, Haddenham and Sutton Railway opened in June 1864 and was at first independent of the GER. The company could see, however, that there was a risk of the GNR muscling in, so they paid a third of the capital, £36,000, to secure it. This had been finally implemented by April 1866.

In 1876, on 7 April, the Ely, Haddenham & Sutton Railway obtained powers to construct a line from Sutton to Needingworth Junction near St Ives on the line from Cambridge to St Ives. The Company was also authorised to change its name to the Ely and St Ives Railway.

Following an inspection of the line by Major-General Hutchinson for the Board of Trade on 3 May 1878, the line was ready for opening to passenger traffic. This took place on 10 May 1878. By an Act dated 21 July 1878 the Ely and St Ives Railway was leased to the GER for 999 years. In 1898 the GER absorbed the company.

The Wisbech and Upwell Tramway was not the only standard gauge roadside tramway in England to be able to provide a through service for goods traffic from the main line. The other one was the Wantage Tramway in Oxfordshire.

The first proposal to build a railway from Wisbech to Upwell was in 1873 when a Mr W.L. Offard obtained parliamentary powers to build a railway between the two places. Unfortunately, because of difficulties in raising the necessary capital, the scheme was not carried out. In 1880, the GER resurrected the proposal, but, rather than build a railway, decided to reduce the construction and operating costs by constructing a tramway to be worked by steam locomotives under the Tramways Act 1870. The Bill for the construction of the tramway was promoted in 1881 and in its original form included not only the line from Wisbech station via Elm Bridge and Boyce's Bridge and Outwell to Upwell but also a branch from Elm Bridge to Friday Bridge. This latter was abandoned as it did not comply with the Standing Orders of parliament. Another proposal for which the GER sought powers was for a line through the streets of Wisbech to the Market Place and there was much ill feeling locally at the Company's decision to abandon it and at a meeting of the Town Council Mr W.S. Collins remarked that the extension was vital to the trade of Wisbech. In fact, goods traffic was mostly sent directly on to the main line at Wisbech station for conveyance to London and other major markets. The Act for the construction of the tramway received its Royal Assent on 24 July 1882. Construction was soon put in hand and on 20 August 1883, the tramway was opened from Wisbech station to Outwell station. It is stated that 960 people travelled on the tramway on the first day of operation. The *Cambridge Independent Press* of Saturday 25 August reported that 'the Great Eastern Tramway, which is intended to be constructed to Upwell, was opened on Monday to the basin at Outwell'. On 8 September 1884, the tramway was extended from Outwell station to Upwell station. The *Lynn Advertiser* of Saturday 13 September reported that 'The Tramway to Upwell is now completed and on Monday trams commenced running the whole distance'.

As the tramway was intended as a goods line as well as a passenger line, it was built to the standard gauge of 4ft 8½in, with bull-head rails, rather than the grooved tramway rails favoured by many British tramways. This allowed standard goods wagons to run along it, without the need to tranship goods into wagons suitable for operating on tramway rails.

A reason for building the line as a tramway as opposed to an ordinary railway was to demonstrate that such construction could bring railways to rural areas which could not otherwise benefit from the new mode of transport. In doing this the GER had the support of the Board of Trade. Whilst goods rolling stock was normal railway goods rolling stock, passenger rolling stock was special tramway carriages of which four originally were built for the Millwall Extension Railway and another four built by the GER in 1884. All of the carriages except for the last two were four wheeled vehicles, but the last two were eight wheeled vehicles carried on two four-wheel bogies. The Company also built a new baggage van at the same time as the new carriages and allocated a brake van built in 1875 to the tramway. Motive power was provided by three 0-4-0 tram engines built in 1883 for the tramway and which had their wheels and motion enclosed by side

The Wisbech and Upwell Tramway was the GER's most celebrated branch line. Class G15 0-4-0 tram locomotive No 132 is seen on a passenger train on the tramway near Wisbech on 12 July 1912. (Ken Nunn).

plates and were fitted with cowcatchers. In appearance they looked rather like guard's vans, but with self-propulsion. Initially, trams were limited to a speed of 8 miles per hour and passengers could be picked up or dropped off at any point on the line. Most trains were mixed, with the passengers often having to wait while goods wagons were shunted.

In 1892, the Duke of York (later King George V) along with a distinguished list of well-known racing personalities signed a memorial to the Chairman and the Directors of the GER requesting the re-opening of the closed section of the former Newmarket and Chesterford Railway from Great Chesterford to Six Mile Bottom so that they could get to and from Newmarket directly without having to go via Cambridge. The memorial failed – bypassing Cambridge was a mortal sin.

Lines in Norfolk

The Lynn and Hunstanton Railway opened for traffic on 3 October 1862, just over two months after the formation of the GER. The success of the Lynn and Hunstanton Railway led businesses in north Norfolk to consider whether the north Norfolk coast east of Hunstanton could be developed by the construction of a railway.

Plans were drawn up for the construction of a railway from Heacham, which was the first station south of Hunstanton, to Wells via Docking, Burnham Market and Holkham. The West Norfolk Junction Railway, as the Railway was known, received its Act of Parliament on 23 June 1864. The Company had powers to run trains from Hunstanton to Wells Harbour. The GER subscribed £30,000 of the authorised capital of £75,000 of the Company and agreed to work the Railway for 50 per cent of gross receipts. The construction of the line went well and on 13 January 1866 (some sources say 8 January), several months prior to the official opening, the Prince and Princess of Wales made a private journey over the line to Holkham to visit the Earl of Leicester. There were shortcomings in the signalling arrangements and at first the Board of Trade's inspector refused to allow the line to open, but once the issues were overcome, the line opened to all traffic on 17 August 1866. The Railway was seriously affected by the failure of Overend, Gurney and Company's bank and an outbreak of cattle plague in north Norfolk, so in the final quarter of 1866 receipts amounted to only £1,355 and no dividend was paid.

Whilst the Railway rescued north-west Norfolk from isolation and saved it from the worst effects of the agricultural depression, it did so without stimulating any economic development of note. This in part was due to the fact that the course of the line was some distance from the coast and the towns and villages situated on it. In 1872, the West Norfolk Junction Railway amalgamated with the Lynn and Hunstanton Railway to form the Hunstanton and West Norfolk Railway, which in turn was acquired by the GER in 1890 on 1 July.

At Hunstanton in 1876 on 1 May the Sandringham Hotel was opened. It was built by the Lynn and Hunstanton Railway, but was not acquired by the GER until that company took over the Hunstanton and West Norfolk Railway in 1890.

1862 saw the opening of a short branch in King's Lynn, about three-quarters of a mile long, connecting the docks by the King's Lynn Docks and Railway Company. 1869 saw the completion of the Alexandra Dock which was linked by rail in 1870. According to Cecil J. Allen in *The Great Eastern Railway*, the King's Lynn Docks Branch opened on 10 June 1870.

In 1874 on 10 September there was a head on collision between two trains on the line from Norwich to Yarmouth at Thorpe St Andrew, involving the 8 40 pm mail train from Yarmouth to London and the 5 pm express from London to Yarmouth. The *Eastern Daily Press* of 11 September carried an article commencing:

Appalling Railway Accident At Thorpe. Fifteen people killed and 30 or 40 injured. Last night one of the most fearful railway accidents that has ever taken place in Norwich or its neighbourhood occurred at Thorpe, near this city, by which as far as can be ascertained at the time we left the spot, at least 15 persons were killed and 30 or 40 wounded.

The *Morning Post* of Saturday 12 September carried a similar report. 'Appalling Railway Accident. Norwich Friday. Last night one of the most appalling accidents which ever occurred took place on the GER between Norwich and Brundall.' Prior to 1866, the whole line had been single track, but in that year the section from Brundall to Reedham had been doubled. John Robson, the telegraph clerk, had, contrary to the rules, transmitted to Brundall permission for the mail train to proceed without having first obtained Alfred Cooper, the night inspector's signature to verify the instruction. On a technicality this perhaps cleared Cooper, except that he then returned to Robson specifically to cancel the previous message. On the two trains, the crews set off making speed in the belief that the other had been held for it. At about 9.45pm, near Thorpe village, they met head on with a crash that was described as like 'a peal of thunder'. Both locomotives reared into the air, and the carriages were reduced to wreckage. In the collision, the drivers and firemen of both trains were killed as were seventeen passengers and a further four who later died from their injuries. Seventy-three passengers and two guards were seriously injured. There was difficulty in apportioning blame for the accident. Norwich City Coroner's jury first indicted both Cooper and Robson for manslaughter, then the Norfolk County Coroner found against Robson only, but at Norwich Assizes in April, Robson was acquitted and Cooper was imprisoned for eighteen months.

Prompted by the Norwich accident, the engineer Edward Tyer developed the tablet system in which a token is given to the train driver which must be then slotted into an electric interlocking device at the other end of the single-track section before another train is allowed to pass.

In 1883 the Great Eastern Railway opened an alternative route from Norwich to Yarmouth via Acle. The line opened from Breydon Junction to Acle on 12 March, and through to Brundall on 1 June.

1 October 1879 saw the opening of the Wensum Curve at Norwich to enable trains to bypass Norwich Thorpe Station.

At Norwich itself, with traffic growing it became apparent that a new station was required. The new station was built to the north of the original station and opened on 3 May 1886, the old terminus becoming part of the expanded goods facilities. It cost £60,000 and was built by Messrs Youngs and Son, of Norwich, from the designs by Messrs J. Wilson and W.N. Ashbee, the Great Eastern Railway's engineer and architect respectively.

The East Norfolk Railway's ancestry goes back to 1859 when plans were deposited for a railway to serve Aylsham, Cromer and North Walsham, but nothing came of this. The East Norfolk Railway was incorporated in 1864 for a line from Whitlingham Junction to North Walsham. The GER offered to work the Railway for 50 per cent of its receipts. During the passage of the Company's bill through parliament, strong objections were raised by the Yarmouth Haven and Pier Commissioners and the North Walsham Dilham Canal, which regarded the Railway as unfair competition. Their objections were dismissed by parliament. Construction of the Railway began in 1865, but a snag arose; firstly, money was short, but secondly, the contractor, W.S. Simpson, died and work ceased. A new contractor, Messrs Lucas Brothers, was found and work recommenced in 1870. In 1872 it was found necessary to ask parliament for an extension of time to complete the Railway. Coupled with this request was authorisation of an extension of the Railway to Cromer, which was then a market town and rather select seaside town for those seeking peace and quiet and for whom the joy of being 22 miles from the nearest railway and the curse of excursionists was a particular recommendation for the town. *Bradshaw's Handbook* for 1865 describes Cromer thus: 'Cromer, a pleasant bathing place on the cliffs of the North Sea, is suffering from its encroachments, by which the land fast swallowed up, and converted into numerous shoals for coasters. Crabs, lobsters, amber and shells are got.' The decision to authorise the extension of the Railway to the town was not popular. The Railway was opened to North Walsham on 20 October 1874 and was extended to Gunton on 29 July 1876 and finally to Cromer on 26 March 1877. At Cromer, the terminus station, which came to be known as Cromer High, was situated to the south on the outskirts of the town on a steep escarpment. As to whether this gave some small comfort to those in the town who objected to the extension of the Railway there is not known. The GER worked the extension on the same terms as under the original Act. In 1881 the GER absorbed the East Norfolk Railway.

Under the Company's Act of 1864, plans were included for a line diverging south of Wroxham station to Aylsham, but in 1876 the plan, which had lapsed, was revived and modified, to leave the main line north of Wroxham station. The line was to run via Aylsham to a junction with the line from East Dereham to Fakenham and Wells. The line was built in a leisurely fashion. It opened to Burton Lamas on 8 July 1879, to Aylsham on 1 January 1880, to Reepham on 2 May 1881 and to the junction with the line to Fakenham and Wells on 1 May 1882. Trains ran through to East Dereham. Initially there was not a station at the junction, but on 1 March 1886 one was opened. It was called County School and was built to serve the private school from which it took its name.

In 1879, the East Norfolk Railway proposed building a branch line from Cawston to Cley and Blakeney, with an intermediate station planned for Holt. It was estimated that the cost of the line would be £300,000 but would generate only £7 per mile per week. The main intention of the proposed line was to block access by rival companies, not necessarily to make money. Not surprisingly, there was very little support for the proposed line, especially in Holt, especially as the station was going to be in Letheringsett, more than a mile away. Nothing came of the proposal.

On 2 May 1881, the GER opened a connecting line from Wymondham on the Norwich to Ely line to Forncett on the Ipswich to Norwich line, the intention being to give the line from Wells-next-the-Sea a connection into the Norwich to Liverpool Street trains at Forncett and vice versa; again, the intention was also to block any threats from rival companies in the area of north Norfolk. On 1 August 1882 the nominally independent Downham and Stoke Ferry Railway opened to Stoke Ferry from Denver on the line from Ely to Kings Lynn.

The railway was worked by the GER and taken over by it on 1 January 1898.

Lines in Metropolitan Essex

The NLR used the Fenchurch Street terminus of the L&BR as its London terminal. As the years progressed, the Company found that its passenger traffic from north-west London was increasing so much that a terminus in the City of London approached by a more direct route than that to Fenchurch Street was becoming desirable. In 1861, an Act was obtained for a line from Kingsland to Liverpool Street in the City of London. The L&NWR, which subscribed two-thirds of the NLR's stock and appointed 16 of the Company's 24 directors, was empowered to subscribe and make arrangements with the NLR for the use of the terminus by its own trains. The L&NWR demanded a half share of Broad Street station, as the new terminus came to be known, and in fact paid more towards the terminus than the NLR did. The new station and its associated extension line was formally opened on 31 October 1865 with public traffic beginning the next day. The NLR still also used Fenchurch Street station until 31 December 1868. The GER put on a replacement service to Bow on the NLR which ran until 3 April 1892. On 1 September 1870 the North London Railway extended a number of their Poplar trains to Blackwall. This ceased on 30 June 1890 and the connecting curve at Poplar, seeing little use after the cessation of the Blackwall trains from the NLR, was removed in August 1890, the connecting curve having lost much of its value after the opening of the Limehouse curve which was opened on 5 April 1880 and enabled trains to run direct from the L&BR to the GER at Bow Junction and via Gas Factory Junction on to the NLR at Bow.

Apart from being used by passenger trains between 1 September 1880 and 1 March 1881, it was only used by goods trains.

Following the creation of the GER in 1862, negotiations followed which led to the GER leasing the L&BR for a period of 999 years from 1 January 1866 under the L&BR Lease Act of 1865 guaranteeing the L&BR shareholders dividends of 4½ per cent on its ordinary stock. On 17 June 1864, the GER, with the assistance from the London and St Katherine's Dock Company, had opened a short branch line from the south side of the L&BR viaduct to a goods station called East Smithfield. When the goods station opened, the branch line terminated at a goods station on the north side of Upper East Smithfield, but this was changed when the lines were extended across the road into the dock premises on 1 September 1865. Rather than serve the entire dock, the line came to a halt at the Wool Warehouses and no further extensions were made.

Around 1870 the GNR constructed a goods station on the north side of the branch line to the East India Docks.

The Millwall Extension Railway's origins began in 1863 when the L&BR directors suggested the line, but their bill was refused the necessary parliamentary authority. The area for which it was intended to run the proposed line was described by Jim Connor in *Stepney's Own Railway* (Connor and Butler 1984) as 'desolate swamps' and that the entire district had once been known by the name 'Stepney Marsh'. Things however had begun to change with the development of the docks and, the L&BR being canny, decided to get their branch line built before the price of land rose higher than it was. So the Company made another application to parliament and this time it met with success. By an Act of 19 June 1865, the London, Blackwall and Millwall Extension Railway became a reality.

According to Jim Connor, the line was jointly promoted by the L&BR and the Millwall Canal Company, and that the latter was then actively engaged in the completion of their new Millwall Docks. Charles Hadfield in *Canals of the East Midlands (including part of London)* (David and Charles 1970) says that in 1864 a bill was introduced and passed by parliament to authorise the Millwall Canal Company to build a canal across the Isle of Dogs from Limehouse Reach, nearly opposite the Greenland Dock, to Blackwall Reach near Cubitt Town pier and from it a branch north towards the West India Docks, the purpose being to provide shipping wharves and other business accommodation for shipbuilding and other businesses needing waterside premises. In part following the authorisation of a railway branch line in 1865 from the L&BR, the plan was much changed. In March 1868 the western half of the original plan and the branch, both much enlarged, were opened as a dock and in 1870 the Company's name was changed to the Millwall Dock Company.

According to Jim Connor, the railway branch line was designed to leave the main line at a junction near Harrow Lane, Poplar and then run southwards to a riverside terminus in Johnson Street, which was about 200 yards from the jetty that was used by the Greenwich ferries. Apart from serving trade and industry around Millwall, one of the principal aims of the new line was to link Fenchurch Street with those ferries. The name given to the terminus of the branch was North Greenwich.

The Millwall Canal Company's General Manager was the brother of the GER's General Manager, which meant that the two companies were on good terms with each other. Not so in the case of the Railway Company and the East and West India Docks company, which saw the new line as a threat to them. During the passage of the Railway Company's Bill through parliament, the Docks Company made numerous technical objections about the line's construction. Its real complaint was that its existence would give the Millwall Canal Company a right of way over its property. Eventually, after a lot of arguing and following the intervention of an arbitrator, the opposition dropped from 21 March 1865, when the companies concerned reached an agreement concerning the line's operation. Under this, the sections of the line which passed through the Dock Company's premises was built, owned and controlled by that Company and not to be worked by locomotive power. The agreement also stipulated that if the L&BR wished to operate a locomotive hauled passenger train service to the Isle of Dogs, another line would have to be built under the Dock Company's premises instead of the proposed surface railway. Both the Canal and the Dock companies eventually contributed to the construction of the line, controlling it through a joint committee on which the GER was also represented. Ownership of the line was as follows: the first 110 yards were owned by the Railway Company; the next 902 yards were owned by the East and West India Docks Company; then 1,144 yards owned by the Millwall Docks Company; and finally 682 yards by the Railway Company, making a total of 1 mile and 1,078 yards.

Construction of the line was a bit of a protracted affair. By the end of 1867 only a short section between the junction and the south side of the West India

Docks was ready for use. The following year, parliament granted an extension of time for the completion of the Railway until 1871. On 18 December 1871 the Railway was opened to Millwall Docks and the following year it was extended to North Greenwich on 29 July.

Initially, at least, operation of this very short railway was a somewhat complex affair. When the line first opened in 1871, both passenger and goods traffic was worked by horses. The passenger service using single carriages. The complex bit started with the extension to North Greenwich in 1872. The section from the junction at Millwall to the southern boundary of the Millwall Docks was worked by horses, but on the final section a small steam locomotive took over. The first was a small 2-4-0 tank locomotive, which had originally been built in 1851 as a 2-2-0 tank locomotive named *Ariel's Girdle* and had been exhibited at the Great Exhibition of that year. It had been rebuilt to a 2-4-0 tank locomotive in 1868. In 1878 it was replaced by a 4 wheeled steam tram locomotive, this having been hauled over the line with its fire out by horses. In 1874, the GER, which owned the Blackwall to Greenwich steam ferry, took over the operation of the long-established ferry boat service between North Greenwich and Greenwich itself. The Railway Company had acquired the ferry from the Poplar and Greenwich Railway and Steam Ferry Company. In 1877 the Company's pier was replaced by a new one near the station. The mixture of horse and steam traction continued until 1880 when the Millwall Dock Company purchased three small 2-4-0 tank locomotives from the locomotive building company Manning Wardle. These small lightweight locomotives had tall chimneys and were fitted with spark arresters to stop any stray sparks setting fire to anything in the docks. Carriages were provided by the GER.

The Tottenham & Hampstead Junction Railway (T&HJR) was an independent company that was incorporated by its Act of 28 July 1862 to build a railway from Tottenham North Junction on the GER to Highgate Road. According to G.H. Lake in *The Railways of Tottenham* (Greenlake Publications 1945), this was the first tangible result of the many proposals for linking the Cambridge main line at Tottenham with the western districts of London. Prior to the Company receiving its Act, at a meeting of the Norfolk Railway in June 1862 at which a number of Bills were submitted to parliament including one for the amalgamation of the Eastern Counties, Eastern Union and Norfolk railway into the GER, there was also the Bill for the incorporation of the T&HJR. At the meeting of the Norfolk

Railway, the Chairman said that the T&HJR Bill was an important one and that the united companies would work the railway for 46 per cent of the receipts. The Railway opened on 21 July 1868 and the first service over the line was from Fenchurch Street to Highgate Road. Unfortunately, the T&HJR were soon in financial troubles and on 31 January the GER declined to continue working the Railway any longer for passenger traffic.

Meanwhile, in 1868 the MR had opened a new line from Bedford to St Pancras station in London to which there was a connection from Kentish Town to the T&HJR at Junction Road. This opened on 3 January 1870. In August, a local act was passed which abandoned the railway in its original form. On 3 July 1870, the MR started a service from Moorgate on the Metropolitan Railway to Crouch Hill.

In 1870, the MR, having been granted running powers to run its goods trains over the GER to the docks at Poplar and other points in the docklands, gave the GER running powers for its passenger trains into St Pancras station. This had the effect of giving the GER a west end terminus. GER trains started running into St Pancras on 1 July 1870. On 1 May 1871, a station was opened at South Tottenham, to which on that date the MR extended its service from Moorgate. In that year an attempt was made to transfer the T&HJR to the GER and MR, but it was thrown out by parliament. Although the GER and MR did not jointly own the T&HJR, from 1 January 1885 the working of the Railway was put on a joint basis. In that year a curve was opened between Hall Farm Junction and Copper Mill Junction on the GER and 1 August of that year a service was started between Chingford or Wood Street, Walthamstow and Highgate Road. On 4 June 1888, an extension of the Railway to Gospel Oak on the Hampstead Junction Railway was opened. In 1902 the GER and the MR jointly acquired the T&HJR.

Bradshaw's Railway Guide for August 1887 shows the GER operating services over the line from Highgate Road to Chingford, whilst the MR operated services over the line from Moorgate to South Tottenham.

Bradshaw's Railway Guide for December 1895 shows the GER operating services over the line from Gospel Oak to Chingford, whilst the MR operated services over the line from Moorgate to South Tottenham.

The principal piece of construction during the period was the building of Liverpool Street and its subsequent enlargement. Bound up with this is the construction of the line from Bethnal Green to Edmonton to link up with the line to Enfield. Additionally, there were the construction of the lines to Chingford and later to Palace Gates and from Edmonton to Cheshunt. In the docklands there were the lines from Custom House to Beckton and Custom House to Gallions. There was also the link to the ELR and the involvement or rather attempts of the Metropolitan Railway to get running powers over part of the GER.

Bishopsgate station was not the most conveniently situated London terminus. But then none of the London termini apart from Fenchurch Street were. Paddington was probably the worst situated. Paddington's bad location was not the actual cause of the building of the Metropolitan Railway – the world's first underground railway – but it did however improve its communication with the rest of London.

According to *Liverpool Street Station* (Academy Editions 1978), following the NLR obtaining its Act in 1861 to build a line from Kingsland to Liverpool Street (Broad Street) in the City of London, the ECR presented a Bill to parliament in 1862 for a line from the Cambridge main line at Tottenham to the NLR at Kingsland and then share the extension line to Broad Street. The ECR's case for the scheme was both ill prepared and unimpressive. The problems of crossing the NLR on the level at Kingsland had not been thought out and no one had found out if Broad Street station could accommodate the extra trains. The engineer William Baker, speaking on behalf of the NLR, said that there would be no room for the ECR's trains and that the Eastern Counties Railway ought not to force its traffic over the NLR's line to save itself at the latter's convenience. The ECR ought to have an independent line and an independent station. While it is true that the ECR was trying to save money, the joint line would have disturbed less property. But it would have only solved half the problem as the Stratford and Colchester lines would have still been using Bishopsgate, making sensible working of the Railway even more difficult. The Commons committee that examined the Bill rejected it.

According to Alan A. Jackson in *London's Termini* (David and Charles 1968), in a report to the GER Board dated 17 December 1862 the manager and engineer recommended the construction of a new passenger terminus inside the City of London, the development of suburban traffic by the construction of new lines and the conversion of Bishopsgate station to a goods station.

At the first half yearly meeting of the GER on 27 February 1863, the Directors reported that they had given 'their most serious attention to the position of the GER in the metropolis, and to the necessity which exists for an improved and more conveniently situated Terminus'. They found that 'all the Great Railway Companies entering London are making efforts to obtain new and central Stations'.

In their report, the Directors said that they found Bishopsgate 'objectionable in almost every feature'. It was remote, its approaches were inconvenient and it was restricted for space so that traffic could only be carried with great delay and with an absolute restriction on the number of trains that could be despatched. According to the report, the station did not afford the accommodation which was necessary for the public convenience or more especially for the conduct of the Company's goods traffic. Accordingly, the Directors, having carefully considered the best position for the site of the new terminus, decided that Finsbury Circus would be the best position for the new terminus, where there was a large amount of land available, and that the existing terminus should be converted to a goods station. They felt that a Finsbury Circus terminus would be convenient for the Bank of England, the Royal Exchange and all principal places of business and would ultimately be placed in immediate connection with the proposed extension of the Metropolitan Railway, the latter having opened the previous month from Paddington to Farringdon. The Directors said that they were anxious to remedy the inconvenience to local traffic which had resulted from the original laying out of the Cambridge line a long distance from the high road along which the course of the suburban traffic flowed. They therefore proposed an extension from Bishopsgate station to Finsbury Circus and an extension commencing at Enfield and following the course of the direct high road from there to London collecting traffic from the districts of Enfield, Edmonton, Tottenham, Stamford Hill and Stoke Newington and 'discharging the same at Finsbury Circus'. The extension by avoiding the detour to Stratford would save 3 miles on the journey out of London to the Lea Valley and beyond. It would also remove the complications which existed at the Stratford and the Shoreditch stations and would enable arrangements to be made for the increase of local trains on that part of the system. The report said that the Directors, having resolved on proposing the extension, had been in communication with the London and North Western and North London railway companies and were happy to report that they were promoting the extension with the other companies' agreement on terms which would result in considerable saving to all the companies. The estimated cost of the extensions would be £1.2million. In this latter, given what was said earlier, there does appear to be some contradiction.

It is quite clear that even before the half yearly meeting of 27 February, the Directors of the GER had decided to press ahead with the proposed new terminus in Finsbury Square, as the *Norwich Chronicle* of 21 February 1863 reported that a Bill was before parliament for the extension of the GER to Finsbury Circus, but that it was meeting violent opposition from the inhabitants of the neighbourhood of the proposed terminus. This effect of opposition was confirmed at the second half yearly meeting of the GER on 13 August 1863. It was reported that the Bill for the construction of the Metropolitan Extensions and new Terminus had met powerful opposition from various quarters and had been thrown out in the Second Reading and had therefore not been submitted to a Committee of either House. According to the book *Liverpool Street Station*, an additional reason for the bill being thrown out was that being on a viaduct it could not make a connection with the Metropolitan Railway when its underground railway was extended east from Moorgate Street, the Metropolitan Railway having obtained its Act to extend eastward from Farringdon to Moorgate Street on 6 August 1861. However, the Select Committee appointed by the House of Lords to enquire generally into the system of Metropolitan Railway Communication had reported in favour of such a station by the GER Company alone and had recommended 'that for the present no other of the great Companies should be allowed to bring their stations farther into the Metropolis'. The Directors said that 'the question of a central station will therefore occupy the serious attention of your Directors before the next meeting of Parliament, the necessity for that accommodation as well as for the more convenient conduct of the goods traffic becoming daily more urgent'.

At the third half yearly meeting of the GER held on 18 February 1864 the Directors said that they were seeking powers to build a line from the Enfield branch to Mile End, connecting with the main line at Tottenham and carrying the present line to a new City terminus at the back of Broad Street, with an approach from Bishopsgate Street at the corner of Wormwood Street. They were also seeking powers to build a line from near Leyton (Loughton Branch Junction), Stratford, through Walthamstow and Chingford Green to High Beech Green. High Beech was and is a village in Epping Forest and is the only settlement inside the Forest. They said that the NLR was applying for powers to construct a line from Hackney to Walthamstow which afforded an additional inducement for the construction of the line. There was also mention of the Tottenham and Farringdon Railway. This was an independent company proposing to build a railway from the GER at Tottenham to a junction with the London, Chatham and Dover Railway (LC&DR) at Farringdon. If the company was successful, the GER would provide one third of the capital of the Company; nothing came of this latter proposal – or the NLR's proposal.

Regarding the Wormwood Street proposal, during its passage through parliament it was subject to all kinds of objections, forcing the railway back to Liverpool Street. However, the idea of putting the line on a viaduct was retained even though this put the proposed station thirty or forty feet above the Metropolitan Railway, so preventing any physical connection with it. Whilst any scheme for the new terminus would either have to go over or under the existing roads, that for going over would at least have the advantage of not having difficult gradients. The Act of 29 July 1864 – the GER (Metropolitan Station and Railways) Act – authorised not only the construction of the new line from the old ECR viaduct at Tapp Street (just west of Bethnal Green station) but also the lines from Bethnal Green to Lower Edmonton and Hackney Downs to Copper Mill Junction on the Northern and Eastern Railway (N&ER) line (the detour avoiding Stratford). At this stage the new terminus was going to be built as a high level station. Other features of this scheme were the doubling of the Enfield branch outwards from Lower Edmonton, links with the then proposed Tottenham and Hampstead Junction Railway (T&HJR) (both of these being completed) and a link with the North London Railway (NLR) at Hackney, which was never built, although a footway connection between the two companies' stations at Hackney was opened on 1 December 1885. Another Act obtained in 1864 was for the earlier mentioned Leyton (Loughton Branch Junction) Stratford, through Walthamstow and Chingford Green to High Beech. In 1865, under the GER (Additional Powers) Act of 19 June that year, the GER obtained powers for a branch line from Tottenham to Winchmore Hill and a loop line from Lower Edmonton to Ordnance Factory (Enfield Lock). Neither of these lines was ever built. On the same day that the GER obtained its Act to build the new terminus and the associated lines and the Metropolitan Railway obtained an Act to build a line from Moorgate to Trinity Square, Tower Hill via

Liverpool Street – as the new terminus has always been known – and Aldgate. As the line to the new terminus involved the destruction of a lot of properties, the former Act required the GER to run one 2d return train daily from Lower Edmonton and one also from Walthamstow. William Birt, the General Manager of the GER, in evidence on 16 May 1884 to the Royal Commission on the Housing of the Working Classes, said that the construction of the line to the new terminus involved the destruction of 450 tenement dwellings sheltering 7,000 families. Some of the houses had been occupied by as many as seven families and were probably the worst of their kind in London. The construction of the new line also saw the destruction of the City of London Theatre and the City of London Gas Works. Unfortunately, those thrown out of their houses were too poor to afford new houses in the suburbs and travel on the new cheap trains. Instead, they migrated to the adjacent streets and so increasing already pitiable overcrowding that existed in the Shoreditch area.

The building of the new lines was fraught with difficulty. Properties had to be bought up. There were problems raising the money as the GER was going through a rather anxious period of financial stress as mentioned earlier. The book *Liverpool Street Station* quotes an incident recorded by the *Railway Times* in February 1867. A widow who was carrying out the business of a 'paper stainer' in Norton Folgate (the northward extension of Bishopsgate) agreed to sell her property to the Company in October 1865. That December she left the premises and set up business elsewhere. Fourteen months later, the GER had still not completed the purchase of her property. The court ordered the Company to make payment before the end of the month including 4 per cent interest on the original purchase price of £1,300.

To compound matters, in 1870 the Company successfully submitted a Bill to parliament altering the levels of the line into Liverpool Street and making a connection with the Metropolitan Railway.

In building the new terminus as a low level station, there was clearly no thought given to the locomotive crews who were faced with starting heavily laden trains up a rather steep incline.

And then there was the matter of the ELR. The ELR Company was incorporated under an Act dated 26 May 1865 with powers to build a railway from Old Kent Road Junction on the London, Brighton and South Coast Railway (LB&SCR) and from junctions with that Railway and with the South

Eastern Railway (SER) at New Cross, through Surrey Dock, the Thames Tunnel, Whitechapel and Shoreditch to a link with the GER at Liverpool Street. Without the alteration of Liverpool Street station from a high level to a low level station, the connection to the GER would have been rather difficult and would have involved a rather steep incline. According to Charles E. Lee in *The East London Line and the Thames Tunnel* (London Transport 1976), 'tentative arrangements were made to build the Shoreditch – Liverpool Street section jointly, but the plan fell through. Eventually, an agreement with the Great Eastern dated 17 December 1869, secured to the East London running powers into Liverpool Street'. Lee also mentions an associated company called the East London (Eastern Extension) Railway which was incorporated by an Act of 6 August 1866 to build a 3½ mile long line from the ELR at Whitechapel to West Ham. This project failed to materialise. The ELR took over the pedestrian-only Thames Tunnel from Wapping to Rotherhithe and which had been designed by Sir Marc Isambard Brunel. It had originally been intended for both vehicles and pedestrians. Work had started in 1825 and suffered a number of accidents. Sir Marc's son, the famous Isambard Kingdom Brunel, was the engineer in charge from 1825 to 1828. After an accident in 1828 work was suspended on the tunnel for over seven years and did not resume until 1835. The tunnel was eventually completed in 1835 – but without the intended roadway access. The ELR acquired the Thames Tunnel on 25 September 1865 from the original owners, the Thames Tunnel Company. Under the new owners the tunnel continued in use as a public footway and was not closed until 20 July 1869. Following a formal opening on 6 December 1869 the ELR was opened between Wapping and Shadwell station and a temporary station alongside the LB&SCR at New Cross on 7 December 1869 and was worked by the LB&SCR with its own locomotives and rolling stock under an agreement dated 17 November 1869. On 13 March 1871 the section of line from Deptford Road Junction to Old Kent Road Junction was opened. This section was also worked by the London, Brighton and South Coast Railway.

Liverpool Street Station gives a description of the route to the now level Liverpool Street Station. The line left the existing line to Bishopsgate at what was then called Winchester Street, passed under the approach tracks to Bishopsgate Station, then under Commercial Street and Shoreditch High Street. As it descended, the line turned south so that all of those crossings were at unusual angles which required carefully designed brickwork. Having turned south, the new line ran parallel with Norton Folgate and Bishopsgate into the terminus, passing under Worship Street, Primrose Street and what was then called Skinner Street and Sun Street. The GER obtained permission to remove the last named street once work on the station had started. As the new terminus was seventeen feet below ground level and even lower from the level of the tracks of the adjacent Broad Street Station, the contractors, Lucas Brothers, had the problem of not only excavating the site, but also under-pinning the NLR's viaduct as they did so. They also had to shore up houses on the east side of the site. At this time Liverpool Street only had the thirteen platforms of the west side.

The GER (Metropolitan Station and Railways) Act of 1864 allowed the building of a line from Leyton via Walthamstow and Chingford to High Beech Green and the connection to the line from Hackney Downs to Copper Mill Junction at Clapton Junction. As mentioned earlier, the GER's difficult financial situation in 1867 had led to the appointment of a receiver. On the line to Walthamstow, Chingford and High Beech Green, work had progressed to the point where an embankment had been built from west Walthamstow down to the Lea Valley, but work ceased when the GER had been unable to pay Lucas Brothers. In 1868 it became necessary for the GER to apply for an extension of time to complete the works authorised under the acts of 1864. At Walthamstow, James Higham, who had built some houses in Walthamstow, wanted to get the railway built to Walthamstow. Higham had objected to the provision in the GER (Metropolitan Station and Railways) Act of 1864 that required it to offer one 2d return train daily from Lower Edmonton and one also from Walthamstow. It should be explained that the new lines were in essence directed at a middle class market and Higham did not want what I suspect he would have described as 'the lower orders' invading his new development for 'the middle orders'. Higham had unsuccessfully promoted a competing scheme to that from Hall Farm Junction via Walthamstow and Chingford to High Beech. His line would have run from a junction just north of Stratford station. Higham went to the GER and offered to muster cash to secure a railway as far as there. According to Alan A. Jackson in *London's Local Railways*, 'all this no doubt influenced Parliament for its granting the extension of time, it insisted the GER build a branch into Walthamstow from its Lea Valley line'. Somehow money was scraped together for this line which was a single track branch over the alignment used by the contractors for building the earlier mentioned embankment. On 26 April 1870, trains began running between Lea Bridge station and a temporary terminus in Walthamstow called Shern Hall Street.

On the new lines authorised under the Metropolitan Station and Railways Act, although the construction of Liverpool Street station had been delayed by financial difficulties, the section of line from Bethnal Green Junction to Stoke Newington was opened on 27 May 1872, followed on 22 June by the section from Hackney Downs Junction to Clapton and to Copper Mill Junction. On the same day, the Enfield branch from Bury Street Junction to Enfield became doubled. On the remnant of the original branch to Enfield, the only passenger services to remain were workmen's trains. Also, on 1 August 1872 it became possible to work a half hourly service from Bishopsgate to Shern Hall Street (Walthamstow) over the newly completed double track between Hall Farm Junction and Hackney Downs. From the information in the February 1875 working timetable, Bishopsgate main station seems to have become known as Bishopsgate (North).

In 1869, powers were granted to abandon the planned branch Walthamstow and Chingford line from Leyton to High Beech Green subject to the presentation

In some ways, Bethnal Green Junction was the most important junction on the GER. It was here, just east of Liverpool Street, that the Cambridge and Colchester main lines divided. The Cambridge line is on the left and the Colchester line on the right. (Author's collection).

in the following session of parliament for a Bill to extend the line from Shern Hall Street (Walthamstow) over the northern end of the High Beech alignment as far as Chingford Green. This was duly sanctioned in 1870 together with the Lea Bridge-St James's Street (Walthamstow) spur which had been built in advance of parliamentary authority. At Wood Street (Walthamstow) the extension deviated to the east from the original 1864 alignment, possibly for reasons connected to land purchase. On 17 November 1873, passenger trains were extended over a newly doubled line between Hall Farm Junction and Shern Hall Street to a terminus in Bull Lane, Chingford. Not all trains ran through to Chingford. With the extension to Chingford, Shern Hall Street station was closed and replaced by one in Wood Street, serving the eastern part of Walthamstow. To finish the story of the Chingford branch, on 2 September 1878 the line was extended a short distance north to a new station in Chingford. The final act, if you like, was in 1883 when a Bill was promoted for a line from Chingford via Sewardstone to a point three-quarters of a mile north of High Beech. On 6 May that year, Queen Victoria travelled to Chingford in the Great Western Railway's royal train hauled by a GER 0-4-4 tank locomotive (No 189) to declare Epping Forest open to the public. Opposition to the desecration of the Forest by a railway was very easily aroused and so the extension was killed for all time.

On 2 February 1874 the section of line from Bishopsgate (Low Level) to Liverpool Street station was opened for suburban traffic. The *Pall Mall Gazette* of that day carried an announcement which said that on and after Monday 2 February 1874 local passenger trains from Enfield, Walthamstow, Edmonton via Stratford and Forest Gate would run to and from Liverpool Street station.

On 1 February 1875, the Metropolitan Railway was extended from Moorgate into Liverpool Street station. The railway ran via a connecting curve into Platforms 1 and 2. This curve had the name 'Queen Victoria's Curve', although Queen Victoria is never known to have used it in any of her railway journeys. On 12 July 1875, the Metropolitan Railway opened its own station at Liverpool Street named Bishopsgate (for the Bank) and trains of the Metropolitan and also the Metropolitan District Railway which jointly ran a service from Mansion House via Victoria, South Kensington, High Street Kensington, Edgware Road and King's Cross to Bishopsgate (as I shall call the Metropolitan station) ceased running into Liverpool Street main line station. After that, only the occasional goods, special or excursion train used the connection.

Monday, 1 November 1875 saw the opening of Liverpool Street station to all passenger traffic and the *Evening Standard* of that day carried an announcement to that effect and that Bishopsgate (High Level) station would be closed for all passenger traffic on that day. The *Daily News* of that day said that 'The GER Company will open its new passenger terminus at Liverpool Street today. The Bishopsgate terminus is to be used as a goods depot'. The same newspaper of the following day in reporting the opening carried a brief description of the new terminus. The *Morning Post* of 2 November also carried an article on the new terminus.

Just over a year later, on 18 November 1876, the Metropolitan Railway extended its line from Bishopsgate station to Aldgate station.

According to Alan A. Jackson in *London's Metropolitan Railway* (David and Charles 1986), the original intention of the Metropolitan Railway had been to run its trains over the GER through to Walthamstow, but after initial disputes over the terms of working, the Metropolitan Railway and the GER argued over the routes for the through service. The Metropolitan Railway wanted to run its trains to south London via the ELR, but the GER not unreasonably argued that

The exterior of the West Side of Liverpool Street station in the 1900s showing a plentiful array of hansom cabs in the cab roads. To the left of the station can just be seen part of the NLR's Broad Street station. (Author's collection).

The Great Eastern Railway From its Formation in 1862 to the End of 1895 69

An interior view of the Western train shed of Liverpool Street station in the 1900s showing the carriage sidings between Platforms 9 and 10 and the footbridge connecting the two parts of the station. Observe the horse box attached to the carriages at Platform 9. (Author's collection).

this would have involved crossing all the approach tracks to Liverpool Street on the level. From a reading of the Directors' Reports of the GER, it is clear that had Liverpool Street station been built as a high level station, the ELR was to make a low level connection with the Metropolitan Railway at Liverpool Street. The Report to the 12th half yearly meeting of 7 August 1868 says that 'By a contract made in 1865, and confirmed by parliament, the East London Company, wishing to construct an underground railway under that portion of the Great Eastern extension which takes the present Great Eastern line to a station in Liverpool Street, bound themselves to pay for half the land taken by the Great Eastern'. From reading the Directors' Reports, the GER and the ELR had a bit of a long running dispute over the payment for the use of Liverpool Street station.

Returning to the Metropolitan Railway, the GER suggested either a service to Chingford or along the main line and on to the Loughton branch. The discussions ran into the sand. Following the extension of the ELR from Wapping to a junction with the GER on 10 April 1876, through bookings were started between Metropolitan Railway stations and the LB&SCR via the ELR with passengers having to walk between the Metropolitan Railway and GER stations at Liverpool Street.

The ELR was extended north from Wapping to a junction with the GER on 10 April 1876, following an agreement with the GER dated 17 December 1869. Initially, the service was worked by the LB&SCR using its famous Class A1 0-6-0 tank locomotives known popularly as 'Terriers'.

Meanwhile, in the latter part of 1874 a line had been constructed from Deptford Road Junction to a point on the Up side of New Cross (London, Brighton and South Coast Railway) station and both Up and Down junctions with the SER at its New Cross station. These do not appear to have been brought into regular use immediately. Following the opening to the GER, the LB&SCR introduced through carriages from Liverpool Street to Brighton from June 1875 which became a daily through train between 1 November 1876 and September 1884, although it only comprised through carriages from June 1883. A regular service was begun between Liverpool Street and New Croydon, which was then the name of the local side of East Croydon station. The use of the ELR station at New Cross (London, Brighton and South Coast Railway) ceased on 1 November 1876 and all trains used the LB&SCR station.

In building the extension to the GER, the ELR had experienced serious financial difficulties in raising the capital and its Chairman, William Hawes, approached the financial house of Grant Brothers and Company in 1872.

The south-western terminus of the Railway at Old Kent Road was a wayside two platform station and was rather inconvenient as a terminus. This was one of a number of differences between the ELR and the London, Brighton and South Coast Railway about the working and the development of the Railway's traffic and an appeal was made to the Railway Commissioners who gave judgement in favour of the ELR on 1 August 1876; on 1 August 1877 the Old Kent Road service was extended to Peckham Rye.

The ELR's acute financial difficulties resulted in a reorganisation of its board of directors and Sir Edward William Watkin was appointed Chairman. Watkin was also the Chairman of the MS&LR, the Metropolitan Railway and the South Eastern Railway. The new policy that was adopted by the ELR was to bring it into closer connection with the Metropolitan Railway and to build a line from Aldgate to Whitechapel. The Chairman of the Metropolitan District Railway was James Staats Forbes, who was also the Chairman of the LC&DR and was the opponent of Watkin. It would be quite true to say that the two chairmen conducted a feud which involved the construction of a large number of railway lines in Kent which otherwise might not necessarily have been built. The railway map of Kent was rather crowded compared to that of Essex on the north side of the Thames. The two chairmen may not have exactly been the greatest of friends, but the pressure of events induced them to work more or less harmoniously in the completion of the Inner Circle which in 1879 extended from Mansion House via Victoria, South Kensington, High Street Kensington, Edgware Road and King's Cross to Aldgate. On 11 August 1879, the Metropolitan and Metropolitan District (City Lines and Extensions) Act was passed authorising the two companies to build a jointly owned line from Aldgate to Mansion House and an extension from the neighbourhood of Aldgate to effect a junction with the East London at Whitechapel.

Meanwhile, under the agreement of 1869 with the London, Brighton and South Coast Railway, it was provided that the South Eastern and the London, Chatham and Dover might participate on the giving of six months' notice in the ELR. The LC&DR never did as it did not have any junctions with the SER which would have allowed it to do so. The SER did participate in the ELR. On 30 June 1879 it gave due notice and commenced running from Liverpool Street to Addiscombe Road station in Croydon on 1 April 1880.

Prior to the development of the Kent coalfields in the early part of the twentieth century, house coal from the north of England for distribution in both south London and further afield including Brighton and Maidstone was an important source of revenue for the ELR. Access to the northern end of the Railway was rather difficult and trains were limited to 26 wagons and had to be shunted into Liverpool Street station and then drawn forward to the ELR. It was also difficult for any excursion train to or from the Great Eastern and the London, Brighton and South Coast and South Eastern railways. To avoid this reversal, a line which was intended primarily for goods traffic was planned from the ELR north of Whitechapel to the GER at Bethnal Green. Acts for this were passed in 1866 and 1868. Work was actually begun on the tunnel which had been passed under the 1866 Act, but was abandoned for lack of funds. When the GER route to Hackney Downs Junction was constructed in 1872, the route was altered to connect at Cambridge Heath. A short length of the tunnel authorised under an Act of 1877 was built.

The connecting line between the three railways (ELR, Metropolitan Rky & MDR) was somewhat modified from that authorised in 1879. The junction was not at Whitechapel, where a separate station was built by the Metropolitan District Railway, but at a higher level to the ELR station. East of the Inner Circle, the new line passed through two stations – Aldgate East and St Mary's Whitechapel. Under an Act dated 10 August 1882, the East London Railway obtained powers to build a curve called the Whitechapel Junction Railway from a point south of its Whitechapel station to near the new St Mary's Whitechapel station.

The Act of 1882 also established the ELR Joint Committee comprising the London, Brighton and South Coast, the South Eastern, the London, Chatham and Dover and the Metropolitan and the Metropolitan District railways, which should lease the ELR in perpetuity. The lease came into effect on 1 October 1884. Power was also given to the GER to join the Committee, which it did in 1885. Under the Act of 1882, provision was made for the maintenance and staffing of the East London to be undertaken by the London, Brighton and South Coast Railway. In 1885 the maintenance work was taken over by the South Eastern Railway. The first section of the new lines to be opened was the Whitechapel Junction Railway on 3 March 1884, when the SER diverted its Addiscombe Road trains to St Mary's Whitechapel instead of Liverpool Street.

On 1 October 1884, the Metropolitan and the Metropolitan District railways began local services on the ELR to New Cross (SER) and New Cross (ELR) as a temporary arrangement. For this the ELR station at New Cross had to be reopened and continued to be used until 31 August 1886 when trains were transferred to the adjacent London, Brighton and South Coast Railway station. 1 October 1884 also saw the Whitechapel Junction Railway transferred to the Metropolitan and the Metropolitan District Railways Joint Committee under the powers of an Act dated 14 July 1884. On 6 October 1884, the Inner Circle was finally completed and Metropolitan Railway trains began running between Hammersmith (Hammersmith and City Joint Railway) and New Cross (South Eastern Railway) via the northern part of the Inner Circle whilst Metropolitan District railway trains began running between Hammersmith (Metropolitan District Railway) and New Cross (London, Brighton and South Coast Railway) via the southern part of the Inner Circle.

On 1 August 1895, a direct stairway was opened at Shadwell between the ELR station and the L&BR station.

On 31 December 1885, the London, Brighton and South Coast Railway ceased running into Liverpool Street station and on 1 January 1886 the GER took over the service from there to New Cross (LB&SCR). From 1 February 1887, some of the trains were extended on weekdays to New Croydon. Goods traffic was transferred to the London, Brighton and South Coast and South Eastern railways at their respective New Cross stations.

Something that is sometimes overlooked is that certainly after the creation of the South Eastern and Chatham Railway (SE&CR) in 1899, on at least three occasions royal trains were worked by locomotives of that Company from Dover into Liverpool Street station via the ELR. Ken Nunn photographed D Class locomotive No 740 at Liverpool Street in 1912 on such a working and it is known in August 1910 and August 1913 E class locomotive No 19 was similarly employed on such a working. The only other company's locomotives to work in to Liverpool Street were those of the LT&SR and later the MR on boat trains from Tilbury Docks.

The 'Palace of the People', renamed Alexandra Palace to commemorate the popular new Princess of Wales, was first thought of in 1863 when the Alexandra Park Co. Ltd. acquired the land of Tottenham Wood Farm for conversion to a park and to build the Palace; the grounds were opened to the public on 23 July 1863. Construction of the Palace began in September 1865. On 24 May 1873 the Palace was opened to the public on the same day that a branch line from Highgate to the Palace from the GNR's line from Finsbury Park to Edgware and High Barnet was opened. The branch line had been promoted by the Muswell Hill Estate and Railway Company incorporated in 1866. Sixteen days later the Palace was destroyed by fire and did not reopen until 1 May 1875.

Under its Act of 1866, the GER, wanting to get a slice of the excursion traffic to Alexandra Palace and Park, included powers for a line 1 mile 2 furlongs and 9 chains that curved west and then north through Alexandra Park to a point just south of what later became Friern Hospital where it would have made an end on junction with a 3 mile, 1 furlong 7 chains branch line that had been authorised by the GER Act of 1866 from the proposed Enfield (Town) line at Seven Sisters. The loop line round the back of Alexandra Palace included a chord that would have allowed through running from Highgate to Seven Sisters. According to Alan A. Jackson in *London's Local Railways*, this would have involved some interesting engineering to bring the tracks down from the top of the hill into the Lea Valley. Amongst the proposed lines of what Jackson describes as 'dubious merit' that the GER went to parliament in 1869 with a Bill to discard, was this one. In 1871, the Muswell Hill Estate and Railway Company obtained powers to abandon the bits of its 1866 Act that were rendered unnecessary by the GER's withdrawal.

Although the GER was not interested in building what Jackson calls 'a mountain railway up to the Palace', it did feel the need to fill in the gap that existed between the Enfield (Town) branch and the GNR main line should another rival company show an interest in building a line there. In the GER's Act of 1874 there was included a short branch from Seven Sisters following more or less the alignment of that included in the 1866 Act to a point in Bounds Green that was very close to the GNR's Wood Green station, although there was no provision for a connection between the two companies. As there was clearly still some intention of catering for the Alexandra Palace traffic, the terminal station named 'somewhat deceitfully' Palace Gates was rather extra spacious. The double track branch was opened in two stages. From Seven Sisters to Green Lanes on 1 January 1878 and then to Palace Gates on 7 October 1878.

As early as 1864 the GER had considered a second line up the western side of the Lea Valley in the hope of attracting business from the ribbon development that grew up along the Hertford Road, the adjacent market gardens and the popularity of the Lea Valley for holiday trips and retirement homes. In the Company's Additional Powers Act of 1865 there was what was called an 'Ordnance Factory Railway' to run from Lower Edmonton on the already authorised Bethnal Green to Edmonton line and to make a junction with the original 1840 N&ER line at what was then called Ordnance Factory, which was named after the Royal Small Arms Factory in the area. Sadly, nothing came of this. Nor did proposals in the 1870s to link the Enfield branches of the Great Northern and Great Eastern railways. By the early 1880s, the Board of the GER, noting how its direct line from Enfield to Liverpool Street had worked wonders in enlarging Tottenham and Edmonton, reconsidered the position and in 1882 obtained powers for a line from Lower Edmonton to Cheshunt on the Cambridge line. Unfortunately, construction of the line was somewhat deferred and it was not until 1 October 1891 that the line was opened for passenger and goods traffic.

Two branches off the North Woolwich line were opened in this period. The first of these was from Custom House to Beckton, which was opened on 18 March 1874. The line was built to serve what may be described as a small village in itself built to serve the large riverside works of the Gaslight and Coke Company as well as the gasworks itself. The works which, situated on desolate marshland to the south-west of Barking Creek, were well placed to receive coal by sea but were poorly served by land, with at first nothing more than a rough road from Barking. Work on constructing the gasworks and associated village commenced in November 1868 with the first gas being produced on 25 November 1870, full production beginning the following month. Under the Gaslight and Coke Company Act of 1871 the Company was authorised to construct a line from Custom House Junction, which was about a quarter of a mile east of Custom House station. The construction of the line was to be done at the Company's expense. From Custom House Junction to East Ham Manor Way the line was single, but beyond there to the terminus the line was double, being on the Company's own land. Goods traffic started on 14 October 1872, with passenger traffic starting on 17 March 1873. The line was originally worked by the Gaslight and Coke Company, which had its own internal railway system extending to a length of about 70 miles of track. In 1874, the branch line was leased to and worked by the GER from 18 March that year. A clause in the Gaslight and Coke Company Act of 1871 required the operation of a 1d workmen's train each way on weekdays between Barking Road, as Canning Town was then called prior to its renaming on 1 July 1873, and Beckton before 6am (Down) and 6pm (Up). In practice, these and other passenger trains worked mostly from Stratford Market or Stratford Low Level at times to suit the changes of shifts at the gas works.

The other line was from Custom House to Gallions. The London and St Katharine Docks Company in the latter part of the 1870s planned to build the Royal Albert Dock in the uninhabited marshes to the east of Canning Town. It realised that the normal dock railways that were appropriate for goods traffic were not so for passenger traffic and therefore built on its own land a double-tracked line of 1 mile and 61 chains in length from near Connaught Road on the North Woolwich branch to the river edge at Gallions. When the Royal Albert Dock was opened on 6 May 1880, the Royal Albert Dock Railway was not ready for opening but a limited train service commenced on 3 August 1880. One slight problem was that the Railway had been constructed without parliamentary approval and so in 1882 an Act was obtained for the Docks Company to 'maintain and use' the railway as if it had been authorised by the Act. The Act also gave powers for the Dock Company to make working arrangements with the GER and restricted the line's traffic to passengers and parcels. It also required that a 1d workmen's train be run in the Down direction before 7am and in the Up direction after 6pm. At Custom House, the GER built a bay on the Up side of the line for the Gallions trains and rented it out to the Dock Company. The line had four stations which were fully staffed by the Dock Company. These were Connaught Road, Central, Manor Road and Gallions. According to Jackson, it is probable that for the first few weeks of operation trains only ran to a station called Central, but soon after were extended to Gallions. Trains either ran to and from Custom House or to Fenchurch Street.

When Liverpool Street station opened, although the station offices reached the street the train shed stopped short, leaving a space between it and the street for a hotel. For long distance travellers arriving at any great city such as London, a hotel convenient to the railway station that they arrived at was important. Euston had one, St Pancras had one, King's Cross had one, Paddington had one, Charing Cross had one. There was one near Victoria. Waterloo did not have one, but Waterloo was situated just south of the Thames and one could, after the opening of the SER from London Bridge to Charing Cross, relatively easily get to the latter station and its hotel by getting a train from what was then called Waterloo Junction, that is the SER station adjoining Waterloo London and South Western Railway (L&SWR) station.

It was the space between the train shed and the street that began to attract attention only months after the final plans of the station were settled. In October 1873, William Bridge of the Green Dragon Hotel in Bishopsgate asked the GER whether it was going to build a hotel – perhaps because he feared competition. In 1875, Henry Heath contacted the GER to say that he was willing to take the site on a 99-year lease of £1,000 a year for the purpose of erecting a hotel and appurtenances, shops, offices or warehouse to the plans approved by the Company's Engineer. It is probably as a result of that inquiry that the Company's Land and Construction Committee asked the Company's Engineer, Edward Wilson, to prepare plans for the site. When Wilson presented the plans to the Committee a month later, he did not refer to them as his own but said that they had been prepared by the Company's Land Agent, Mr Dobbin.

Although the GER Company had plans prepared in 1875, it was not in a particular hurry to start work on the hotel itself. During the delay, offers were received from a number of people. Chapman and Kemp offered to take the site for 80 years at £2,000 a year. J.W. Bedford of Threadneedle Street offered to take it for

£3,500 a year. Arthur Allom, the son of Thomas Allom who designed the Great Eastern Hotel at Harwich, offered to take the site for £3,400 a year. In November 1877, Allom failed to confirm his offer, so the GER's Land and Construction Committee began to recommend to the Board of the Company that the Company carry out the work. In March 1878, the Company accepted a tender from William Bangs and Company for the erection of six shops, followed in September by a second agreement from the same company for the construction of the platform on which the hotel was to be built. Just when work appeared to be starting, the minutes of the Land and Construction Committee go silent on the subject beyond a reference to a letter from Bangs explaining the delay in completing the shops and a mention of a further outside offer to take on the project which was rejected. The reason for the delay is not clear. It could have been financial reasons, or it could have been that the plans were found to be unsatisfactory. Equally, if the Company's Engineer, Edward Wilson, had been responsible for the plans, his death in October 1877 would have added to difficulties in revising them.

The silence was broken in December 1879 when the Board of the GER appointed Charles Barry and his son Charles Edward Barry as joint architects for the work. Charles Barry was to be paid 100 guineas for inspecting the plans and drawings that had already been made and to make whatever revisions he thought necessary. Charles Edward Barry was to be paid £400 a year for two years as superintending architect. Mr Dobbin, the Company's Land Agent mentioned earlier, was to be granted 300 guineas 'for designs and services' in connection with the hotel.

The Barrys were quite a famous family of architects. Charles Barry senior's father was Sir Charles Barry, who had designed the rebuilt Houses of Parliament and the Reform Club. As to how the Barrys obtained the commission for the hotel is unclear, but it was almost certainly not as the result of a competition, which, had it been held, would have delayed the project even further and led to confusion and sour feelings. Most likely, the GER decided to act decisively and appoint two members of an architectural practice which had a strong tradition in designing public buildings.

As the alterations that the Barrys had to make to the existing hotel plans took four months, they must have been quite radical. Meanwhile, the alterations were progressing. William Bangs was told to start work on the shops that were to fill most of the ground floor façade in Liverpool Street. These were completed and occupied before the work of building the hotel itself had barely started with the result that the *City Press* complained that the effect was an odd one. According to the *City Press* 'the unfinished state of the building, with portions of the scaffolding standing, is incongruous in the extreme, and detracts from the effect of the spacious station building'. It was not until 1882 that evidence of real progress could be seen. Charles Edward Barry reported in May 1882 that the block of the hotel nearest Bishopsgate was well advanced, most of the cellars were already being filled by the hotel manager, but that the main hotel block had only been erected to just over the first floor. Barry blamed the Company for the delay on that section. He said that they had great difficulties to contend with at the beginning of building operations owing to the decision of the Company's Directors to set aside the original scheme of a great meeting hall when the foundations of that had already been laid. By the autumn of 1883, details of the decorations were being discussed – mosaic and parquet flooring, a tilework frieze and scagliola columns for the restaurant, papier-mâché architectural ornament, which the Company's Board wanted to be of the plainest possible character. Charles Edward Barry submitted designs for the stained glass in the dome of the restaurant in November 1883. Maple and Company supplied the furniture for the hotel.

The *East Anglian Daily Times* of Monday 26 May 1884 announced that the Great Eastern Hotel at Liverpool Street station, London would be opened on Monday 26th of that month and that it would be under the management of the Company. The following day's edition announced that the hotel was now open. The opening took place with a dinner attended by the Directors and Officers of the GER Company. In his report to the shareholders at the 44th half yearly meeting of the Company held on 29 July 1884, the Chairman said, 'the new Hotel at Liverpool Street Station, which was opened at the end of May last … is becoming much used in connection with the Railway'.

By the mid-1880s, traffic in to Liverpool Street station was flourishing to the point that it had become inadequate. The Company's General Manager, William Birt, told the Royal Commission on the Housing of the Working Classes in 1884, 'We scarcely know what to do at Liverpool Street for want of room'.

The idea of enlarging Liverpool Street station seems to have gone back to 1881 as at the 40th half yearly general meeting of the shareholders of the GER on 28 July 1882, the Chairman in his report said that the 'GER Bill has passed both Houses of Parliament. It contains amongst other provisions powers to construct two additional Lines of Railway into Liverpool Street Station and to purchase additional land for the enlargement of that Station. The exercise of these powers may require the early consideration of the Directors'. According to the book *Liverpool Street Station*, the powers obtained under that Act had to be renewed in 1887, requiring a fresh Act.

Under the Act of 1882, the GER obtained powers not only to enlarge Liverpool Street station, but also to build an additional pair of tracks from Bethnal Green Junction into the terminus. This need to enlarge Liverpool Street was emphasised in the Chairman's Report to the 41st half yearly meeting held on 30 January 1883 in which he said that the suburban traffic had outgrown the accommodation at Liverpool Street station and that new train services were urgently demanded, but that the margin of time and space for additional services was very small. He said that the Company proposed to raise the money to finance the work by issuing extra Stock. The purchase of land and of properties required for the enlargement of Liverpool Street station was expensive and it was because of this that the Act of 1887 was needed in order to renew the powers to do so.

Demolition of the buildings acquired for the enlargement of the station started in 1890. The contractors for the enlargement were John Mowlem and Company. In addition to the enlargement of the station there was, as mentioned, the construction of additional lines of railway into it from Bethnal Green Junction and this work had been completed by early July 1891.

The Chairman of the GER in his report to the 59th half yearly meeting of the Company held on 26 January 1892 said that work had made great progress during the previous half year and it was expected that erection of the building would commence in the following few weeks.

At the 62nd half yearly meeting of the Company held on 31 July 1893, the Chairman in his report said that works for the enlargement of Liverpool Street were nearing completion.

At the 63rd half yearly meeting of the Company held on 30 January 1894, the Chairman in his report said that satisfactory progress had been made with the construction of the new portion of Liverpool Street station.

According to the *East Anglian Daily Times* of Tuesday, 3 April 1894, the new portion of Liverpool Street station was opened the previous day.

The enlargement was certainly necessary as in early 1895 there were, according to the Chairman of the GER, 873 trains into and out of the station daily.

Liverpool Street, as widened, was flawed. Platforms 1 to 10 were separated from Platforms 11 to 18 by a cab way. The whole station was a bit of a mess from a passenger's point of view. Because of the connection to the Metropolitan Railway, Platform 1 could only be reached by a footbridge from Platform 2. The tracks between Platforms 9 and 10 extended underneath part of the hotel and then there was the cab way separating the western part of the station from the eastern part. The easiest way to get round the station was by using a footbridge that extended throughout the station – not the most satisfactory situation and not very helpful for anyone who was infirm and who had problems walking through injury or amputation or was in a wheelchair. But then one could argue that the needs of those people were not thought about at that time and that from the point of view of the GER, there were plenty of porters about.

The Cheap Trains Act of 1883 removed the passenger duty on any train charging less than a 1d a mile and obliged the railway companies to operate a larger number of cheap trains and marked the beginning of workers' train services. The background to the Act was that the period in which it was passed was one of extreme overcrowding in the major cities of Britain. This was a major political issue and one of the solutions sought by the authorities was to encourage working people to move to new housing outside of the cities. However, this required availability of cheap transport as even a fare of 1d a mile was beyond the reach of most people. The Act applied to all trains charging less than a penny a mile, even those trains that did not stop at all stations.

Since the Railway Regulation Act 1844, third class coaches were provided on what became known as 'Parliamentary trains'. The Act included the right of passengers in this class to take up to 56lb of luggage with them free of charge so facilitating travel in search of work. In return, the railway companies were exempted from paying duty on these passengers.

The duty was collected by the Board of Trade and gradually, as services improved, the Board allowed more and more exemptions, even on trains which did not stop at all stations, as required by the Act. However, as the duty collected rose to around £500,000 in the 1860s, the Inland Revenue became involved and in 1874, a test case against the NLR confirmed that trains must stop at all stations for the duty to be remitted.

The duty had always been irksome to the railway operators, who felt that it hindered their development. The railway operators formed the Passenger Duty Repeal Association in 1874, followed in 1877 by another group, the Travelling Tax Abolition Committee. Between them they lobbied for the complete abolition of the duty. The Board of Trade could decide whether a railway company's services were adequate and reasonably priced and if it felt otherwise, it could remove the company's exemption on all its services. Under the Act, the GER was one of six companies that were obliged by law to run workmen's trains.

In fact, the GER was already running workmen's trains. Its public timetable for March 1882 showed four workmen's trains a day from Enfield, three from Walthamstow and four starting from Hackney Downs. The return fares on these services were 2d. Workmen's return tickets at 2d were available to Liverpool Street on trains leaving Stratford (Main Line) at 5.30 and 6.14am, from Stratford Market at 5.15 and 6.18am and Coborn Road at 5.22, 5.36, 6.20 and 6.25am.

The GER's London suburban service was the heaviest in Britain with many routes worked by 0-6-0 side tank locomotives. Class C72 0-6-0 side tank No 50 is seen passing Bethnal Green on the 2pm Liverpool Street to Enfield Town on 11 June 1915. (Ken Nunn).

It was not only Liverpool Street station that was enlarged. There was also the widening of the lines into the station. In 1884, widening of the line between Coborn Road station and a point west of Devonshire Street was completed. At the same time, a new station called Globe Road and Devonshire Street was opened. In connection with the extension to Liverpool Street station, an additional pair of tracks had been opened between Bethnal Green and the terminus. By the end of 1891, the line out of Liverpool Street via Stratford had been quadrupled as far as Ilford. On the line via Hackney Downs, quadrupling had been completed between Bethnal Green and Hackney Downs in June 1894.

On the L&BR, the viaduct between Fenchurch Street and Stepney was again widened to accommodate an additional Down line in 1895-6.

Under its Act of 1862, the LT&SR became a separate Company. The bill prior to it becoming an Act was opposed by the Chairman of the ECR. The LT&SR was leased by its promoters to the contractors who built it – Peto, Brassey and Betts. The operators arranged for the ECR to provide the engines, carriages and waggons.

Whilst the GER had a majority of Directors on the board of the LT&SR, the independent Directors had only little opportunity to influence or run the Railway. An attempt in 1872 to negotiate a way was rejected by the GER and in 1874 a bill presented on behalf of the shareholders of the LT&SR to gain independent control of the Company was rejected by parliament. The shareholders elected Charles Bischoff and Henry Doughty Brown as Chairman and Deputy Chairman at a meeting on 15 September 1874. During 1873/1874, another shareholder named Eley had approached various other railways such as the NLR, the London and North Western Railway and the GNR, none of whom were interested in the LT&SR. On 4 November 1874, there was a change of Chairman on the GER when Lightly Simpson was replaced by Henry Charles Parkes who was on the London, Tilbury and Southend Railway board, a significant shareholder in that company and was sympathetic to getting the problem resolved.

The LT&SR employed outside assistance to understand the state of the railway and a report was delivered on 31 March 1875. In 1875, the lease under which the LT&SR was worked expired. The GER could have taken over the London, Tilbury and Southend Railway at this time, but for some unknown reason this did not happen. By the end of May that year, an operating agreement had been reached between the two railways and the arrangements were applied from July, although due to legal reasons everything was not sorted out for another year. Most importantly, the LT&SR was granted running powers into Fenchurch Street. In terms of rolling stock, the LT&SR was now the customer rather than the lessee and any GER staff operating on the LT&SR were to be treated as LT&SR staff for rules purposes. As far as is known, only one photograph exists of a GER locomotive on the LT&SR during the time that the former company provided the motive power for the latter Company.

In 1876, the LT&SR acquired its first rolling stock, followed in 1880 by its first locomotives. The locomotives were built to the design of William Adams, who was the Locomotive Superintendent of the GER from 1873 to 1878.

Following the LT&SR gaining its independence, the period 1880 to 1895 saw the construction of a number of new lines by the Company, but also the construction of Tilbury Docks by the East and West India Docks Company under an Act of 1882. Also, in 1882 the LT&SR obtained Acts itself. These were for an extension of the line from Southend to Shoeburyness where the Royal Artillery had a school of gunnery and for the construction of a new goods depot in Whitechapel and associated short branch line off the L&BR. This was known as Commercial Road. The most important was for a new line from Barking to Pitsea via Upminster. The reason for the latter was that as the LT&SR began to move away from GER influence, there was a perceived need to claim the area between the GER main line and the line to Tilbury. Additionally, it was recognised that with the opening of Tilbury Docks more goods trains might render the two track section of line to Tilbury inadequate. A direct line would see most Southend trains diverted from the Tilbury line and improved journey times.

It was perfectly natural for the GER to want to prevent the LT&SR intruding into the part of south Essex that it perceived to be its territory. There was also the matter of gaining independent access to Tilbury Docks.

It has not been established when the GER decided to apply for powers to build its own line to Southend. Without such a line, the GER would be dependent on the LT&SR conveying through coaches from Liverpool Street via Barking.

Peter Kay in Volume One of his *History of the LT&SR* says that the GER, having 'lost' the LT&SR, wanted a line of its own to Southend and decided on the Shenfield-Billericay-Wickford-Rayleigh-Hockley-Rochford route. John

Wilson, the company's Chief Engineer, was asked in late 1881 to do a survey for the line for a Bill to be promoted in time for the 1882 parliamentary session, but, owing to the difficulty of surveying the terrain, was unable to put the Bill forward in time.

A linen and woollen draper in Billericay, H.J. Emerson, claimed at a meeting held in the town on 20 March 1883 in support of the proposed railway from Shenfield to Southend that he was responsible for the line being built. He said that twelve months previously, he was thinking what steps could be taken for the improvement of the town and he came to the conclusion that nothing but a railway would have that effect. So he wrote to the General Manager of the GER and he received a reply back asking him for the route that he proposed. He replied that the line should commence midway between Brentwood and Ingatestone, passing through Billericay, Ramsden Crays, Wickford, Rayleigh and Rochford to Southend. He forwarded his correspondence to the editor of the *Essex Chronicle* which was published in the edition of 24 February 1882. There, it came to the attention of the Rev Beresford Harris, who was the Rector of Runwell near Wickford and the Rural Dean of Danbury, and who then 'took up the gauntlet'. Obviously one should not pass judgement but given what Peter Kay says it is likely that Emerson was unaware of what the GER was proposing.

Having failed to get its Bill for a line to Southend in the 1882 parliamentary session, it was decided by the GER to put it forward for the 1883 session. What was proposed were lines from Romford to Tilbury to enable the GER to gain direct access to Tilbury Docks, from Shenfield on the Chelmsford and Colchester main line to Southend via Wickford, Wickford to Southminster via Woodham Ferrers and Woodham Ferrers to Maldon to join up with the existing branch from Witham. In connection with Tilbury, there had also been an independent Romford and Tilbury Railway which had been designed to give the GER access to Tilbury Dock and which secured the GER's support; but the Romford and Tilbury Railway's Bill of 1882 failed on financial grounds.

At the same time, the LT&SR could not avoid hearing about the GER's proposals and put forward its own. These were for new lines from Romford to Tilbury and from Pitsea to Southend via North Benfleet, Rayleigh, Hockley, Rochford and Prittlewell. The junction at Southend would have been east of Southend station in the direction of London. The LT&SR also backed an independent Mid-Essex Junction Railway from Ingatestone to Pitsea via

Mountnessing, Buttsbury, Great Burstead, Laindon and Basildon. The junction with the Great Eastern Railway at Ingatestone would have been just south-west of the station facing in the direction of the station and Chelmsford. At Pitsea there would have been a Y-shaped junction with the LT&SR. One side of the Y would have been to the west of Pitsea station and would have been facing in the direction of Stanford-le-Hope and Tilbury and the other side of the junction would have been at a point 325 yards east of Pitsea station facing in the direction of Benfleet and Southend. The station at Great Burstead would have actually been in Billericay as for many years Billericay and Great Burstead were intertwined. The railway would have been operated as a joint railway. However the Bill for this Railway was not proceeded with. The *Chelmsford Chronicle* of 30 March 1883 reported that it was one of 41 Parliamentary Bills that were 'either withdrawn, not proceeded with or thrown out'.

According to Peter Kay, neither of the General Managers of the GER and the LT&SR wanted conflict between the two Companies and tried to reach a mutual agreement. In late September or early October 1882, the two companies' General Managers had come to an agreement that the Great Eastern Railway would build the sections of line from Romford to Upminster, Shenfield to Rayleigh and the LT&SR those from Upminster to Tilbury and Rayleigh to Southend. However, at this point the Great Eastern Railway's Chairman approached the LT&SR's Chairman with the proposition that the former company might take over the latter. The LT&SR rejected the offer. Apparently, whilst the GER was definitely enthusiastic about the Shenfield to Southend line, it was not as keen about the Wickford to Southminster and Woodham Ferrers to Maldon lines. The LT&SR was not particularly enthusiastic about the Romford to Tilbury line, which as finalised joined the existing line to Tilbury just west of Grays. In building the lines south of Shenfield, the GER had built a new station at Shenfield, on the site of an earlier station which had been open from October 1847 to March 1850.

Even before it had fully committed to building a line from Shenfield to Southend it does seem that the GER was considering a new station there, as the *Chelmsford Chronicle* of 15 July 1881 carried a report of a meeting held at the Spread Eagle Hotel in Ingatestone the previous Wednesday on a proposal to remove the town's goods station from there to Shenfield. Understandably, those attending the meeting were less than happy with the proposal and angry scenes developed during which one person was assaulted. The proposal to close Ingatestone's goods station was not carried out by the GER.

In parliament, the Great Eastern Railway's proposal for a line from Romford to Tilbury was rejected but it did obtain an Act dated 8 July 1883 to build lines from Shenfield to Southend via Wickford, Wickford to Southminster via Woodham Ferrers and Woodham Ferrers to Maldon. The London, Tilbury and Southend Railway's proposal for a line from Pitsea to Southend via Rayleigh, and Rochford was rejected, but it did obtain an Act dated 20 August 1883 to build a line from Romford via Upminster to Grays.

The Great Eastern Railway's line from Shenfield to Southend was originally going to be double track as far as Billericay and then single track to Prittlewell where double track would recommence, with the provision that the section from Billericay to Wickford have provision for an extra pair of rails to be laid at a later date. However, in 1887 it was decided that the section from Shenfield to Wickford should be double track throughout.

This is the best photograph that I have been able to find of a line under construction. It shows engineers building part of the New Essex Lines from Shenfield to Wickford and Southend near Wickford in the mid-1880s using a steam navvy. Essex people called them 'Devil Diggers'. (Christopher Corbin).

The Great Eastern Railway From its Formation in 1862 to the End of 1895 87

According to the *Essex Standard* of 4 October 1884, on 26 September the Chairman and the General Manager of the Great Eastern Railway had inspected the route of the new railway from Shenfield to Billericay, on which work was to shortly begin.

The sod cutting ceremony was held at Upminster Windmill on 11 October 1883 to mark the start of work on the LT&SR line from Barking to Pitsea. The line between Barking and Upminster opened to all traffic on 1 May 1885, followed on 1 May 1886 by the section from Upminster to East Horndon; full opening to Pitsea was on 1 June 1888, although a storm on 1 August caused the partial closure of the new line until 1 October. During that time, trains from London and Barking via Upminster terminated again at East Horndon and a shuttle service ran from Pitsea to Laindon, which was the intermediate station between East Horndon and Pitsea. The extension from Southend to Shoeburyness opened on 1 February 1884. Commercial Road goods station opened on 17 April 1886, the line from Upminster to Grays 1 July 1892 and the line from Upminster to Romford on 7 June 1893.

The first of the GER's new lines to be opened was the new Shenfield station on 1 January 1887. The next section was that from Shenfield to Wickford on 19 November 1888, but only for goods traffic and without any public ceremony. The reason that the section was not opened for passenger traffic was that the Board of Trade's Inspector, Major General C.S. Hutchinson, was concerned about slippage of earth in the cuttings. The cutting at Billericay was particularly deep. Following another inspection in December, permission was given for the section to be opened for passenger traffic. This took place on 1 January 1889, with much rejoicing including lunches for invited guests held in Wickford and Billericay. On 1 June 1889, the section of line from Wickford to Southminster was opened for goods traffic without official public ceremonies, although at Southminster a large number of inhabitants turned out to see the arrival of the first train. On 1 July 1889, the section from Wickford to Southminster was opened for passenger traffic with much rejoicing including lunch for invited guests at Southminster. On 1 October 1889, the sections of line from Wickford to Southend and Woodham Ferrers to Maldon were opened for all traffic. On the Southend line, there was a number of celebrations including a public lunch at Rochford. Whilst there was a lunch for invited guests at Southend there was nothing at Maldon, the Mayor and Corporation of which town went to that at

Southend and the Mayor on his return to his home town was followed from the new West Station at Maldon by a mob of about 200 people who hooted and hissed and pelted him with mud.

As opened, the new lines had a number of spurs off them as did the Witham to Maldon branch. The purpose of these at Wickford, Maldon and Witham was so that trains could travel between Southend and Colchester without having to travel to Shenfield and reverse and travel to Colchester via Chelmsford.

Whilst the station at Southend was built as a terminus, that at Southminster was built as a through station. Although I have never found evidence in the surviving records of the GER of there being an intention to extend the line beyond Southminster, it is clear that the Company could have done so had it wished to. At the time of the opening of the lines to Southminster and to Southend there were calls for the line to Southminster to be extended to Bradwell-on-Sea.

The new lines were all single track with passing places except between Shenfield and Wickford, Prittlewell and Southend and the two Maldon stations. As the GER's route to Southend had a large portion of single track, this put it at a disadvantage compared to the LT&SR which had double track lines to Southend via both Tilbury and Upminster.

It was not that the GER did not try to compete for the Southend traffic. In fact, it resorted to skulduggery as far as excursion traffic was concerned. The GER put on through trains from Fenchurch Street to Southend via Shenfield. Leasing the L&BR meant that the ticket clerks at Fenchurch Street station were employees of the GER who would be instructed to influence traffic to the Company's trains rather than those of the LT&SR. This happened in August 1890. Another piece of skulduggery happened in August 1890, to be precise on August Bank Holiday Monday, which at that time was the first Monday of the month. On that day, the GER suspended the train service from Liverpool Street to Barking, where it connected with the LT&SR for most of the day, so forcing anyone wishing to go from Liverpool Street to Southend to go via Shenfield. The GER alleged that this was due to a mistake by an Inspector. The LT&SR did not think that a mistake had been made. It is worth pointing out that both railways were in competition for the excursion traffic with the excursion steamers plying from London down the Thames to places on the Essex and Kent coasts. North Woolwich was tried in 1891 and Gospel Oak was another. This last lasted a bit longer. The Southminster line had an advantage over the

Southend line in that at Burnham-on-Crouch, the GER had a monopoly as the town was served neither by the LT&SR or by pleasure steamers.

One advantage that the GER had over the LT&SR was that at Liverpool Street station, passengers had direct access to the underground railways, whereas at Fenchurch Street station the nearest station on the underground railways was Mark Lane. Even though the underground railways were at this time worked by steam traction, having access to them was an advantage. The LT&SR tried in 1891 to get running powers into Liverpool Street station, albeit only for eight trains a day, the idea being that they would replace the existing GER service to and from Barking. The GER would have none of it and the idea was thrown out. All that happened was that the GER agreed to charge the same fare from Liverpool Street to Southend as the LT&SR did from Fenchurch Street to Southend. Naturally, the GER had been charging lower fares to Southend even though its route via Shenfield was longer than the LT&SR's route via Upminster at 41½ miles as opposed to 35¾ miles.

What the GER did not do was compete with the LT&SR for the lucrative business traffic from Southend. According to *Bradshaw's Railway Guide* for December 1895, the earliest that one could reach Liverpool Street from Southend via Shenfield was 9.1am by leaving Southend at 7.35am. On the LT&SR, the earliest that one could reach Fenchurch Street from Southend was 7.50am by leaving Southend at 6.38am.

Whilst the GER was failing with the Southend business traffic, there was another area in which it was also failing. Between the opening of the lines to Southend and Maldon in October 1889 and the end of February 1895 there was on Saturdays only a through train in each direction from Southend via Rayleigh, Woodham Ferrers, Maldon (West station), Wickham Bishops and Kelvedon to Colchester. At the end of the summer of 1891, the through train from Colchester to Southend was diverted to call at Maldon East station, as the original station at Maldon had been renamed. With the end of the through service on 23rd February 1895, the spurs which enabled this service to operate were removed by the end of 1895. The reason why the GER did not try to run a couple of trains a day from Liverpool Street to Colchester or beyond via Wickford and Maldon is not known.

Returning to Southend, in July 1894 the GER faced a new competitor for the Southend traffic in the form of the MR following the opening of the Tottenham and Forest Gate Railway (T&FGR) from the Tottenham and Hampstead Joint Railway at South Tottenham to the LT&SR to Woodgrange Park on the section of the latter Company's line from Forest Gate Junction to Barking. Off the latter line, a spur was put in to East Ham on the LT&SR's line from Barking to Gas Factory Junction and Fenchurch Street. The T&FGR was jointly owned by the MR and the LT&SR. It was not long before the MR started running some through trains from St Pancras. In 1894, these were summer only, but from 1895 they ran throughout the year.

The Metropolitan Outer Circle Railway was promoted by Charles Grey Mott, who was a director of the Great Western Railway and the Chairman of the City and South London Railway. The Metropolitan Outer Circle Railway obtained its Act on 7 August 1888. It was authorised to run from a junction with the Metropolitan District and Great Western railways at Ealing and to go to a triangular junction with the GER Cambridge line at Tottenham, joining on the way the North and South Western Junction Railway, the Metropolitan Railway, the MR at Hendon and the GNR at Southgate. The time given for the completion of the works was five years, but in 1891 permission had to be sought for an extension of time for completion and in 1893 a further application was made for an extension of time until 7 August 1896. Before that date, the Company made an application to abandon the works granted under its Act of 1888 and this was granted under an Act of 14 May 1895.

As mentioned at the beginning of this chapter, the GER was dependent for its income on the agricultural and rather limited passenger traffic of the Eastern Counties which produced rather low revenue in return for high operational costs. It was more akin to the railways operating south of the Thames – the L&SWR, the London, Brighton and South Coast, the South Eastern and the London, Chatham and Dover than those operating into London from the north – the London and North Western, the Great Northern, the MR and the Great Western.

In 1863, the GER promoted a Bill for a line from March to Spalding where it hoped to obtain running powers over the GNR to Doncaster. The GNR was having none of this and promptly promoted a Bill for a line from Spalding to March. Whilst the GNR's Bill was passed, the GER's Bill was rejected. The GER was, by way of a consolation prize, given running powers over the GNR's proposed line as far as Spalding, but no further. In 1864, the GNR promoted another Bill which planned to authorize it to continue its Lincoln Line from Gainsborough directly to Doncaster and not to Bawtry as originally proposed by the promoters of the Railway. The GER's response in 1864 was to seek powers to construct a completely independent line called the Great Eastern Northern Junction Railway, which was to run from Long Stanton between Cambridge and St Ives via Peterborough, Bourne, Sleaford, Lincoln and Gainsborough to a junction with the authorised, but as yet unbuilt, West Riding and Grimsby Railway at Askern Junction north of Doncaster. Naturally, the GNR opposed the Bill for the proposed Railway and after a long and projected fight it was thrown out by parliament.

In 1864, the L&YR, having become disturbed by the fact that the North Eastern Railway (NER) had obtained powers to build a direct line from York to Askern Junction, Doncaster via Selby, over which GNR trains at that time travelling over the Lancashire and Yorkshire (L&YR) between Knottingley and Askern would be diverted, tried to join hands with the GER in reviving the Great Eastern Northern Junction Railway. The name of this new projected railway was the Lancashire and Yorkshire and Great Eastern Junction Railway and as far as Sleaford it would have followed the course of the Great Eastern Northern Junction Railway and then take a more easterly course until it joined the L&YR at Askern. The proposed Railway was supported by a proposed Goole, Keadby and Haxey Railway to connect with it at Haxey and join the L&YR at Goole. This new railway would not only have been for the conveyance of coal but would also have been a new trunk railway between London and Lancashire and Yorkshire and would threaten not only the GNR, but also the MS&LR which used the GNR to haul its trains from Manchester through to London. Under an agreement dated 23 September 1864 between the GER and the L&YR, the latter company would have been given running powers over the whole of the GER. From reading it one gets the impression that the GER would have been subservient to the L&YR. The Bill for the Lancashire and Yorkshire and Great Eastern Junction Railway made little progress in parliament. According to the Directors of the GER in their report to the 6th half yearly meeting on 24 August 1865, the Bill encountered so serious an opposition in the House of Commons at the Second Reading on the part of the GNR that it was thrown out. At the same time, the Goole, Keadby and Haxey Railway proposal was abandoned. Following the defeat of the Bill, the feeling of the Directors of the GER was, according to the earlier mentioned report, 'in the first instance to renew an arrangement with the Lancashire and Yorkshire Company, but, after considerable discussion and consideration, that Company declined to co-operate with this Company upon the footing of their previous agreement'. The earlier agreement was understandably dropped with the failure of the Bill.

The sequel to this was that the GNR opened talks with the GER about providing it with the route to the north of England that it desired. The GER agreed to bear half of the cost of the constructing of the GNR's lines from March to Spalding and from Gainsborough to Doncaster and to become joint proprietors with the GNR of its line from Spalding to Lincoln, which if it was found necessary would be shortened at the expense of both companies. By an agreement with the Manchester, Sheffield and Lincolnshire Railway (MS&LR), the GER secured a means of conveying its traffic from Doncaster to Wakefield and other northern districts. The GER was given the right to fix the rate for the conveyance of coal and for all other traffic, the rates between the GER and the MS&LR were to be the same. Any disagreements were to be submitted to arbitration. The agreement between the GER and the GNR was signed on 20 June 1865, as was that between the GER, the GNR and the MS&LR, but that between the GER and the MS&LR was not signed until 3 August 1865. There was an unhappy sequence to this. In 1866, preparations were made for a Bill in parliament to sanction this just at the time that the GER's finances were at their lowest and following a change of Directors on the GER the new Directors refused to sanction the scheme, so the Bill was withdrawn. In January 1867, the GER recommenced negotiations with the GNR when the respective General Managers worked out a new agreement. Under the new agreement, the GER was to have running powers to Doncaster as soon as the GNR's new Spalding to March and Gainsborough to Doncaster lines were ready and would pay the GNR a minimum toll of £25,000 a year for this. The GER could exchange traffic for the West Riding of Yorkshire with the Lancashire and Yorkshire Railway (L&YR) at Doncaster, but traffic for Liverpool and Manchester had to be worked over the MS&LR via Sykes Junction (near Saxilby, between Lincoln and Gainsborough) and Retford or Doncaster and Penistone. When the Chairmen of the two Companies met on 12 March 1867 to complete the arrangements, they were not able to agree about L&YR exchange traffic and in consequence the agreement fell apart as the GNR Directors felt that such an arrangement would be prejudicial to the MS&LR with which they had at the time very friendly relations.

Just to make things interesting, whilst all this was going on, in 1865 there was a project for a Hull, Lancashire and Midland Counties Railway which would have given the MS&LR, the GNR and the GER completely independent access to the important north-east port of Hull. The new railway had the support of the Corporation of Hull but was regarded as a threat by the NER, which at that time had a monopoly on railway traffic to Hull. The cost of the proposed railway, which would have run from Bardney on the Boston to Lincoln Loop Line of the GNR to Hull, would have included a large viaduct across the Humber which would have been enormous and in consequence the lack of financial support caused it to be dropped.

Just about this time there was a rift in relations between the GNR and the MS&LR. Briefly, the rift was over the rates charged for the conveyance of coal, resulting from a public statement in 1868 by the Chairman of the GER, Lord Cranborne, that the Company was still determined to have its own line to the north of England; the Chairman of the MS&LR, Sir Edward Watkin, who was also a Director of the GER, threatened to build a new line to London in conjunction with the GER from Market Rasen on the MS&LR to Long Stanton on the GER. Watkin actually took a share in depositing a Bill in Parliament to that effect in 1871. The Bill was supported by the MS&LR and GER and was opposed by the GNR and MR. Following a very short contest, the Bill for the proposed railway was thrown out by a Committee of the House of Commons.

In the mid-1870s there was a possibility of the GER amalgamating with the GNR. Negotiations opened in May 1876. At a meeting on 4 November 1876, the GNR offered the GER the following terms. Using 6 per cent of the GNR dividends for a basis for calculation, the following would be the dividends payable to holders of GER ordinary stock: in 1878, £1 5s; in 1879, £1 10s; in 1880, £1 15s; in 1881, £2; in 1882, £2 5s; and in 1883, £2 10s, all to increase or decrease x per cent according to the sum available for division. In 1884, GER ordinary was to be converted into GNR ordinary stock at 50 per cent GNR for every 100 per cent GER. The GER declined the proposals.

The Directors of the GER in their report to the shareholders of the Company at the 29th half yearly meeting of the Company held on 20 January 1877 said that on behalf of the Great Eastern it was proposed that the ultimate fusion should be by the holders of Great Eastern Ordinary Stock receiving for every £100 Great Eastern Ordinary Stock 60 per cent, of Great Northern Ordinary Stock. The Great Northern Directors offered 50 per cent — the Directors of the Great Eastern subsequently proposed a reduction of the amount to 55 per cent — but did not feel justified in making any further abatement, unless the Great Northern would make modifications on their side. Also:

> The Directors much regret that the negotiation was unsuccessful, they believe that if the amalgamation had been carried out on the basis they proposed it would have been highly beneficial to the Shareholders of both Companies, and also would have conduced greatly to the advantage of the public.

In what I assume to be the early part of 1877, the GNR's main line to Doncaster and York was getting a bit crowded and the Company, being desperate for an alternative route to relieve it, resolved to deposit Bills with parliament with lines from Shepreth on the Hitchin to Cambridge line where it joined the GER to March and Spalding to Lincoln. The two Bills did not comply with Standing Orders, but the GNR was informed that as they were of public importance, they could be re-submitted with the objections removed. At this point the Deputy Chairman of the GER, Lord Claud Hamilton, requested an interview with the GNR and no further actions were taken about the Bills. However, fresh proposals were made for an amalgamation of the Great Eastern and the Great Northern railways. Under the new proposals the GNR agreed to the amalgamation of the two companies taking place in 1883 instead of 1884, but it required that its engineers be allowed to make a thorough examination of the GER's permanent way and plant. As the two Companies could not agree on the amount that the GER should spend on renewals, so it was proposed that the matter should be referred to the arbitration of T.E. Harrison, the Chief Engineer of the NER, that 'the railway was handed over in good order'. All seemed settled for the amalgamation to take place when the GER demanded that the 6 per cent assumed as the average GNR dividend should be guaranteed for ten years. As the dividend had slipped to 5½ per cent, the GNR broke off negotiations on 7 July 1877. Negotiations resumed six days later on 13 July and on 19 July the GNR offered the GER terms for joint lines. The terms were that the GNR would: sell to the GER half of the March to Spalding line and half of the Spalding to Boston via Lincoln line and a new direct line from Spalding to Lincoln to be made jointly when needed; grant the GER running powers from Lincoln to Doncaster and the use of Lincoln and Doncaster stations; carry to and from Doncaster GER traffic for all places on or beyond the GNR by reasonable direct routes; allow the GER to have full access to lines of other companies with which the GNR connected at Doncaster and Lincoln for exchanging traffic. Additionally: the GER would sell to the GNR half of the existing Shepreth to March line (via Cambridge and Ely), the proposed direct line to be made jointly when needed; the GER would grant running powers to the GNR from Huntingdon to Cambridge and Newmarket, and Ely to Norwich and Yarmouth; and the GER would double the St Ives to Huntingdon line and to make a new junction at Huntingdon at joint expense.

Understandably, the GER was not happy with the terms offered and declined them. It was unwilling to become part of the GNR's original Spalding to Lincoln line and rejected the extensive running powers that the GNR sought. The company counteracted by reviving the 1864 Great Eastern Northern Junction Railway on a slightly different route and undertook to offer some special rates. The project was put in the hands of the solicitor Robert Baxter and the engineer Sir John Hawkshaw. The GNR responded by submitting a Bill to parliament for a Spalding to Lincoln direct line. A strenuous tussle took place in the 1878 session of parliament. The House of Commons' Committee was not prepared to pass the GER's Bill for its line but thought that the Company should have access to the north by a joint line from March to Doncaster, as the GNR had proposed. The Committee approved the GNR's Bill (which became an Act on 17 June 1878) and the GER's Bill only as a 'money' Bill, with clauses binding the GNR and GER to come together the following year for a joint scheme. A money bill is a bill that in the opinion of the House of Commons Speaker is concerned only with national taxation, public money or loans. The Act authorising the formation of the Great Northern and Great Eastern Joint Committee was passed on 3 July 1879. The Joint Committee was not a corporate body. It was run by a joint committee of three representatives of each Company. The Act transferred to the Joint Committee certain existing authorised lines of the GNR and the GER. Since the greater mileage was owned by the GNR, the GER had to pay that company £415,000 to equalise the value of the joint property. Under the

Act, the GNR lines from Black Carr Junction to Lincoln and Spalding to March and the GER lines from Huntingdon to St Ives and Needingworth Junction (1 mile 68 chains north of St Ives) to March and the new Spalding to Lincoln direct line were all to be joint. The junctions at Huntingdon and St Ives were to be improved. The first meeting of the Joint Committee took place on 11 August 1879 with C.H. Parkes of the GER in the chair. In November of that year, tenders for permanent way materials for the new Spalding to Lincoln direct line were opened. Richard Johnson of the GNR was appointed Engineer for the northern section of the line and Alfred Langley of the GER was appointed Engineer for the southern section of the line. The contracts for the building of the line were let at the beginning of 1880. In building the line it was necessary for the GNR's line from Sleaford to Boston to be lowered where the Joint Line crossed it. At Sleaford and Spalding, temporary junctions were laid in connection with construction of the new line and the stations at those places were rebuilt and re-signalled. Much of the St Ives to March lines and about 3 miles of the St Ives to Huntingdon line required renewal.

Although the Great Northern and Great Eastern Joint Committee's Act was passed on 3 July 1879, the respective lines of the two Companies were not transferred at that time. Arrangements had been made for the opening of the line from Spalding to Ruskington on 1 February 1882, but subsidence delayed this until 6 March when the GNR March to Spalding line and the GER Huntingdon to St Ives and Needingworth Junction to March lines were transferred to the Joint Committee. The passenger service on the March to Ruskington line was provided by the GER whilst the GNR provided the goods service. The GER undertook to pay the GNR £33,330 – half the value of GNR property in excess of that of GER lines transferred to the Joint Committee. On 1 July 1882 the section of the line from Ruskington to Sincil Junction, Lincoln was opened for goods traffic. The GNR extended its goods service to Lincoln. On 1 August the section opened for passenger traffic and on the same day avoiding lines at Sleaford and Lincoln were opened for goods traffic. The GER extended its passenger service to Doncaster and the GNR was able to divert traffic over the new lines. On 2 August the GER paid the GNR £383,760, the balance of purchase money of lines to become joint and the GNR Pyewipe Junction to Black Carr Junction line was officially transferred to the Joint Committee. The MS&LR agreed to the GER's use of its Trent bridge at Gainsborough on the

The Great Eastern Railway From its Formation in 1862 to the End of 1895

The GER ran to York via the Great Northern and Great Eastern Joint Line. Class T19 4-4-0 No 777 is seen arriving at Doncaster on 30 July 1914 with the 6.35am Harwich to York train. This was the famous North Country Continental. (Ken Nunn).

payment of tolls. On 20 March 1883, the Board of Trade sanctioned the use of the avoiding lines for passenger trains when required.

In 1865, the GER had obtained powers to build a line from Somersham to Ramsey. In 1875, it acquired the Ramsey Railway, which ran from Holme on the GNR main line to Ramsey, and which the GNR worked. The plan was to join the two branch lines. The Ramsey Railway had been authorised in 1861 and was opened on 22 July 1863. In acquiring the Ramsey Railway, the GER never attempted to work its isolated section, leaving the GNR to continue working it and to which the GER leased to the latter Company for 21 years on payment of 2 per cent per annum, on agreed capital of £43,000, such dividend to increase at the rate of ¼ per cent per annum until a maximum of 3¼ per cent was reached. The GER's line from Somersham to Ramsey was not opened until 16 September 1889. Although the line linking the two branch terminals at Ramsey was authorised, it was never implemented. In October 1895, the GNR and the GER decided to make the line part of the joint line with the GER, working it for 30 per cent of receipts, balance to be divided. The lease of the Holme to Ramsey section of the GER to the GNR was renewed for 21 years from 1 July 1896. An Act of 29 July 1896 authorised all this with the Somersham to Ramsey line being transferred to the Joint Committee on 1 January 1897.

On 1 November 1892 the GER obtained running powers over the NER from Shaftholme Junction to York and extended its through services to Doncaster from Liverpool Street and Harwich to York.

Other than the London, Tilbury and Southend Railway the GER's main competitor was what became known as the Midland & Great Northern Joint Railway (M&GNJR). At the time of the formation of the GER all that existed was a line from Spalding to Sutton Bridge owned by the Norwich and Spalding Railway and worked by the GNR. The next part of the future M&GNJR to be opened was the Lynn and Sutton Bridge Railway which was authorised on 6 August 1861 to connect with the ECR (later GER) at South Lynn. The line was opened for goods traffic in November 1864 from a junction some distance south of King's Lynn station with passenger traffic starting on 1 March 1866. The Railway was worked by the GNR. The next line to open was the Spalding and Bourne Railway which was authorised on 29 July 1862. The Railway was to make an end-on junction at Bourne with the Bourne and Essendine Railway which was an offshoot of the GNR and had opened on 16 May 1860. The Spalding and Bourne Railway opened on 1 August 1866 and were worked by the GNR.

On the same day that the Spalding and Bourne Railway opened, the Peterborough, Wisbech and Sutton Bridge Railway opened from Peterborough to Sutton Bridge via Wisbech together with its Wisbech Harbour Branch. The Company received its Act on 28 July 1863 and powers were to be sought by the Railway to connect to the GER line at Wisbech. The Norwich and Spalding Railway was given running powers between Sutton Bridge and Wisbech. The Railway was not worked by the GNR, but by the MR and started from the GER station in Peterborough and not the GNR station in that town, calling at the latter en route. In 1864, the Company got authorisation to make a connecting line at Wisbech to the GER, and to the harbour.

The next section of the Midland and Great Northern Joint Railway to be opened was the Great Yarmouth and Stalham Light Railway which received authorization on 27 June 1876 to build a line from Great Yarmouth to Stalham, the terminus at Great Yarmouth later becoming known as Yarmouth Beach. At that stage there was no connection with any other railway. The first section of line to be opened – on 7 August 1877 – was from Great Yarmouth to Ormesby, the section from Ormesby to Hemsby opening 16 May 1878. The Hemsby to

Martham section opened from a temporary station north of the level crossing, on 15 July 1878. On 27 May 1878, the Company was granted powers to extend to North Walsham, and to change its name to the Yarmouth and North Norfolk Light Railway, its status as a light railway was designed to prevent the GER from acquiring running powers over the line. Successive openings took place: to Catfield on 17 January 1880; and on to Stalham on 3 July 1880. On 13 June 1881, the Railway was extended from Stalham to North Walsham.

Next in order of authorisation was the Lynn and Fakenham Railway, on 13 July 1876 (in the face of bitter opposition from the GER), to run from the GER- operated Lynn and Hunstanton Railway at Gaywood Road near King's Lynn to near Fakenham. For some reason, the GER did not make any attempt to take control of the Lynn and Fakenham Railway but did make obstructions during its construction, for example by refusing to allow material used in the construction to pass over Gaywood Road Junction so that it had to be carted. The Railway was opened to Massingham on 16 August 1879 and extended to Fakenham on 16 August 1880. The Railway operated itself.

On 12 August 1880 the Lynn and Fakenham Railway got approval to extend to Norwich, so creating a much sought-after independent line to the city. The line was to pass through Melton Constable, and from there a branch to Blakeney Harbour was planned but never built. On 11 August 1881, the Lynn and Fakenham Railway and the Yarmouth and North Norfolk Railway together managed at last to get powers to build a line from Melton Constable to North Walsham, which would connect their systems. In the same Act the Lynn and Fakenham Railway got powers to build from Holt via Kelling on the proposed line to Blakeney, a line to Cromer (not completed at that time), and the Yarmouth and North Norfolk Railway was converted from a light railway to a full system, avoiding the speed and weight restrictions imposed by light railway status. The Lynn and Fakenham Railway opened from Fakenham to Guestwick on 19 January 1882, and from there to Lenwade on 1 July 1882. The final section to Norwich was opened on 2 December 1882. The Norwich station was named Norwich City from the outset. Melton to North Walsham was opened in April 1883.

The short Yarmouth Union Railway was authorised on 26 August 1880 to extend from the Yarmouth and North Norfolk Railway station at Yarmouth Beach to the quay, where it became effectively a tramway, joining the Great Eastern Railway tramway there though it did not create any through running between the two systems. The capital was £20,000. The Yarmouth Union

Railway itself was slow to start work, but the Yarmouth and North Norfolk Railway helped out and the work was completed on 15 May 1882.

In 1866 the Lynn and Sutton Bridge Railway and the Spalding and Bourn Railway amalgamated to form the Midland and Eastern Railway, the reason being to push forward to Saxby where it would join the MR. Following opposition from the GNR, the scheme was dropped, and a compromise was reached that the MR was given running powers over two GNR sponsored lines from Bourne to Essendine, and (by reversing there) from Essendine to Stamford; this route was neither direct or fast. The arrangement was agreed and ratified by the Midland and Eastern Railway Act of 23 July 1866. The Midland and Eastern Railway was jointly operated by the GNR and the MR and was authorised by an Act of 1867.

The minor railways in Norfolk that were independent of the GER realised that amalgamation with one another was desirable and on 18 August 1882 the E&MR Act was passed. Under the Act, on 1 January 1883 the E&MR was created by amalgamating the Lynn and Fakenham Railway, the Yarmouth and North Norfolk, and the Yarmouth Union Railway. Shares in the Companies generally were transferred to Eastern and Midlands Railway (E&MR) stock, but some preference shareholders retained their rights. By the same Act, a second stage arranged that the E&MR take over the Midland and Eastern Railway on 1 July 1883. The MR and GNR working arrangements were to continue on those affected routes, and the E&MR could only run trains on those sections with the consent of those larger railways. The whole line from Bourne to Great Yarmouth was now under the control of the E&MR.

On 5 April 1883 the E&MR had opened a section from Melton Constable to North Walsham, followed on 1 October 1884 by a section from Melton Constable to Holt.

At Lynn, the E&MR access to the town was inconvenient, involving reversal at the GER station for through trains coming from the east and reliance on the GER's grudging acquiescence. There had been plans to create an independent through route for a while and on 2 November 1885 the Lynn Loop, from South Lynn to Bawsey, was opened for goods traffic; passenger services followed on 1 January 1886. The line ran south of Lynn, connecting from South Lynn goods station to Bawsey. At South Lynn, a new passenger station was provided close to the old goods station. The former connection from Gaywood Road Junction, north of King's Lynn, to Bawsey was closed. King's Lynn station had always been known simply as 'Lynn' but from this time 'Lynn Town' was used instead.

After a suspension of work, the section of line from Holt to Cromer was finally completed and opened on 16 June 1887. This gave Cromer a second station, which was more convenient for the town. The GNR started a through service from King's Cross to Cromer, competing with the GER's service to the town from Liverpool Street. This route was quicker at approximately 3½ hours as opposed to 4½ hours. At the same time, the decision was taken not to proceed with the Blakeney Harbour branch from Kelling.

On 20 June 1888, a branch line from North Walsham to Mundesley, a small seaside resort on the Norfolk coast, was authorised by parliament. The GER opposed the line as it was also interested in the district and had an arrangement with a Mr Palmer who provided horse buses or what the Great Eastern Railway's publicity called 'conveyances'.

For some years there was continuing friction between the E&MR and its predecessors and the MR over the routing for goods traffic. The former company contended that the latter company was obliged to route its goods traffic to Norwich over it and not the GER, notwithstanding the inferior times. The MR repeatedly protested at tribunals that no such obligation existed.

However, in 1888 a Bill was to be submitted to the session of parliament for that year to build a connecting line from the MR near Ashwell (in the vicinity of Oakham) and Bourne. The E&MR was to build this with financial help from the MR and in the following year the MR would take over the entire western section. Traffic from the eastern section would be directed via the MR. This would have cut the GNR out of much of the traffic, even though it had constantly been friendly and supportive of the E&MR when the MR had treated it shabbily. In the circumstances this was 'extraordinary conduct' by the E&MR.

A.J. Wrottesley in *The Midland and Great Northern Joint Railway* (David and Charles 1970) attributed the schemes to R.A. Read who was a director of the E&MR and was friendly to the MR but prone to 'rash and elaborate schemes'.

The new line was sanctioned on 28 June 1888, although to mollify the GNR, a junction with the latter was inserted at Little Bytham. Following the passing of the Act, wiser counsels prevailed, and the E&MR, MR and GNR boards negotiated a more congenial arrangement. The MR and GNR would become joint owners of the western section whilst the eastern section would be unaffected for the time being.

The route of the Bourne connecting line to the MR would be varied, to meet the Midland at Saxby; the connection to the GNR main line at Little Bytham would be retained; and the connecting line west of that point would be the property of the MR and not the E&MR. Ordinary shareholders in the E&MR would get £47 for every £100-worth. A joint committee of the Midland and Great Northern railways met at King's Cross station on 5 March 1889. Whilst it was a Midland and Great Northern Joint Committee, at this stage no such designation was applied to the railway itself. It was not until 1890 that the words M&GNJR appeared in public timetables.

Just at the moment when the future seemed secure, the E&MR was plunged into crisis. For some years the Company had been paying only modest dividends, and profitability had not always been adequate to support outgoings. A Mr W. Jones had been hiring carriages to the Company and for some time had not been paid. On 27 June 1889 he obtained judgment in his favour, but the Company had no money to comply. At the time there was a system which had been established in 1867 and was intended to keep a railway in operation for the convenience of the public in this situation: in effect to trade out of bankruptcy.

R.A. Read was appointed receiver. At a shareholders' meeting held on November 1889, it was stated that the Company had liabilities of over £108,000 on working costs as well as £71,645 on unpaid debenture interest and guaranteed share dividends. At a further meeting held on 2 May 1890, the debenture stock holders accused Read of being to blame for getting the Company into this situation, and demanded his removal, as well as a declaration that their debenture payments should rank equally with the railway operating costs, contrary to normal practice when a railway company was in receivership. Appeals were eventually dismissed and, despite the legal and financial difficulties, the railway kept running. It was not until 16 August 1892 that a scheme of financial arrangement was finalised.

In 1891, the MR and the GNR indicated that they now wished to acquire the eastern section too. This was agreed in October 1892, and a Bill was submitted to the 1893 session of Parliament. The consideration was £1.2million of MR and GNR 3 per cent rent stock, although there were complicated provisions for preference and debenture shareholders. Both eastern and western sections transferred to the M&GNJR.

With only minor interference from the GER, the new arrangement was passed by parliament on 9 June 1893 and the M&GNJR became an incorporated entity and not just a committee delegated by the two principals.

Meanwhile, on 25 July 1890, an avoiding line at Spalding was authorised, enabling through running past the south of the town. It opened for goods traffic on 5 June 1893, and on the same day the Saxby to Bourne section opened, also for goods only. Both sections were opened for passenger traffic on 1 May of the following year. At Saxby, additional platforms were provided. Here the formation was made for a southward connecting curve there, but track was never laid on it. The boundary with the Joint Line was at Little Bytham as planned, and the formation of the connection to the GNR was also made, and here too track was never laid on it.

Changes to the GER

In 1869, the Ipswich District Sorting Carriage ceased running. It was succeeded by the Ipswich Sorting Tender which commenced running in 1872. Meanwhile, in 1863 the Cambridge District Sorting Carriage had succeeded the Cambridge District Sorting Tender. However this ceased running in 1869 and was replaced by the Peterborough Sorting Tender which lasted until 1916.

It was during the period covered by this chapter that the GER commenced the operation of slip coaches, special carriages that could be detached from a moving train. The first use of slip coaches was at Chelmsford in July 1872 when a carriage was slipped off the 10am train from Bishopsgate to Yarmouth, which ran non-stop to Colchester. For the inauguration of slip coach working, two first and second class composite slip coaches were built. In December 1873, the Chelmsford slip was withdrawn, but was reinstated in February 1874, but only on Tuesdays and Fridays. Following their initial introduction, further slip coaches were introduced so that by July 1885 there were no less than 19 slip coach workings on the GER on both the Ipswich and the Cambridge lines. Control of the slip coach was undertaken by a special slip coach guard, who travelled in a special compartment in the slip coach and was responsible for detaching the slip coach from the main train and for bringing it under control into the station for which it was destined. Co-operation was required with the driver and the guard of the main train. Technically, a slip coach was breaking railway regulations as it involved what was, after the slip had taken place, two trains in operation on the same section of line.

In the early 1870s, the GER started to show what might be called democratic leanings when from 1 September 1870 it abolished 'express' or extra fares for the use of its fast trains. Amongst other newspapers, the *Essex Herald* in its edition of 30 August 1870 under the heading 'GREAT EASTERN RAILWAY – DISCONTINUANCE OF EXPRESS FARES' carried an announcement that 'on and after 1st September the charging of express fares by any of the trains of the company will be discontinued, and the ordinary fares charged by all trains'.

On 1 April 1872 it went a step further and admitted third class passengers to all of its trains. In this it was following the example of the MR which had done the same thing on that day. The *Eastern Daily Press* of Monday 1 April 1872 carried the following announcement:

GREAT EASTERN RAILWAY THIRD CLASS PASSENGERS BY ALL TRAINS. ON and after MONDAY, APRIL 1st 1872, THIRD CLASS PASSENGERS will be convoyed ALL TRAINS the GREAT EASTERN RAILWAY. S. SWARBRICK, General Manager. London. March, 1872.

However, unlike the MR which abolished second class on all its trains in 1875, the GER retained second class on all its trains until 1 January 1893 when it was abolished on all trains other than London suburban and continental boat trains.

Carriage Lighting

Originally carriages were lit by oil lamps, but later oil gas replaced oil as the method of lighting. In the early 1880s many of the GER's carriages were lit by oil gas and at Stratford a special plant for its production had been built for the supply of carriages in the London area. Unfortunately, the production of the oil gas left a tarry waste product which was run into the Channelsea River, a tributary of the River Lea. After a time the local sanitary authorities came to the conclusion that this contamination was a nuisance and, using the force of the law, compelled the GER to abate it.

The problem for the GER and in particular its Locomotive Superintendent, James Holden, lay in turning the waste product from the production of oil gas into fuel for the Company's locomotives. A steam locomotive can be made to run on most sorts of fuel and in 1887, Holden, as an experiment, converted an 0-4-4 tank locomotive, No 193, to run on this oil fuel. The experiment proved successful and other conversions followed. The most famous was 2-4-0 locomotive No 760 which was named *Petrolea*. The locomotives that were either converted or originally built to run on oil fuel were mostly but not exclusively express locomotives. Eventually about 60 locomotives were burning oil fuel and suitable oil fuel was purchased to supplement the limited supply from the oil gas plant at Stratford. Then two things happened. Firstly, coal gas started to

The GER was one of the pioneers of the use of oil fuel in steam locomotives and here we see Class P43 4-2-2 No 14's tank being fuelled with oil at Ipswich about 1898-1900. Class P43 were the last single driver locomotives built by the GER. (Harold Hopwood).

supplant oil gas for carriage lighting and then the price of oil rose so that oil firing became more expensive than coal firing and so all the oil burning locomotives were converted to coal burning.

Record breaking construction!

In December 1891 the GER's Stratford works set a world record for the construction of a locomotive. The locomotive in question was Y14 0-6-0 No 930. The time taken for the building of the locomotive was 9 hours and 47 minutes. Prior to the construction of the locomotive all the parts required had been machined, prepared and laid out in readiness: although no actual work had been done. At 9am on Thursday, 10 December 142 men and boys started work. Of these, 85 worked on the locomotive and 57 on the tender. Each was allocated a particular duty to perform. Including an hour's lunch break, work continued until 5.30pm when work finished for the day. Work resumed the next morning at 6am and by 7.40am the tender was completed. Twenty-five minutes earlier both the locomotive and the tender had begun to receive a workshop coat of grey paint. After the men had a break for breakfast between 8.15 and 9am, the locomotive was completed

The Class Y14 0-6-0 was both the largest and the most useful class of locomotives on the GER. Built between 1883 and 1913 the class numbered 289. No 930, seen here, was built at Stratford in 9¾ hours in December 1891, a world record for building a locomotive. (Ken Nunn).

at 9.10am Following this the locomotive and tender were coupled up, the boiler and the tender were filled, the fire laid and after No 930 had been photographed outside of the erecting shop, it was in steam by 10am Following adjustments of weights on the weighbridge, No 930 made a trial trip to Broxbourne and back and was then handed over to the Running Department and put into service hauling coal trains between Peterborough and London.

Braking

In the early 1870s, the only braking that trains had was the handbrake on the engine and a handbrake in one or two carriages. All of these were under individual control, those on the engine that of the driver and those in the carriages under the control of the guard or an under guard. This did not apply just to Great Britain but to the whole world. It was the American George Westinghouse who came up with the idea of a continuous automatic air brake for trains. From having the original idea in 1866, it took him until 1874 to perfect his system. Following this, a number of British railways sat up and took notice, the LB&SCR and the NER being amongst them. In 1878, the GER adopted the Westinghouse air brake. The adoption of a continuous automatic brake took some time and it was not until 1899 that an Act was passed that compelled all railways to fit automatic brakes to all trains. The only problem was that whilst some such as the GER, the NER and the LB&SCR adopted the Westinghouse compressed air brake, others such as the GNR, the L&SWR and the L&YR adopted the vacuum brake which meant that not only some carriages, but also some locomotives had to be dual fitted.

Signalling

When the GER was formed, block signalling was still very primitive and two systems were in force. One was Time Interval and the other Electric Telegraph. The Time Interval worked in conjunction with semaphore signals; the instructions laid down stated that the 'Danger' signal was to be shown for five minutes or for such longer periods as might be considered necessary in the event of the line being obstructed from any cause. After the passage of a train and the necessary time interval had lapsed, the signal was moved to the 'Caution' position for five minutes then to the 'All Right' position. The signal arm was moved by a small lever at the base of the signal post. Only a hut, or at junctions a tower, was provided for shelter. The first signal boxes date from 1857 following the invention by John Saxby of the mechanical interlocking between points and signaling , which he patented in 1856. At night, a lamp was lit to indicate the three positions: 'All Right' showed a white light; 'Caution' (proceed slowly with care) showed a green light; 'Danger' (Always to stop) showed a red light. In general, there was one signal for each line at a station. Were the line to be blocked either for shunting or for an emergency, a man was sent with flags and hand percussion signals and stopped an approaching train. At certain stations Auxiliary (or Distant) Signals were provided for each line 600 yards to the rear of a semaphore post. The Auxiliary signal showed just two positions, 'All Right' and 'Danger'. Auxiliary (or Distant) Signals worked as follows; the Auxiliary signal was placed to 'Danger' as soon as a train passed it and was kept at 'Danger' until the train had passed the Semaphore signal post in advance. If a train arrived at an Auxiliary signal before the line ahead was clear, it was brought to a stand outside the signal and the arm was then lowered to allow the train to pass within its protection. Later on, signalling was improved so that at an ordinary passing station, there would usually be three signals per line, 'Distant', 'Home', and 'Starting'. In some cases, there would be an 'Advance Starting'. The 'Distant' (which had replaced the Auxiliary signal) was usually placed 800 to 1,000 yards to the rear of the 'Home Signal' and could be passed when at 'Danger'. To distinguish it from the 'Home Signal', the end of the Distant arm was cut out like a fish tail. All signal arms were painted red.

The earliest type of telegraph in use was the same as which was used for sending messages and were simply 'Stop' and 'Clear' instruments. This used a single needle. There was no audible signal given with the indications which meant that a signalman had to listen for the clicking of the telegraph machine needle. Signalmen used various methods of attracting attention. These included pieces of paper tied to the bottom of the needle, or a piece of metal placed so that when the needle moved, it tapped it like a sounder. The best was balancing a marble so as soon as the needle moved, it dislodged the marble which rolled down an improvised chute and fell into a bucket. In 1865 'Clarks Recording Double Needle' was in use. This gave audible warning from a bell or gong which worked independently of the needles. They were worked by clockwork released by electricity. The bells and gongs were merely for drawing attention to the needles and could not be used for code. Not all of the GER's lines were controlled by Clarks Recording Double Needle system. Of those that were not, time interval was used on double track lines and on single lines, fixed crossing places for the passing of trains. If late running or the cancellations of trains occurred, problems arose. The dangers of the system were highlighted in the Thorpe accident of 1874, mentioned earlier, when two trains collided head-on due to the misunderstanding of telegraph messages.

In 1870, Tyers Block Instruments were introduced. By 1884, nearly all double lines and some single lines had Tyers Two position Block Instruments.

By the 1890s, because of the dense traffic, there was need for a more advanced form of block, and Sykes Lock and Block was installed in the London area between 1893-94 with the expansion of Liverpool Street and its approaches. Sykes Lock and Block's unique feature is that the lever controlling the signal protecting the section ahead is released by the signal box in advance and that the release cannot be given until the previous train has passed clear out of the section. Sykes was fitted in all signal boxes from Liverpool Street to Seven Sisters and Ilford, and between Hackney Downs and Coppermill Junction, Stratford and Woolwich, Bow Junction and Salmons Lane Junction and in the North Thorpe area.

GER signals were interesting in that from new they had a white metal band put on them. This was done to stop the wooden blade of the signal splitting. On other railways this was done after several years' service.

The Great Eastern Railway From its Formation in 1862 to the End of 1895   109

The GER had a number of signal gantries crossing all lines in the London area. Here we see Class S46 4-4-0 No 1880 coming under the signal gantry at Stratford Western Junction on 6 March 1913 on the 9.02am Norwich to Liverpool Street. (Ken Nunn).

Industrial relations

By the standards of Victorian England, the GER in 1891 was somewhat benign. F.A.S. Brown in *From Stirling to Gresley 1882-1922* (Oxford Publishing Company 1974), in writing about a request on 22 July 1891 by the men at the Doncaster works of the GNR for three days' holiday per annum with pay and three passes, says that the management of the company contacted a number of other companies. These were the Caledonian, the GWR, the L&YR, the LNWR, the MR, the North British, the NER, the SER, the MS&LR and the GER. Of the companies consulted, only the GER provided a sympathetic reply. James Holden, who was the Locomotive Superintendent and a Quaker, said that each man employed in the Locomotive, Carriage and Wagons Department of the company was allowed three days' annual leave with pay and a pass for himself, his wife and family under the age of fourteen years of age to any part of the GER and that arrangement had come into operation the previous year.

Natural hazards

The Great Eastern Railway, like practically all the railways in Great Britain, was affected by the Great Blizzard of January 1881. On 17 January 1881, weather systems in the Channel created a gale force easterly wind with heavy blizzards and drifting snow. The blizzard paralysed all transport, communication, trade and industries. Hundreds of miles of rail track were blocked by drifting snow, dozens of feet high in places. Even in central London, there were 3-foot drifts in places. Around 100 people are believed to have died as a result of the blizzard. Traffic on the GER suffered greatly. Practically all railway traffic ceased. Those trains that were able to move during the blizzard suffered severe delays.

Finally, there was an earthquake. The earthquake in question occurred at 9.18am on 22 April 1884 and was centred round Colchester, but it was felt elsewhere. It did considerable damage. In relation to the GER, the *Lynn Advertiser* of 26 April reported that at the main station in Colchester, the 9.20 train which was about to start rocked so much that the driver fell off the engine on to the platform.

Sea water

Starting in the late 1870s the GER started selling sea water from Lowestoft for domestic use. The sea water at Lowestoft was pumped by a redundant steam locomotive into a number of fish and open carriage wagons converted to salt water tanks . The trains carrying the sea water ran to Liverpool Street where the sea water was distilled into the kegs (barrels). According the GER's advertisement the sea water was delivered daily except Sundays to any station or any address within the ordinary carriage delivery area of the Company in London and the Country at the uniform price of 6d for every 3 gallons payable on delivery. Within the London area the water was delivered by horse drawn van or later also motor van. Elsewhere the kegs would have been taken by train to the nearest station to the recipient or recipients and delivered from there. The kegs containing the sea water were perfectly tight, well corked and fitted with a handle so that they could be easily carried upstairs; they would be left by the GER's carmen (van or cart driver) if required by the consignee and called for afterwards for no extra charge. Orders could be sent by post or given verbally to any station master or carman when delivering or fetching the kegs or at the Sea Water Office, Liverpool Street Station. The seawater was used in baths. Thus you could wash in the sea in your own house.

Laundry

In 1888 the GER built a laundry at Colchester, which at one time employed 70 people and supplied the Company's hotels with bed linen, tablecloths etc.

Section 2

The Great Eastern Railway 1896 to 1922

The period 1896 to 1922 saw the GER reach its peak and sadly start a decline. Its last branch line to be built was opened in 1913 when the Thaxted branch was opened. There had however been contractions as far as passenger services were concerned with the Lower Edmonton to Cheshunt line losing its passenger service in 1909 as the result of tramway competition and the Metropolitan Railway taking over the working of passenger services on the ELR in 1913 and the withdrawal of the passenger service from Liverpool Street to Shoreditch. There was competition from electric tramways and the threat of competition from electric underground railways. The GER, had it been wealthier like the L&SWR, would have electrified its London suburban services, but it did not have the money to do so and so had to make do with steam. The motor bus was developed of which the GER was a pioneer in the use of in the 1900s. Later motor bus companies independent of the GER threatened to become competitors. There was co-operation with the MR and GNR in the formation of the Norfolk and Suffolk Joint Railway (N&SJR). Later there was a thwarted proposal from the GER to join with the GNR and the GCR in a joint working arrangement. In south Essex, the GER found that the MR had become a competitor when the latter took over the LT&SR in 1912. In mid-Suffolk, a possible competitor arose in the form of the MSLR, which, had it been completed in full and joined up with a re-gauged Southwold Railway, could, in the form of a direct route from Haughley to Halesworth and an alternative route from Westerfield to Halesworth via Kenton, have given the GER competition. However, the MSLR was never completed in full and the Southwold Railway was never re-gauged. The GER provided financial help to the Lancashire, Derbyshire and East Coast Railway, which Company was later taken over by the GCR. Of the railways in east London and the eastern counties, only the Corringham Light Railway on the Thames estuary did not connect with the GER. After the war came the Railways Act of 1921 which put the GER, along with the GNR, the GCR, the NER, the North

British Railway and the Great North of Scotland Railway, in the London and NER group.

It was during the period covered by this chapter that the N&ER was taken over by the GER. Notice of the GER's intention to acquire the former company was given at the 75th Half Yearly Meeting of the latter Company held on 30 January 1900. The authorisation was part of a wider Bill to be introduced into parliament. Things did not go to plan, though, as at the next Half Yearly Meeting of the GER, held on 31 July 1900, the Chairman Lord Claud Hamilton reported that 'the Clauses relating to the purchase of the N&ER were also withdrawn in consequence of the negotiations between the two Companies not having been completed'.

At the 79th Half Yearly Meeting of the GER held on 28 January 1902, the Chairman reported that a Bill had been deposited with parliament for the ensuing session that included amongst other things the purchase of the N&ER. At the following Half Yearly Meeting of the GER, held on 29 July 1902, the Chairman reported that:

> The Company's Bill in Parliament, which was approved by the Proprietors at the Special General Meeting on the 28th January, 1902, received the Royal Assent on the 23rd June, 1902. The Act confirms the Agreement for the purchase of the N&ER, which became vested in the GER Company from the 1st instant.

The Chairman's report at the following Half Yearly Meeting of the Company held on 28 January 1903 said that the purchase of the N&ER had been completed and that it would not entail an additional burden on the shareholders of the GER as the rent that had been previously paid for the lease of the N&ER would in future be represented by Debenture interest.

GER New Lines

On 17 May 1896, the Newmarket curve was opened at Cambridge. In north western Cambridgeshire, the area of Benwick was poorly served by road and rail and during the 1880s local farmers lobbied the GER board for a new railway. Initially the GER very reluctantly provided a siding and a goods shed at Three Horseshoes. The farmers continued lobbying and the GER opened a single track goods only line from Three Horseshoes to Burnt House on 1 September 1897 and to Benwick on 2 August 1898.

At Felixstowe on 1 July 1898 the GER opened an extension of the branch line to a central site in the new town that had grown up on the cliffs away from the docks to a station named Felixstowe Town, and the two original stations (originally Town and Beach, but then changed to Beach and Pier) that were intended to act as the nuclei for the development of the town. The *(Ipswich) Evening Star* of 1 July 1898 reported that:

'PROGRESSIVE FELIXSTOWE. OPENING OF THE NEW RAILWAY STATION.

The new town station at Felixstowe, of which a description has already been given, was formally opened this morning for the purposes of railway traffic. Although no formal ceremony was organised, the event was rightly and naturally regarded one of first-rate importance in the history of this rising seaside resort, and all sections of residents—official, trading, and private— were represented in the crowd which gathered at the terminus, to await the arrival of the GER Company's officials who came down by special train at 12.57, to make a formal inspection of the new work.

In the London area in the last quarter of the nineteenth century, suburban growth around Ilford and the lack of a railway in the area of Barkingside and Chigwell prompted the promotion in 1895 of an Ilford, Barkingside and Chigwell Railway. Whilst the bill for the railway was deposited with parliament for the 1896 session, it was withdrawn when the GER promised to build a similar railway – so fulfilling what was probably the real intention of the promoters. The GER obtained powers in 1897 under its General Powers Act of that year to build a railway from Woodford on the Epping and Ongar line via Chigwell and Barkingside to near Ilford where the line divided in two, one curve going west in the direction of Ilford and the other going east in the direction of Seven Kings. The railway opened for goods and passenger traffic on 1 May 1903. Only the west curve was regularly used for passenger trains with the east curve being used for goods trains. The *Barking, East Ham & Ilford Advertiser, Upton Park and Dagenham Gazette* of Saturday 2 May reported:

THE NEW ILFORD AND WOODFORD RAILWAY.

The Great Eastern Railway Company opened on Friday for passenger traffic a new 'loop' line, six miles in length, connecting the Colchester main line at Ilford with the Loughton and Ongar branch at Woodford. The district opened up by the line can be served by a circular service of trains from Liverpool Street or Fenchurch Street, running over the main line to Ilford, thence by the loop line to Woodford, and back over the Loughton line to Liverpool Street or Fenchurch Street, and vice-versa. Between Ilford and Woodford the new railway runs practically east and west, describing a curve which at all points is within the 12 miles City radius. It traverses what, for the most part, is at present open country, considered ripe and eminently suitable for residential development.

Not all of the stations on the line proved successful. Hainault, between Fairlop and Grange Hill, closed on 1 October 1908 due to lack of custom.

Light Railways

Both of the remaining new lines built by the Great Eastern Railway were light railways built under the Light Railway Act of 1896. The purpose of the Act was to facilitate the construction of railways in rural areas, especially to facilitate the transport of goods. The Act did not specify any exceptions or limitations that should apply to light railways, nor did it even attempt to define a 'light railway'. However, it gave powers to the Light Railway Commissioners to include 'provisions for the safety of the public … as they think necessary for the proper construction and working of the railway' in any light railway order granted under the Act. These could limit vehicle axle weights and speeds. A number of municipal and company-owned street tramways were built or extended by the Act, in preference to the Tramways Act 1870. The procedure of the 1896 Act was simpler and permission was easier to obtain. Under the Tramways Act 1870, local authorities had had the right to veto lines. There was a 75 per cent savings on rates payable as compared to a tramway. An example of this was in Southend where the tramways were built under the Light Railway Act. In Colchester they were built under the Tramways Act.

Only two railways were built by the GER under the Light Railways Act. The first was the Kelvedon, Tiptree and Tollesbury Light Railway which opened to Tollesbury on 1 October 1904 and was extended to Tollesbury Pier on 15 May 1907, the intention being to build bungalows and houses and a yachting station nearby and a yachting resort, as well as tapping the resources of the local shrimp, oyster beds and other fish traffic with easy access to the London market. There was even talk of using the pier as a point for steamer services to the Continent.

The *Chelmsford Chronicle* of Friday, 7 October 1904 reported 'AN ESSEX LIGHT RAILWAY. OPENING OF THE KELVEDON TO TOLLESBURY LINE. The long-looked-for light railway from the main line at Kelvedon, over Tiptree Heath and on to Tollesbury and the Blackwater estuary, is now fully accomplished, and was opened for the public service on Saturday'. The same newspaper of Friday, 17 May 1907 merely reported that 'Tollesbury Pier was brought into use on Wednesday'.

The second light railway was the Elsenham and Thaxted Light Railway which was authorised and constructed under the Light Railway Order of the same name dated 19 April 1911 and which opened on 1 April 1913. The *Chelmsford Chronicle* of Friday, 4 April 1913 reported 'TO THAXTED BY RAIL.

Tiptree station on the Kelvedon, Tiptree and Tollesbury Light Railway, seen here in 1910, presented a marked contrast to the splendour of Liverpool Street station. The locomotive is R24 Class 0-6-0 side tank No 267. The Light Railway had been opened in 1904. (Ken Nunn).

Here is a mixed train on the Kelvedon, Tiptree and Tollesbury Light Railway just after leaving Kelvedon in 1910, hauled by Class R24 0-6-0 side tank No 267 running as a 2-4-0 with the front coupling rods removed. (Ken Nunn).

OPENING NEW LIGHT RAILWAY IN NORTH ESSEX. Monday was a red-letter day in the history of ancient Thaxted, for it saw the entry into that famed North Essex town of the first official train along the newly constructed railway line from Elsenham to Thaxted'. This was the last new railway opened by the GER.

It has to be said not all of the light railways that obtained orders were constructed. To give some examples, the Coggeshall Light Railway which obtained its order on 20 November 1899 to build a railway from Kelvedon to Coggeshall and which appeared as a projected railway on the Railway Clearing House Map of England and Wales of 1904 was never built, neither was the Long Melford and Hadleigh Light Railway which obtained its order on 8 February 1901 to build a railway from Long Melford on the Stour Valley line to join the Bentley to Hadleigh branch at Hadleigh. Another light railway proposal which obtained its order was the Central Essex Light Railway. George Woodcock in *Minor Railways of England and Their Locomotives* (Goose 1970) says that the Central Essex Light Railway had originally obtained its order on 3 July 1901 and obtained an amendment order in 1905, an extension of time order in 1907 and an amendment and extension of time order in 1908 to build a railway from

Ongar via Dunmow to Yeldham on the Colne Valley and Halstead Railway. By the early part of 1914 nothing had been done, but according to the *Chelmsford Chronicle* of Friday, 22 May:

> CENTRAL ESSEX RAILWAY. The Board of Trade have sanctioned a further extension of time for the Central Essex Light Railway. No railway is more required to open up the county of Essex than this one. It will commence 22 miles from London, at Ongar Station, G.E.R. and pass through numerous villages and through Dunmow and Great Bardfield to Castle Hedingham. There are said to be great hopes of seeing the construction begun very shortly.

The same newspaper of Friday, 4 September reported:

> CENTRAL ESSEX RAILWAY. A correspondent informs us that a contract has been signed for the construction of the Central Essex Railway, and eminent engineers have been appointed to supervise the works. In consequence of the heavy motor traffic, the County Council have stipulated that £15,000 for extra bridges should be set on one side to make these bridges when required, but this will not alter the level of the railway, as the bridges will go over the line. The Great Eastern Railway have offered to work the line on favourable terms when constructed.

This seems to have been the source of a report in the *Locomotive Magazine* of October 1914 which stated that 'the contract for the construction of the Central Essex Light Rly has recently been signed. It will form a continuation of the Ongar branch of the GER.' The last that one hears of the Central Essex Light Railway is in the *Chelmsford Chronicle* of 8 January 1915 in its report of the Essex County Council meeting of 5 January 1915. It seems that the extension of time granted to the Railway was due to expire on 30 April 1915 and that a sub-committee of the Highways Committee of the County Council had questioned the Company's financial position with its Secretary and had felt that the information that it had received was of an unsatisfactory nature. It was felt that requests by the Light Railway Company for further extensions of time could not be supported by the County Council. The County Council approved the sub-committee's recommendations and forwarded its report on the Light Railway Company to the Board of Trade and the Treasury. Nothing further can be found about the Central Essex Light Railway, although it is shown on the Railway Clearing House Map of the East of England for 1917.

Another light railway was the South Norfolk Light Railway which obtained its order on 13 February 1899 and was granted an extension of time order in 1902. The Railway was to start from a siding with the Great Eastern Railway's Ely to Norwich line at Trowse and to run via Arminghall, Poringland, Brooke, Seething, Loddon and Gillingham. Nothing came of this. The Great Eastern Railway was not particularly enthusiastic about this Railway.

One other light railway in this area was the Wissington Light Railway which opened in 1905. It ran southwards for about five miles from Abbey and West Dereham station on the Denver to Stoke Ferry branch. It was a sort of a cross between a private siding and a farm railway and as such it was not a public railway and was a purely industrial railway.

The Corringham Light Railway ran from the village of Corringham in Essex to Kynochtown (later Coryton) which was situated at Shell Haven, a small creek off the river Thames and near Thames Haven. There was a branch to the LT&SR's Thames Haven branch. The Railway opened to goods traffic on 1 January 1901 and to passenger traffic on 22 June 1901. Although it operated a passenger service, this did not connect with the LT&SR's passenger services and was principally for the inhabitants of Corringham who worked at Kynoch's munitions works at Kynochtown. As to how much goods traffic Corringham received via the Light Railway and the LT&SR is not known. It was the only railway whose only connection to the rest of the railway network was via the LT&SR. The Corringham Light Railway remained independent following the 1923 Grouping.

Unbuilt Lines

The Canvey Island Deep Water Port proposal went back to 1911 and in 1912 a bill was presented to parliament for a Canvey Deep Water Wharf and Railway. The early proposals of 1911 and 1917 envisaged a connection to the LT&SR (MR after 1912). The proposal for 1919 envisaged a connection to the GER's Southend line at Fanton Junction. The GER opposed the scheme as it would have preferred a flyover rather than a flat junction at Fanton Junction. The MR opposed the scheme because it did not want their line crossed on the flat and the Port of London Authority opposed the scheme as it would have meant competition. Both the LT&SR and later the MR and the Port of London Authority had opposed the earlier schemes. Nothing came of the proposals or later ones in 1921 and 1922, whilst a proposal in 1924 was thwarted by the Ministry of Transport.

The Greater London Railway was promoted in late 1910 to run from a junction with the L&SWR at Feltham with junctions with the GWR near to Southall, with the Metropolitan District Railway, with the GCR, with the L&NWR, and with the Metropolitan Railway at various points in the district of Wembley, with the MR at Hendon, with the GNR at Southgate and Wood Green, with the GER at Tottenham and Ilford and the LT&SR at Ilford and East Ham, before terminating at Tilbury with a junction with the Port of London Authority's Tilbury Docks Railway with a branch railway to the Victoria and Albert Docks. Charles Klapper in *London's Lost Railways* (Routledge and Kegan Paul 1976) says that there was to be a junction with the then proposed extension of the Charing Cross, Euston and Hampstead (tube) Railway north of Golders Green on its way to Edgware. On 16 June 1911, the Select Committee of the House of Commons sanctioned the section from Northolt to the Victoria and Albert Docks and only that section. Worse was to follow. On 3 August 1911, the Select Committee of the House of Lords rejected the remainder of the Company's Bill so it was not proceeded with.

After the end of the First World War there were a number of proposals for light railways that came to nothing. For example, in Essex plans were deposited with the Clerk of the Peace in 1919 for a Bradwell-on-Sea Light Railway running from Southminster station to Bradwell-on-Sea as an extension of the Southminster branch, an Ongar and Shenfield Light Railway running from Ongar to Shenfield with a spur running alongside the main line, but only a connection to the branch line to Southend and the Braintree and Marks Tey Light Railway running from Braintree to Marks Tey.

N&SJR New Lines

On 20 June 1888, the E&MR had obtained powers to build a railway from North Walsham to Mundesley. The GER was granted running powers over the proposed line. Nothing happened. In fact, when the M&GNJR was formed, the two owning companies wanted to abandon the branch line, but parliament refused to allow it. The GER got so dissatisfied with the delays in building the Mundesley branch that it considered applying for powers to build it itself or at the very least make sure of running powers over it. The Company also proposed building a line from Mundesley south along the coast through Bacton to Happisburgh (pronounced Haysboro'). The GER wanted to build a line from Yarmouth to Lowestoft along the coast. This line would have been somewhat more direct than its line between the two places via the Haddiscoe curve. The M&GNJR wanted to serve Lowestoft and also the up-and-coming resort of Gorleston, which was on the coast just south of Yarmouth harbour. The GER wanted to serve the seaside town of Sheringham, which was served by the M&GNJR. On 21 May 1896, the GER obtained powers to build a line of 3 furlongs in length from its North Walsham station to join the authorised M&GNJR line at Antingham Road. Meanwhile the M&GNJR had asked for tenders for the construction of the Mundesley line, for which a Mr Mousley's was accepted and work began on building the line in December of that year. Under an Act obtained by the MR on 7 August 1896, the M&GNJR was authorised to extend the Mundesley line from Mundesley through Overstrand and under the GER just to the south of the latter's Cromer Beach station and curve round to join its line from Cromer to Melton Constable three quarters of a mile west of Cromer Beach station at a point which was later called Runton East Junction. In the same year, the GER's board considered a scheme to extend its proposed branch to Happisburgh south along the coast through Palling and Horsey to Yarmouth. The M&GNJR was not happy about this as it would have been parallel to its own main line about four miles away and would have catered for Cromer to Yarmouth traffic which the M&GNJR was already carrying via Melton Constable and was proposing to carry via Mundesley and North Walsham. At this point the GER's Board felt that there was not enough potential traffic to justify building the line and so only sought powers from parliament for the line from Mundesley to Happisburgh. In the autumn of 1896, the competing Companies deposited their Bills for Yarmouth to Lowestoft lines. At the same time, at Lynn there was a dispute between the two Companies about the extension of the Great Eastern Railway's goods shed for M&GNJR traffic at King's Lynn. The M&GNJR proposed a line from Hardwick Road to Austin Street where the Railway had its offices in order to use that place as a separate goods station.

At this point something unusual happened – co-operation started. On 18 March 1897, the GER and the M&GNJR reached an agreement about the extension. The M&GNJR would not oppose the GER's Yarmouth to Lowestoft Line Bill and the former company's proposed line would be cut down to run from Caister Road in Yarmouth, where it was to leave the old 'Union' line to the west side of the GER's East Suffolk main line into Yarmouth Southtown.

In the following year, an extension of the line, to join the Yarmouth to Lowestoft line, was to be authorised by the GER. The M&GNJR was to be given running powers into Lowestoft station from Coke Oven Junction. The M&GNJR would not oppose the GER's bill for a line from Mundesley to Happisburgh. In 1898 an application would be made to parliament to construct a junction between the M&GNJR's proposed Mundesley to Cromer line and the GER and also if it was found to be practical for another junction to give the GER access to Sheringham and running powers granted to that Company. A new committee, the N&SJRs Committee, was to be formed to control the North Walsham to Mundesley Road Junction, the Mundesley to Cromer line, the Mundesley to Happisburgh line and the new Lowestoft to Yarmouth line from the junction at Gorleston. The new joint system would have four GER directors and four M&GNJR directors. The dispute about Lynn goods station was to be referred to arbitration and the M&GNJR's Bill for a line from Hardwick Road was withdrawn. The GER's Bill was passed by parliament on 3 June 1897 and the M&GNJR's Bill on 6 August 1897. This latter Bill also gave still more time for the completion of the North Walsham to Mundesley line.

On 20 June 1898, the line from North Walsham to Mundesley was opened by the M&GNJR for goods traffic. On the same day, the GER's connecting line was also opened for goods traffic. Passenger traffic followed on 1 July 1898. The *Eastern Evening Press* of 1 July 1898 reported.

MUNDESLEY LINE OPENED. The extension of the Midland and Great Northern (Joint) Railway to Mundesley over which the Great Eastern will have running powers was opened to-day. A party of gentlemen left King's Cross by special train at 9-30, and on their arrival at North Walsham they passed over the new line to Mundesley where luncheon was served.

The Act establishing the N&SJRs committee was passed on 25 July 1898. This meant that until the passing of the latter Act, the GER's access to Mundesley was over the M&GNJR. On the proposed Happisburgh line, powers to divert the line further inland were obtained in 1898, but nothing more was heard of the scheme and the powers to build it were repealed in 1902.

Further openings were on 13 July 1903 when the section of the M&GNJR from Caster Road Junction, the section of the N&SJR from Coke Oven Junction in Lowestoft to Gorleston North Junction and the section of the GER from Yarmouth South Town to Gorleston North Junction were opened.

In 1906 on 23 July the following sections of line were opened. The M&GNJR from Runton East Junction to Newstead Lane Junction; the N&SJR from Roughton Road Junction to Runton West Junction; and the GER from Roughton Road Junction to Cromer Junction. On 2 August 1906, the N&SJR opened the section from Roughton Road Junction to Mundesley.

The Lancashire, Derbyshire and East Coast Railway

This, although later taken over by the GCR (as the Manchester, Sheffield and Lincolnshire Railway had become following a change of name in 1897), had been provided with financial help by the GER.

The Lancashire, Derbyshire and East Coast Railway (LD&ECR) was planned to create a railway to connect coalfields in Derbyshire and Nottinghamshire with Warrington and a new port on the Lincolnshire coast at Sutton-on-Sea. The route was surveyed by November 1890 and the plans for it were published and submitted to the 1891 session of parliament. The Railway's Bill was opposed by the MS&LR as much of the new Railway's route ran parallel to its own lines.

The MR also opposed it, mainly because of the new Railway's proposed running powers in the Manchester area. The GER supported it because it had, via the Great Northern and Great Eastern Joint Railway, access to Lincoln which the new Railway would serve and saw that it would give it better access to the collieries.

During the parliamentary stages of the Company's Bill, the GER indicated that it would give financial support to the line in exchange for running powers over the entire system. The LD&ECR Act was passed on 5 August 1891. This was the largest railway scheme ever approved by parliament in a single session.

Its main line from Warrington to Sutton-on-Sea amounted to 170 miles of railway with branches, as well as extensive dock installations. The estimated cost of the construction of the railway alone was £4,542,522, whilst that of constructing the docks at Sutton-on-Sea was £700,000, making a grand total of £5,242,522. The authorised capital of the Company was £5 million. However, it immediately became obvious that subscription for that large sum would not be easy to find and in November 1891 the GER examined the plans for the scheme and agreed to subscribe £250,000. By this, the GER became the dominant force in the Company and insisted on the first construction being limited to the main line between Chesterfield and Lincoln, with a branch to Beighton (near Sheffield), which it was hoped would give it access to Sheffield by running powers over the MS&LR. Although parliament authorised the Beighton line, it refused the GER running powers over it. The first sod of the new Railway was cut at Chesterfield on 7 June 1892.

Construction of the Railway was started, but subscriptions for shares were extremely slow. In February 1894, the Company asked the main contractor to accept shares instead of cash, which he refused, and stated that he would stop work if not paid in cash promptly. At the beginning of May 1894 public subscriptions amounted to about £400,000. The Company's Directors had made themselves responsible for a further £850,000, and a new Director, Mr Perks, and his associates, were to put up £250,000. After protracted negotiations, the GER confirmed their earlier offer to subscribe £250,000 on the condition of the separation of the central section from the eastern section and their constitution as separate concerns. The GER was not prepared to see their money expended on the line to Sutton-on-Sea.

The first section of the line was opened for goods traffic from Barlborough Colliery on the Beighton line, via Langwith to Pyewipe Junction, near Lincoln on the Great Northern and Great Eastern Joint Railway, on 16 November 1896. Barlborough, immediately west of Clowne, was for the time being the northern extremity of the authorised Beighton branch, as there was a colliery there. At Clowne a junction with the MR, and branches to Creswell, Langwith and Warsop Main collieries, as well as the northern curve to the GNR at Tuxford, were brought into use on the same date.

Difficulties in the construction of Bolsover Tunnel delayed opening of the Chesterfield main line, but passenger traffic was started on the line from

Edwinstowe to Lincoln GNR station on 15 December 1896. The GER was quick to make use of their running powers and was soon conveying coal from the line. On 8 February 1897, the line was opened from Chesterfield to Langwith to goods and mineral traffic, followed by the opening for passengers on 8 March 1897. At Duckeries Junction – which was originally to be called Tuxford Junction – the LD&ECR passed over the GNR main line and platforms serving the two railways were connected by stairs.

The Railway realised that as operating as a feeder of coal to the GER its future independence was uncertain and so strong and effective steps were taken to develop tourist traffic. For that purpose, the Railway was designated the Dukeries Route. However, the attraction of having an independent outlet to the sea so enabling a heavy mineral traffic was still prominent in the Company's thinking. It was now plain that the westward route, crossing the Pennines, was clearly out of the question, but in the east Sutton-on-Sea still beckoned. A proposal was formulated by which a subsidiary of the LD&ECR would build the line and the docks. There were other interests active in planning a harbour at Sutton-on-Sea; although a branch line, the Sutton and Willoughby Railway, which branched off from the GNR, was built, opening in 1886, The docks were not. In 1892, powers obtained to build the docks were acquired by the Lancashire, Derbyshire and East Coast Railway, and in 1897 the Lincoln and East Coast Railway and Dock Company was formed to acquire the powers for the docks and the connecting line from Lincoln. The capital of the new Company was to be £2 million, but no progress was made and it was abandoned in 1902.

Langwith Junction was the point at which the Beighton branch left the main line and ran in a northerly direction from the west end of the station. Nearby the MR route passed under the Lancashire, Derbyshire and East Coast Railway, also running towards the north. In 1899 a south to east curve was laid in, connecting the MR towards Warsop, which was used by passenger trains between 1899 and 1912.

The GNR in 1901 completed its Leen Valley Extension line from Annesley and made a connection into the LD&ECR at Langwith Junction. The GNR had been granted running powers over the LD&ECR from Lincoln to Chesterfield and to Langwith colliery, and the LD&ECR got running powers over the GNR to Kirkby colliery on the Leen Valley extension in exchange. On 1 September

1902, the LD&ECR began running over the Leen Valley extension to and from Pleasley, Teversall, Silverhill and Kirkby collieries.

In 1904, the MR built another connecting spur, from south to west which until 1914 the spur and the LD&ECR were used by MR boat trains from St Pancras to Heysham for the Isle of Man ferries on Saturdays. Later the spur was used by passenger trains from Mansfield to Sheffield Midland.

The LD&ECR had always wanted to reach Sheffield, but the MS&LR (later GCR) consistently refused running powers over it from Beighton. As well as the GER, which as mentioned also sought the access, independent business interests urged some means of making a connection. A first attempt at a semi-independent line to Sheffield in April 1894 failed, as the LD&ECR was financially embarrassed. A second application to parliament in 1896 resulted in an Act, of 4 August 1896, for the Sheffield District Railway. This would be a new line running from the LD&ECR at Spink Hill, on the Beighton branch, to a new terminus, Attercliffe, in Sheffield. The new Company had an authorised capital of £400,000, and it was backed by the GER and the LD&ECR which would both have running powers. The Lancashire, Derbyshire and East Coast Railway would work the line for 50 per cent of the gross receipts.

The MR, seeing this, offered the LD&ECR access over its own line into Sheffield. The LD&ECR was to make a junction with the MR at Kilmarsh and would then be given running powers over that Railway to Treeton and could then build its own line from there to Brightside, where it would join the MR's Rotherham line and could have running powers from there to the intended terminal at Attercliffe. Additionally, the MR offered the LD&ECR running powers to its main passenger station in Sheffield. This was an attractive offer, giving a saving of six miles of new construction, at the cost of a more roundabout route. Construction was quickly started, and the variation on the authorised route was passed by an Act of 12 August 1898.

The LD&ECR's Beighton branch was brought into use for coal and goods traffic from Barlborough colliery junction to a new LD&ECR station at Killamarsh, a distance of 4½ miles, on 21 September 1898, and for all traffic on 1 October. Its extension to the connection with the MR at Killamarsh (Beighton Junction), a further 1½ miles, was opened on 29 May 1900 for goods traffic, and the following day for passenger traffic. The GER got access to Sheffield through its running powers agreement with the LD&ECR. The Attercliffe station had been originally conceived as a passenger and goods terminal, but passenger terminal facilities were now provided by the MR at their main station, although a passenger platform was nevertheless constructed at Attercliffe goods station, although it is doubtful whether it was ever used.

In the autumn of 1896, the LD&ECR was able to discard earlier plans to build a branch from Edwinstowe to Mansfield, when the MR agreed to give the Company and the GER running powers for goods and coal traffic from Shirebrook to Mansfield. This involved the construction by the LD&ECR of an east to south curve near Langwith Junction, and the cost of building a Mansfield branch was saved; moreover the Company secured entry to Shirebrook colliery over the MR. In return, the MR was given running powers to Edwinstowe.

Although the LD&EDR's connection over the Sheffield District Railway into Sheffield was something of a triumph, the plain fact was that the Company was a small railway which was dependent on much bigger neighbours. Its Chesterfield terminal was a dead end, and the dreams of reaching the North Sea had long since disappeared. In the circumstances, its absorption by one or other of its bigger neighbours was inevitable. The question was which one. The Railway made physical connection with the GNR at three points, with the MR at Shirebrook and Beighton and of course with the GER. The GNR was very interested in acquiring the LD&ECR in about 1904-5, when the GCR put in a successful bid to outdo the GNR towards the end of 1905. The question as to why the GER did not attempt to buy the LD&ECR is that it had the access it needed by virtue of its running powers, so it had no motivation to purchase it. The Act of the acquisition of the LD&ECR by the GCR was dated 30 May 1906 and came into force on 1 January 1907. At Duckmanton, between Chesterfield and Bolsover, curves were quickly laid to connect the GCR to the LD&ECR as there was no pre-existing connection. Later a spur was laid at Beighton between the GCR and the LD&ECR.

The SE&CR in January 1899 opened goods sidings at Hither Green, to which both the L&NWR and the GER had access. The SE&CR was a working union of the SER and the LC&DR and had come into effect on 1 January 1899. The goods sidings at Hither Green had been planned by the SER, which had begun buying land for them in 1897.

Widening and doubling of lines

On the Colchester main line, the section between Ilford and just west of Romford was quadrupled by the end of 1902.

On the Tendring Hundred lines, the section from Wivenhoe to Great Bentley was doubled in 1898.

On the New Essex lines, the section between Rochford and Prittlewell was doubled in 1896, that from Wickford to Rayleigh in May 1900, from Rayleigh to Hockley some time between October 1900 and January 1901 and from Hockley to Rochford in 1901 some time after February.

In Norfolk on the line to Cromer from Norwich between 1896 and 1900 the track was doubled between Whitlingham and North Walsham.

Closures

The first was from Lower Edmonton to Cheshunt. On 11 December 1907 the Metropolitan Electric Tramways opened a line from Lower Edmonton to Enfield Lock (Freezywater) and on 17 April 1908 extended the line to Waltham Cross. The new electric trams not only provided a cheaper and more frequent service for the local journeys that made up most of the passenger traffic on the line, but they offered the great boon of accessibility as they passed along the centre of the built up area on each side of the main road that ran parallel to the railway. Almost overnight, receipts on the railway fell by half and so the GER decided to withdraw the passenger service. This took place with the last train running on 30 September 1909.

The second was the connection to the Metropolitan Railway at Liverpool Street which was last used by an Aylesbury to Yarmouth excursion in 1904 and was disconnected in 1907. The GER end was first used for a few years for the storage of stock, but was later converted for use as a staff canteen and recreation space.

The other withdrawal of service was that of GER scheduled passenger services over the ELR.

Electrification

Between 1903 and 1905 the Metropolitan District and the Metropolitan railways electrified most of their systems, although some steam working over the northern part of the Inner Circle by steam trains from the Hammersmith and City Railway by the Metropolitan Railway continued until 2 December 1906.

On the Metropolitan Railway steam working continued for passenger traffic on all lines north of Harrow-on-the-Hill and for goods traffic north of Finchley Road. The ELR was not included in the electrification, though, but continued to be worked by steam traction. The reason for this being that despite a decline in traffic over the railway, four of the six lessees of the Railway (the GER, the SER, the LC&DR and the LB&SCR) had refused a proposal from the other two lessees (the Metropolitan and the Metropolitan District railways) that all the lessees should jointly fund the conversion of the Railway to electric traction. Following the cessation of Metropolitan District Railway trains on 31 July 1905, the LB&SCR provided additional trains between Shoreditch and its New Cross station. Following the end of the Metropolitan Railway's trains on 2 December 1906, the SE&CR introduced a limited service between Whitechapel and its New Cross station. At the same time, the Whitechapel curve was closed. South of the River Thames, the LB&SCR electrified its South London line in 1909. This made a reversal of steam trains at Peckham Rye on that line an obstruction to the development of the electric services and the Shoreditch to Peckham Rye service was withdrawn after 31 May 1911 as were GER trains to Croydon. With traffic continuing to decline, Lord Claud Hamilton, who was both the Chairman of the GER and the ELR Joint Committee, became convinced that electrification was the only answer to halt the decline in traffic on the ELR. A decision on electrifying the ELR followed largely from his personal efforts and from the positive attitude of the Metropolitan Railway's General Manager, Robert Selbie. When the General Managers of the lessee companies of the ELR met on 24 April 1911, they had a proposal from British Thomson-Houston proposing to electrify the section of line from Platforms 14 and 15 at Liverpool Street station to the two New Cross stations for £100,944. This included rolling stock on the third and four rail system that was used on the Metropolitan and Metropolitan District railways. The outcome of the discussions was that on 26 April, the six lessee companies of the ELR agreed to share the track equipment costs in proportion to their liabilities under the lease with the Metropolitan and the Metropolitan District railways to provide the trains and the power from their existing resources, charging the Joint Committee only working expenses. In July 1911, the GER agreed to find the capital for the electrification of the ELR on the provision that the lessee companies paid interest on it at 4 per cent a year in proportion to their liabilities under the lease. On 7 August 1912, the GER obtained an Act sanctioning the electrification and the raising of £90,000 by the issue of 4 per cent Debenture stock. Six months later, the contracts for the electrification equipment, automatic signalling and substation plant were in place. Work on the electrification proceeded under the supervision of the engineers of the Metropolitan, Metropolitan District and South Eastern railways. Following further discussion, it was agreed that the Underground Group would supply the electric power through its Whitechapel substation and a new substation at Deptford Road with the Metropolitan Railway providing the whole train service and the operating staff. On 31 March 1913, the scheduled steam passenger trains of the GER, the SER and LB&SCR ran over the ELR for the last time and on the following day, trains of the Metropolitan Railway began running from South Kensington via Edgware Road, and Moorgate Street to the two New Cross stations. There was also a local service from Shoreditch to the two New Cross stations. The section from Liverpool Street (GER) to Shoreditch was closed to scheduled passenger services. The proposal to electrify the section of the GER from Platforms 14 and 15 at Liverpool Street to Shoreditch was dropped. On 1 November 1909, the name of Bishopsgate (Metropolitan Railway) station was changed to Liverpool Street. Thus travel from Liverpool Street to stations on the ELR was still possible, albeit via the Metropolitan Railway from its station at Liverpool Street. The western terminus of the Metropolitan Railway's service was changed to Hammersmith (Hammersmith and City Railway) station from 9 February 1914.

The other underground railway to reach Liverpool Street station was the Central London Railway (CLR). The CLR's origins went back to 1889 when two tube railway schemes were put forward. These were the Central London Subway to run from Shepherd's Bush to a terminus near the present junction of New Oxford Street and Bloomsbury Street and the CLR to run from Queen's Road, Bayswater to a through connection with the City and South London Railway near its terminus at King William Street. The latter Company had obtained powers to build a tube railway from King William Street to Stockwell and was the first electrically operated underground railway in the world when it opened in 1890. The London Central Subway fell by the wayside before reaching parliament and the CLR, although it got to parliament, was cut back to Cornhill following opposition from the City and South London Railway and was rejected by the House of Lords. The following year, the promoters of the CLR returned to parliament with a proposal for a tube railway from Shepherd's Bush to Cornhill. This received its Act on 5 August 1891. In 1892 a further Act was obtained authorising the replacement of the Cornhill terminus with one beneath the Bank intersection and an extension to Liverpool Street station.

New and Branch Lines

Construction of the CLR started in April 1896, but at the end of the year negotiations with the GER and NLR for the Central London Railway's station at Liverpool Street were broken off, but part of the authorised extension to Old Broad Street at Throgmorton Street was built to provide two reversing sidings. The CLR had its ceremonial opening from Shepherd's Bush to the Bank by the Prince of Wales (later King Edward VII) on 27 June 1900 followed by a public opening on 30 July 1900. When the Railway was built it used electric locomotives to haul its trains, but these caused excessive vibration and in 1903, following experiments, the Company replaced the locomotives with carriages at each end of the trains incorporating motors so that the trains became multiple units. Prior to the introduction of multiple unit trains, the Railway, realising the length of time taken to change locomotives at the end of each journey, proposed a loop via Liverpool Street, the Bank, Hyde Park Corner and Hammersmith to Shepherd's Bush to join the existing Railway. Nothing came of this.

Under an Act dated 26 July 1907, the Railway was extended to Wood Lane in Shepherd's Bush and opened on 14 May 1908 – the same day the Franco-British Exhibition opened there. At the other end of the Railway things had been sorted out with the GER and NLR and on 16 August 1909 an Act was obtained authorising the extension of the Railway from the Bank to Liverpool Street. Work began in July 1910 and the extension was opened on 27 July 1912. Under the Act the GER agreed that the CLR could build its station under its property on the condition that the latter Company make no further extension north or north-east into GER territory.

In the 1890s there was the London, Walthamstow and Epping Forest Railway, which was first created in 1891 as the London, Tottenham and Epping Forest Railway, to run from Whitecross Street in the City of London to Waltham Abbey via Tottenham and Walthamstow. The GER was to be given running powers over it. Unfortunately, the company could not find the £100,000 deposit required by parliament and its promoters decided not to proceed with it. The scheme remained stalled for several years until the money for the deposit was arranged, by which time the name of the Company was changed to the London, Walthamstow and Epping Forest Railway (LW&EFR). In the 1894 session of parliament, the Railway was promoted to run from South Place, just off Moorgate, to High Beach, north of Chingford; it would have had three branches. One branch would have provided a west facing connection to the T&HJR at South Tottenham station, a second a north-west facing connection to the GER just to the north of Copper Mill Junction, whilst the third was to the GER at Hoe Street (Walthamstow) where the link was to connect the east end of that station to the LW&EFR in a north facing junction. Although the GER, MR, LT&SR and T&FGR made conditional agreements to subscribe to the new Company's capital, the GER, the MR, the T&FGR and the NLR presented petitions to parliament against the Railway. They were not the only organisations petitioning against the Railway. The London County Council, Hackney Board of Works and the East London Waterworks Company also did. The opposition was resolved by signing an agreement with the GER allowing the latter Company running powers over the LW&EFR. How things would have worked was that electric locomotives would have replaced steam locomotives on the trains at a point just before the commencement of the tunnel section. At this point, the MR got involved. The MR proposed running a service starting from Moorgate, over the City Widened Lines parallel to the Metropolitan Railway, to Kentish Town and from there they would curve east over the T&HJR to South Tottenham before curving to join the LW&EFR to South Place. The LW&EFR received its Act on 25 August 1894. It has to be said that the Railway's financial position appeared to be poor, but in 1895 the Railway promoted a number of alterations in the Leyton area including a connection with the T&FGR. What happened was that the MR agreed to work the Railway. By 1897 nothing had been done and the LW&EFR put forward two Bills to parliament. One was for an extension of time and the other for abandonment of the Railway. By the end of January 1897, the promoters decided to withdraw the Bill for the extension of time and concentrate on the abandonment Bill. However, in 1897, Arnold Frank Hills, the Chairman of the Thames Iron Works Company, replaced the promoters of the LW&EFR. One of his first actions was most likely to withdraw the abandonment Bill. Hills promoted the LW&EFR which sought to extend the time permitted to purchase land and construct the Railway. Royal Assent was given on 1 July 1898.

That year also saw the promotion of the LW&EFR (Abandonment) Bill for some obscure reason. This was read once in the House of Lords, referred to the Examiners of Bills and then discharged.

On 9 September 1899 the LW&EFR obtained another Act. This one abandoned the original junction with the GER Cambridge line and replaced it with a connection to that Company's railway south of Clapton Junction which would allow trains to run to the LW&EFR from either the Cambridge or the Chingford lines. The new line would join the LW&EFR main route at a point 56 feet below the surface and curve beneath Mount Pleasant and Bakers Hill before emerging to the surface and joining the GER. The GER agreed to run a minimum of 60 trains each working day between the stations at Finsbury and either its line or the T&HJR. The agreement of 1896 between the LW&EFR and the MR was also reconfirmed in the Act. Unfortunately, the LW&EFR had problems raising money and it was threatened by proposals by the East London Waterworks Company who were in the preliminary stages of obtaining powers to construct the Lea Valley reservoirs. In 1900 the LW&EFR put forward a new Abandonment bill, which received its Royal Assent on 6 August 1900.

This was not the end of the story as on 3 October 1900 the engineer Douglas Fox wrote to the Board of the GER to say that he had been approached by several influential people who were interested in reviving in some form or other a North Eastern Underground Railway from the neighbourhood of Liverpool Street to serve Clapton and Walthamstow. Fox asked if it would be agreeable to the GER if an independent 'Combination' was formed to build a line which whilst it served the locality might be valuable to the GER for through traffic. The GER declined to be involved. The scheme however went before a Joint Select Committee of Parliament that was examining a proposed Piccadilly and City Railway in 1901. The proposed Railway would run from Cannon Street in the City of London via Liverpool Street to Tottenham where it would terminate beneath the garden of a house called Farleigh Dene in Broad Lane. There was to be a branch that diverged at Stoke Newington and ran to north Walthamstow where it would terminate on the east side of the Chingford Road in an area called Chapel End. This branch would have a connection to the GER's old Cambridge line near Walthamstow Marshes. It was proposed that trains would run every two and a half minutes along the railway south of the junction with the branches probably being served by alternate trains. On 1 March 1901, the Bill for the North East London Railway (NELR), as the Railway was known, received its second reading in the House of Lords. The Joint Select Committee of the Houses of Parliament considered the Railway's Bill. There were objections received, predictably, from other railway companies. The GER was concerned that in placing the NELR under Bishopsgate it would preclude it from constructing its own tube railway in that position. I will mention the GER's proposal for a tube line shortly. The GER was also concerned with potential damage to its existing line and interference with it by the use of electricity, the construction works and the operations. The NLR and the Metropolitan Railway objected in separate petitions as they saw the NELR as unnecessary competition. They also gave similar reasons to the GER with regard to damage and interference. The CLR objected because it believed that the NELR and Piccadilly and City Railway, which latter would have run from Piccadilly Circus to Cannon Street, and whose combined lines would have been similar to its earlier mentioned proposed loop, would have meant that both schemes would not have been approved – and it wanted its scheme to succeed.

A GER tube railway appeared on a map of the GER Metropolitan Lines and connections dated 1901. The proposal originated in 1900 and although no plans were deposited, the tube railway would have run from Queen Street in Romford to Liverpool Street, round a loop and then out to Waltham Abbey. As far as is known there is no record of the GER's Board having discussed the proposals.

In November 1900 plans for another tube railway were deposited with various authorities. This was for the City and North East Suburban Electric Railway, which was to run from the junction of Cornhill, Leadenhall Street, Gracechurch Street and Bishopsgate to Farm Hill Road in Waltham Cross. The Railway was to be built in a combination of tunnels, cuttings and covered ways. There were to be connections to the T&FGR near Lea Bridge Road and to the GER's Chingford branch at Hoe Street, Walthamstow. The railway was not only interested in carrying passengers, but on its surface sections also goods and a spur was to be made to the River Lea on Hackney Marshes so that goods could be transferred from barges on that River to the Railway.

Returning to the NELR, the Joint Select Committee, considering its Bill, said that it would prefer the Railway to be extended north from Tottenham so that it could serve the new London County Council estates that were being planned for the Wood Green area and recommended that the Walthamstow branch be dropped if the C&NESER were to be built.

When the C&NESER came before the Joint Select Committee, its engineer, Richard Hassard, suggested that it and the NELR could share tunnels where the two railways ran parallel between the Monument and Hackney Road. Douglas Fox, for the latter Railway, thought that there would be no problem in superimposing the two lines. For the two companies to share tunnels caused concern that sharing tunnels would block its proposed two and a half minute service.

The Joint Select Committee noted that it would prefer a more easterly route of the C&NESER at the City end of the line in order to serve Whitechapel, but otherwise it allowed the Bill to proceed to the 1902 session of parliament.

According to Cecil J. Allen in *The Great Eastern Railway*, the Joint Select Committee was inclined to recommend both the NELR and the C&NESER to parliament despite the GER's strenuous opposition, but because of the various modifications to which the promoters would have had to submit, the bills were eventually withdrawn. In 1903, a new set of promoters proposed a tube railway of the same name, which was to run from the Monument in the City of London north to Chequers Green and north-east to Waltham Abbey. Naturally the GER opposed the new Railway's Bill. However, before that, in 1902, the GER itself thought about electrifying its lines to Enfield, Palace Gates and Chingford. In that year the Company's Locomotive Superintendent, James Holden, reported on the advantage of electric traction taking over from 36 steam locomotives in use on the aforementioned lines. Electric trains could accelerate more quickly and, in multiple unit trains, having the motors incorporated into the carriages meant that more accommodation could be provided. Holden was supported by the Company's Engineer, James Wilson, who said that it would be possible to increase capacity by 77 per cent and with the higher speed of running a service into Liverpool Street every two minutes. Nothing came of this proposal, possibly because of the GER's financial position.

It has been said that the GER's method of opposing the City and NESER was the somewhat drastic step that it took! The Company's Locomotive Superintendent, James Holden, designed and had built an 0-10-0 three cylinder tank locomotive capable of attaining 30 miles per hour in 30 seconds from a dead start with a train of 300 tons tare weight at a time when Holden's two cylinder

0-6-0 tank locomotives hauling a 15 coach train of about 200 tons unladed weight or 240 tons fully loaded needed 30 seconds to reach 20 miles per hour. The new locomotive was designed to match the acceleration of an electric train of similar weight. The locomotive was nicknamed 'Decapod' on account of its ten coupled wheels. If one assumes that the Company could not afford to electrify its previously mentioned suburban lines, it is not unreasonable that it would take such a drastic step to show what steam could do.

The *Locomotive Magazine* of 10 January 1903 noted, 'The new "decapod" suburban tank locomotive ran a trial trip on 11th inst from Stratford to Romford; other experimental runs will now be made with it'. Other trial runs were run as far east as Brentwood. The final one took place in June of 1903. To test whether or not the locomotive fulfilled the exacting acceleration requirements, a special plant was laid down near Chadwell Heath to give an electrical recording of the actual rate of acceleration. The Decapod never entered service. It was too heavy for the viaducts out of Liverpool Street but that was not the point. The City and North East Suburban Electric Railway Bill failed. At the 82nd Half Yearly Meeting of the GER on 28 July 1903 the Chairman, Lord Claud Hamilton,

The GER's most famous locomotive was the 0-10-0 well tank locomotive No 20, better known as the Decapod, which was built at Stratford works at the end of 1902. The locomotive is seen here at Brentwood on 29 March 1903 prior to the start of a trial run. (Harold Hopwood).

reported 'The Bill for the NESER, which if constructed would have passed through a portion of the district served by this company, was rejected'. As for the Decapod, parts of the locomotive were used in the construction of an 0-8-0 goods locomotive, whilst the boiler became a stationary boiler.

In 1905, a proposal for a railway from Gracechurch Street to Leyton, Walthamstow, Chingford and Waltham Cross called the North East London Railway managed to obtain its Act, but did not attract the investing public and was finally abandoned in 1910.

Trams and Light Railways

Whilst the electric tube railways may not have been built, there was competition from electric traction in the form of electric tramways. Originally there had been horse trams in London, Cambridge, Ipswich and Yarmouth.

By 1924 there were trams of the London County Council Tramways and Metropolitan Electric Tramways from Liverpool Street to Waltham Cross and trams of the London County Council Tramways running from Edmonton and Tottenham to Euston. There were through trams from Aldgate to Ilford operated by Ilford Urban District Council. Walthamstow Urban District Council operated a through service from Liverpool Street to Chingford Mount, whilst the London County Council Tramways ran trams from Aldgate to Leyton. This route had originally been operated by Leyton Urban District Council, but in 1921 the latter's tramways had been taken over by the London County Council Tramways. The London County Council Tramways and East Ham Urban District Council served Blackwall on a route from Bloomsbury to East Ham via Aldgate and the north end of the Blackwall Tunnel.

As a result of tramway competition, Sunday trains between Fenchurch Street and Blackwall were discontinued from 4 October 1908, but the Millwall Docks Company continued to operate a half hourly service from Millwall Junction to North Greenwich. This service was discontinued after 28 December 1913. There had nearly been a tramway in Romford, but although powers to build the tramways had been obtained in 1903, they were never built. It has to be said that whilst trams were all right for short distance journeys, they were in terms of speed slower for a longer distance journey. On the other hand, they were cheaper.

Away from London there were electric trams in Southend, Colchester, Ipswich, Lowestoft, Yarmouth and Norwich. None of these tramways took traffic away from the GER as their place was purely within the immediate area of the towns; for example Colchester's trams probably took some local traffic between the main (North) station and Hythe, whilst Ipswich's took some between the main station and Derby Road station. What was threatened though was in Southend, when the Council started running trams in 1901 including one to Prittlewell (within walking distance of Southend GER station) and proposed routes to Rochford and (via a circuitous route) to Rayleigh.

Worse was to follow. In that same year there was a proposal for a Southend-on-Sea, Burnham and Bradwell Light Railway to run from the LT&SR station in Southend to Bradwell. Although nothing came of this, shortly afterwards there was a proposal for a Southend and District, Bradwell-on-Sea and Colchester Light Railway. This was for a long distance electric tramway between Southend and Colchester via Rochford, Burnham-on-Crouch, Bradwell-on-Sea and West Mersea and would have included a steam ferry from Bradwell-on-Sea to West Mersea. Whilst the Railway would have connected with the Southend trams, it would have stopped short of the Colchester tramways by about a mile. There would have been a connection to the GER at Southminster (between Burnham-on-Crouch and Bradwell-on-Sea) and also at Stanway via a branch off the main line. Originally the track gauge was to be 4ft 8½in, but this was later changed to 3ft 6in, which was the same gauge as the tramways of Southend and Colchester. Naturally, the GER fought the proposal and although the Company obtained a Light Railway Order, no construction ever took place and the powers to build it expired in 1912.

It was not only electric tramways that were a form of competition. In Suffolk there was the threat of competition from the MSLR, which if plans had matured would have joined up to form lines of railway running from Westerfield Junction on the East Suffolk line to Kenton via Debenham, Haughley Junction on the Ipswich to Norwich line to Kenton, from Kenton via Laxfield to Halesworth on the East Suffolk line to join the Southwold Railway re-gauged to 4ft 8½in from 3ft with a branch line from Southwold to Kessingland.

The MSLR grew out of a suggestion in a letter written in October 1898 by Mr H.L. Godden of Messrs Jeyes and Godden, Civil Engineers of London to the parish councils of several villages and the landowners in mid-Suffolk, suggesting that if the local populace would provide some money towards the promotion of a railway, they had clients who would help financially. As there was a large area of mid-Suffolk between the Ipswich to Norwich main line, the East Suffolk line and the Waveney Valley that was not served by any railways except for the branch lines from Mellis to Eye and Wickham Market to Framlingham, the suggestion was enthusiastically received and the first meeting of the interested parties took place at Debenham in February 1899. To cut things short, the Mid Suffolk Light Railway (MSLR), as the Railway was known, obtained its Light Railway Order on 5 April 1900. The Order granted the MSLR to construct the lines from Westerfield Junction to Kenton via Debenham, from Haughley Junction to Kenton and from Kenton to Halesworth. There was however no mention of a connection to the Southwold Railway at Halesworth. The total length of the railway was to be 42 miles. As well as running trains, the Company proposed in its prospectus to run buses from Westerfield station to the centre of Ipswich. This would have been in competition with the GER. Owing to considerable local opposition, particularly in the Mendlesham area, the Company altered its plans many times. The cutting of the first sod of the Railway took place at Westerfield on 3 May 1902 and was performed by His Royal Highness the Duke of Cambridge. Others attending were the Marquis and Marchioness of Bristol, Lord Claud Hamilton, the Chairman of the GER, Lord Rayleigh, Lord Huntingfield and Sir Charles Dalrymple. Although the cutting of the first sod took place at Westerfield, the Company's advertisement saw the Railway running from Haughley to Halesworth via Kenton with a branch from Kenton to Westerfield. On the main line by August 1902 the recognisable shape of a railway was cutting its way across the fields of Suffolk north-east of Haughley, but on the branch line little more than staking out had taken place. By 23 September 1902, work was sufficiently advanced for Lord Kitchener to pay a ceremonial visit to the Railway and travel in a train comprising contractors' wagons and a GER saloon hauled by the contractor's locomotive *Lady Stevenson* from Haughley to Mendlesham, which was the first station between Haughley and Kenton.

Whilst work, at least on the main line, was generally progressing well, there were problems encountered by marshy ground west of Halesworth which effectively formed a barrier to the Railway's progress. The Company applied to the Light Railway Commissioners for the deviation of the route at the

Halesworth end and extension of time to build the Railway as authorised under the original Light Railway Order. The Deviation and Amendment Order was granted and dated 23 April 1903.

It has to be said that the Railway was not in a particularly healthy financial position, as in May 1904 it went to East Suffolk County Council for a loan of £25,000 to complete building the lines to Westerfield and Halesworth. Unfortunately for the Company, the proposal was defeated by 27 to 24 votes when it needed a two thirds majority. At the July Annual Meeting of the Company, the Chairman said that the lines to Laxfield and Debenham would be ready by September and to Halesworth by February 1905. He said that arrangements had been made with the GER for covered ways to join the stations at Westerfield and Halesworth and to use steam rail motors, drawing from the experience of the Taff Vale Railway in Wales, the conclusion being that the operating costs of these would be 5½d a mile.

Work on the branch line had progressed to a bridge over the Aspall Road at Debenham and fencing had reached Otley, whilst on the main line work had advanced so that on 20 September 1904 it was possible to commence goods traffic between Haughley and Laxfield. Fencing had advanced as far as Linstead. The *Eastern Daily Press* of Monday 19 September 1904 carried the following announcement:

> MID SUFFOLK LIGHT RAILWAY. EARLY OPENING FOR GOODS TRAFFIC. In order to meet the noble convenience, and in anticipation of the formal opening of the line, goods can be received or delivered on and after the 20th inst., at owners' risk, at the following Stations HAUGHLEY, MENDLESHAM, ASPALL, KENTON, HORHAM, STRADBROKE, LAXFIELD. Other Stations will be available shortly. Detailed information can be obtained on application to the Traffic Manager. Mr. H.J. REDNALL., or the Local Secretary, Laxfield, Framlingham.

The initial service was one train a day in each direction. At least it was a start. In 1906 the Railway was extended beyond Laxfield to the next station on the route – Cratfield.

On the branch line to Westfield from Kenton, rails had been laid to within 150 yards of Debenham station and some sort of facility for the loading and unloading of goods seems to have been provided. In 1906 there was a complaint that the facility for the public to load and unload at Debenham had been withdrawn.

The Southwold Railway

By the end of the nineteenth century, the Southwold Railway was finding having a gauge of 3ft an inconvenience as any goods traffic had to be transhipped at Halesworth. The Company made two attempts to change its gauge. The first attempt oddly was in 1899 to build a 4ft 8½in gauge line from Southwold to Lowestoft. This proposal was submitted to the Light Railway Commissioners in May 1899. This application was withdrawn before even reaching the stage of a Local Inquiry and it was replaced by an amended scheme in May 1900. The reason for the amended application was that the original scheme would have resulted in a break of gauge at Southwold, which would have killed off any through traffic from the GER which the Directors of the Southwold Railway hoped for. Under a Light Railway Order dated 4 April 1902, the Southwold Railway obtained powers to build a 4ft 8½in gauge railway from Kessingland to Southwold and to convert its existing railway from 3ft gauge to the wider gauge. The reason for stopping 4 miles short of Lowestoft at Kessingland was to obviate opposition from the GER which was contemplating building a line from Lowestoft to Kessingland. The two railway companies were not the only transport companies interested in getting to Kessingland. The Lowestoft Corporation Tramways also gained powers to reach Kessingland by virtue of having taken over on 6 June 1904 the powers of the East Anglian Light Railways to build a light railway between Lowestoft and Kessingland, the original Light Railway Order having been obtained on 30 January 1902. Unfortunately, the Southwold Railway had trouble in raising the money for re-gauging its existing line and whilst some work was done including the widening of the Railway's swing bridge at Southwold and also a few other bridges, the Company ran out of the time allotted for it to carry out the work, despite obtaining a Borrowing Powers Order dated 27 September 1907. On the Kessingland branch no progress was made at all. At this time there was a proposal for the development of a quay on the Southwold side of the River Blyth at Southwold. The construction of the harbour at Southwold included the provision for the construction of a railway connection to link up with the Southwold Railway. In 1913, the Southwold

Railway obtained a Light Railway Order dated 25 September 1913 enabling it to build a branch line off its existing line at Southwold to the harbour and which opened in 1914.

Mid-Suffolk Light Railway

In July 1904 the MSLR announced its intention of applying for a change to the limits of deviation as authorised under the Deviation and Amendment Order of 23 April 1903. The Deviation Order for this, entitled the Halesworth Deviation Order, was obtained on 23 February 1905. At this time the Southwold Railway put forward to the MSLR the idea of the two companies working together in the interests of the district. The MSLR applied to the Light Railway Commissioners in 1907 for another deviation, this time to join the Southwold Railway at Halesworth. The GER was worried as it was known that the fishing trade at Southwold would increase with the construction of the harbour and if such traffic was sent via the Southwold Railway and the MSLR, the Lowestoft fish trade would suffer and the GER would incur reduced receipts. For places such as London, traffic would be lost on the section of the East Suffolk line between Halesworth and Lowestoft. For places west of Haughley Junction, the loss would have been much worse. It was a fact that the MSLR was already abstracting some goods traffic from the Framlingham branch. The previous chairman of the MSLR had been dealing with the MR and the thought of Southwold becoming another Harwich within the MR's empire by taking over both the MSLR and the Southwold Railway was by no means unimaginable. The GER objected. The Light Railway Commissioners at the end of their hearing said that in their opinion there was not enough commercial justification or evidence to support the deviation. They could not consent to the alterations and proved against the scheme.

In May 1909 the MSLR was clearly deciding to have another go at its extension to Halesworth as the *Halesworth Advertiser* of 19 May reported that great satisfaction was being expressed in the district that the Company was depositing plans with the Light Railway Commissioners for an extension of the line to the town. The next one hears is in the *London Gazette* of 7 December 1909 under 'LIGHT RAILWAYS ACT, 1896. The Board of Trade have recently confirmed the undermentioned Order, made by the Light Railway

Commissioners; – Mid-Suffolk Light Railway (Amendment) Order, 1909, amending the Mid-Suffolk Light Railway Orders of 1900, of 1903 and of 1905'.

Meanwhile the MSLR finally opened to passenger traffic between Haughley and Laxfield. On 2 July 1905, Lieutenant-Colonel P.G. von Donop of the Board of Trade had visited the Railway but had declined to allow it to be opened for passengers in the main because the numerous level crossings were not up to the standards that were required by the Light Railway Order. On 25 September 1908 von Donop again visited the Railway and found that the crossings were now satisfactory. There were a few things that needed doing, but he was happy to allow the Railway to open for passengers. This took place on 29 September 1908. The *Eastern Daily Press* of 30 September 1908 recorded, 'MID SUFFOLK RAILWAY FIRST PASSENGER TRAIN. The first train ever run under the Board of Trade regulations for the conveyance of the public over the Mid Suffolk Light Railway started its journey from Laxfield to Haughley Junction yesterday morning'. Originally there were trains every day of the week, but the Sunday service was withdrawn in October 1910.

Beyond Laxfield, traffic on the section to Cratfield did not live up to expectations and was closed beyond Laxfield Mill in February 1912. The rails, along with those from Kenton Junction to Debenham, remained in situ. They were removed during the First World War.

In south Essex the GER faced a definite threat from the LT&SR. This came in several forms. The mid-1890s had seen the development of garden city estates around the area of Romford and Hornchurch. These were not self-contained garden cities as at Letchworth but rather a better form of development than that nearer the centre of London. Another such development was at Highams Park in Chingford. The residents of these estates tended to be city businessmen. The problem with the estates near Romford and Hornchurch was that they had no railway station. Highams Park was all right as it did have one. Considerable agitation grew up amongst the residents of the estates near Romford and Hornchurch for a station. The LT&SR got in first by opening a halt at Emerson Park on 2 October 1909. The GER thought about building one at Great Nelmes to serve the estate at Gidea Park which was developed in the grounds of the historic Gidea Hall, then started building its station to serve the estate at Gidea Park. This opened on 1 December 1910 and was named Squirrels Heath and

Gidea Park station was the last new station in the London suburban area to be opened by the GER and is seen here under construction on 3 July 1910 with Class D56 No 1859 passing with the 7.30am Norwich to Liverpool Street. (Ken Nunn).

Gidea Park. The GER arranged for a local bus proprietor (George Heath of the Bull Inn, Hornchurch) to run a service of omnibuses or brakes on weekdays between Emerson Park, Great Nelmses and Squirrels Heath and Gidea Park station in connection with the GER's trains.

Under an Act dated 6 August 1897, the Whitechapel and Bow Railway was authorised to build a railway from the eastern terminus of the Metropolitan District Railway at Whitechapel to the LT&SR at Campbell Road, a short distance beyond the point where the LT&SR left the GER at Gas Factory Junction. The Railway was owned jointly by the Metropolitan District and the London, Tilbury and Southend railways and opened on 2 June 1902. Metropolitan District Railway trains worked over the new Railway and on to the LT&SR as far as East Ham, with a couple of trains working through to Upminster. In 1905, with the electrification of the Metropolitan and the Metropolitan District railways, electric trains of the latter Company started working through to East Ham on 20 August 1905. Electric working was extended to Barking on 1 April 1908.

Southend

Southend was, along with Brighton, in late Victorian and Edwardian times one of the places on the coast where the better class of city businessmen lived. Both the LB&SCR and the LT&SR provided very good services for their business customers from their respective coastal towns to London. The GER did not provide a good service from Southend to London and there were complaints in the local Southend area press about it. To make matters worse, following the success of a special excursion run by the Metropolitan District Railway from Ealing to Southend on 22 July 1909 to see the flotilla of battleships assembled just off Southend, a daily through service between Southend and Ealing was put on from 1 June 1910. The trains were hauled by LT&SR steam locomotives as far as Barking or East Ham where Metropolitan District Railway electric locomotives took over with the reverse in the opposite direction. From two trains a day the service was built up.

Concern about the level of the GER's service to and from Southend was first raised by Walter Hyde, the General Manager, at the meeting of the Traffic Committee on 16 March 1911. It was a fact that the GER had practically done nothing to cater for the residential traffic to and from Southend and that it was the subject of concern in the local Southend newspapers. The Company was constantly being urged to improve the service to provide an alternative route for business traffic in view of the overcrowding and discomfort of the travelling on the LT&SR. Twenty-one years after the opening of the line, there were only thirty-three season ticket holders from the Southend area. The number using the LT&SR from the Southend area including Westcliff was 6,000, from 27 during the previous 35 years, according to a statement by the Chairman and Managing Director of the LT&SR, Arthur Lewis Stride. In 1891, the population of Southend was 12,333. By 1901 it was now approaching 70,000. The population was not confined to the district adjacent to the LT&SR but also to the GER. The GER did not secure the traffic from the district because of the poor service that it provided. Receipts from bookings at Southend, whilst they had increased by 43 per cent in the first decade after the opening of the line, had shown little expansion in the previous ten years and traffic returns had shown a serious and almost continuous decline. Thus, for a place that was growing by leaps and bounds, the LT&SR was obtaining a greater share of the traffic than formerly. It was evident that unless the GER could secure some proportion of the Southend area season ticket traffic, it could not expect other members of the household of season ticket holders, nor their visitors, to travel by the GER's route. The question of improvements to secure a fair proportion of the residential traffic had been examined by the Superintendent of the Line and proposals were submitted, providing the principal features of the proposed service, compared to the existing service and the service provided by the LT&SR. On Mondays to Saturdays the GER's existing service was three trains from Southend to London between 8am and 11am. The proposed service would be five trains between those times; the number provided by the LT&SR was nine. On Mondays to Fridays, the number of Down trains from London to Southend between 5pm and 9pm under the existing service was five; under the proposed service it would be seven. The LT&SR ran eight trains during that period. There would be a corresponding increase during Saturday afternoons (as people worked half day on Saturdays). There would be Down trains at 9.45pm and midnight and improvements to Up evening trains. The scheme also took into account the requirements of season ticket holders from intermediate stations (Brentwood to Rochford) and the Southminster line (and obviously the Maldon West line). At that time these numbered about four hundred. An additional train was also proposed to and from Southminster. The cost of the scheme was about £7,500 p.a. but of course this expenditure would be more than covered if the result was an additional 500 season ticket holders, which was less than ten per cent of the number travelling on the London, Tilbury and Southend Railway. It was recommended the improvements should begin from 1 May 1911. The Committee resolved that this recommendation be approved by the Directors.

The GER's publicity machine soon got to work as an announcement appeared in the *Southend Standard* at the end of March advertising a 'New Service of Fast Trains for London Businessmen. Southend to Liverpool Street in 58 mins'. Meanwhile, on 7 April 1911 a deputation from the recently formed South-East Essex Travellers Association met with the General Manager of the GER regarding the train service from Southend to London and vice versa. The whole question of a fast and frequent train service was thoroughly discussed. The General Manager assuring the deputation that the suggestions put forward would receive his serious consideration. He also gave his assurance that the new arrangements coming into force would be of a permanent nature. This was reported in the issue of the *Southend Standard* of 13 April 1911. The *Southend Standard* of 27 April said that it was understood that in connection with the new express service of trains between Southend and London it had been arranged to run a service of corridor restaurant car trains which would include breakfast Up by the 8.16am from Southend, tea Down by the 5.03pm train (5.37pm on Saturdays) and supper on the midnight train (12.07 on Saturdays). The new vestibuled train would be open for public inspection at Southend (GER) station from 10am to 7.0pm on Saturday 29 April.

The *Southend Standard* of 4 May contained a glowing description of the new service, giving a description of the restaurant car trains including the engine (of the Claud Hamilton type according to the newspaper) and also the start of the service on Monday 1 May. Whilst the 7.17am departure from Southend did not have a great deal of passengers, the 8.16am restaurant car train attracted at least 100 passengers, not to mention railway officials. The *Southend Standard* said that some passengers had transferred from the LT&SR, one man saying that he had done so as soon as the expresses were promised as his season ticket had expired. Subsequent trains also did rather well. The returns for the other three trains were 30, 50 and 80 passengers. The return trains were also well patronised. There was a genuine feeling of pleasure with the way that the GER was handling the service. A very small point was that whilst the First Class carriages were lit by electricity, the Third Class carriages were lit by gas.

The Times of 26 April reported that from 1 May the GER had arranged to improve their train service between London and Southend. Four express trains would leave Southend and arriving at Liverpool Street before 10am and in the evening a similar number of expresses would run between 5 and 6.30pm. The journey accomplished by the fastest train would be in 58 minutes. A midnight train would leave Liverpool Street for Southend daily.

The newly established *Great Eastern Railway Magazine* had a short article devoted to the new services. According to the magazine, the new services were to 'meet the requirements of the public for a morning and evening express residential service to and from Liverpool Street at times convenient for those engaged in business in the City'. At the same time, the magazine also said that season tickets from suburban stations to London would be obtainable at the suburban station on demand so that passengers would no longer have to fill in a form and forward it to the secretary of the company each time that they wanted a season ticket. Excepting in the case of half rate tickets and those subject to a discount, in future a form would only be required on the first application. This could be filled up and handed in at once and the ticket obtained forthwith. Amongst those places to which the new arrangements would apply would be Southend.

Railway and Travel Monthly for May 1911 carried a short article about the GER's Southend service accelerations, as did the *Locomotive Magazine* of the same month. According to the minutes of the Traffic Committee for 20 July, the improved service had brought in an additional 100 new season ticket holders from the Southend area. By the time of the Traffic Committee meeting of 6 February 1912, the increase in the number of season ticket holders for the period ending 31 December 1911 according to the minutes equalled 749 quarterly season tickets.

In his report of the Directors of the GER to the shareholders at the 98th half yearly meeting of the Company held on 28 July 1911 the Chairman, Lord Claud Hamilton, said 'Consequent upon the rapid growth of the town of Southend, particularly in the neighbourhood of the Company's stations, the Directors decided upon considerable alterations in the passenger train service from the 1st of May last. A new and improved service, including restaurant cars on certain of the trains, has been brought into operation and promises to be successful'.

The following year, at the 100th half year meeting held on 30 July 1912, Lord Claud Hamilton reported that the improved train service between London and Southend had exceeded the Company's anticipations.

However, despite the improvement in the service in the mornings and evenings, the service between 10am and 4pm on Mondays to Fridays was still in need of improvement and was still the same as before the improvements were made. The minutes of the Traffic Committee of 6 March 1913 recorded that deputations of GER season ticket holders from the Southend and District Railway Travellers Association had waited upon the General Manager and the Superintendent of the Line urging a need for earlier and later trains and for an improved service between 10am and 4pm for family members travelling up to London. The service provided compared badly with that provided on the MR (which had taken over the LT&SR in August 1912) from the Southend area between those hours. Various points were put forward by the deputations and were considered by the Traffic Committee. It was found that the deputations' principal requests could be met and that various other improvements could be made in the service including accelerating the Up supper express train at a cost of approximately £176 per month. It was proposed to run additional trains from the start of the summer timetable during which time they would be carefully monitored before a decision was made as to whether they should continue for the winter.

The increases in the number of season ticket holders continued. The minutes of the Traffic Committee of 19 June 1913 record that by the end of April 1913 there were now 800 season ticket holders using the GER service from the Southend area. The minutes of the Traffic Committee for 20 November 1913 reported that there were now 964 season ticket holders from the Southend area; whilst the minutes of 18 June 1914 record that there were 1,011 season ticket holders from the Southend area using the GER's service. At the same meeting, Henry Thornton, the General Manager, said that from 1 June one of the early morning trains from London to Shenfield had been accelerated and extended to Southend to afford better facilities for newspaper and market traffic and he was arranging for several additional trains to and from Southend on Sundays during the summer with a view to further increasing the excursion traffic to Southend by the GER route.

The LT&SR in January 1912, in response to the GER's restaurant car trains, put in to service jointly with the Metropolitan District Railway two eight carriage corridor trains. These trains were the most luxurious trains to be seen on either of the two railways that jointly operated them.

Not all of the proposed alterations to the services initially lived up to their expectations. Those on the Southminster line initially did not meet their running costs and according to the minutes of the Traffic Committee in February 1912 had made a slight loss. However by June 1914 this loss had been reversed. Another improvement that the GER seriously considered doing on the Southend line was in April 1913 when it toyed with the idea of introducing a push and pull service on the line. In addition to serving the existing stations, halts were to be opened at Mountnessing, Ramsden Bellhouse, Down Hall, between Rayleigh and Hockley, and Hawkwell. Some trials were conducted with a small tank engine and a pair of coaches. Unfortunately the idea was abandoned. The trials were reported in the local newspapers and according to the memories of a resident of Ramsden Bellhouse the prospect of a passenger station there influenced their parents' decision to move there. This suggests that other people moved there and possibly some of the other places for the same reason. *Railway and Travel Monthly* of April 1913 mentions the push and pull proposal in a piece which read 'Passengers between Southend and Shenfield Junction are to be provided with additional travelling facilities. A frequent service of rail motors is about to be run over this section of the GER. Rail motors was another term for push and pull trains.'

In August 1912, the LT&SR was taken over by the MR. It was not as if the GER was unaware that the MR wanted to take over the LT&SR. The GER would like to have taken over the LT&SR but had not got enough money to do so. During the period from 1896 to 1912 it had tried in 1900/1 and again in 1905.

The GER was not the only railway company interested in taking over the LT&SR. In 1910, the NLR on behalf of the L&NWR (which had taken over the working of the NLR under a common management arrangement on 1 February 1909) had made an approach to the LT&SR. This was the same year that the MR made its first approach. The earliest mention that I can find of the proposal for the takeover of the LT&SR by the MR is in *The Times* of Thursday, 2 February 1911 in an article headed:

> LONDON, TILBURY AND SOUTHEND RAILWAY, PROPOSED TRANSFER TO THE MIDLAND COMPANY. A provisional agreement has been entered into between the London, Tilbury, and Southend Railway Company and the Midland Railway Company for the transfer of the entire undertaking of the London, Tilbury, and Southend Railway Company to the Midland Company. The consideration for the transfer will be the issue to debenture and preference stockholders in the London, Tilbury, and Southend Railway Company of stock of the same denomination in the Midland Railway Company producing an equal return, and the issue to the ordinary stockholders of £240 Midland Railway-2½ per cent consolidated perpetual preference stock in exchange for each £100 of London, Tilbury, and Southend Railway ordinary stock. The agreement subject to the approval of the shareholders of both companies and Parliament.

The magazine *Railway and Travel Monthly* in its March 1911 edition carried an article about the agreement under the heading 'Will the "Tilbury"

Disappear?' The *Locomotive Magazine* of February 1911 had a brief piece about the agreement. Even the NER was aware of the agreement, as the *North Eastern Railway Magazine* of March 1911 mentions it. The *Daily Telegraph* of 2 February 1911 mentions the agreement; it was hardly a secret.

By the end of June 1911, it was clear what was going to happen. According to *The Times* of Tuesday 27 June 1911:

MIDLAND AND TILBURY DISCUSSION AND ACCEPTANCE OF THE TERMS OF SALE

A special general meeting of the London, Tilbury, and Southend Railway Company was held yesterday, at 41, Trinity-Square, Tower-Hill, to consider the terms Provisionally arranged for the sale of the undertaking as a going concern to the Midland Railway Company. Mr ARTHUR L. STRIDE presided.

Arthur Lewis Stride was the Chairman of the LT&SR.

By the end of January 1912, it was very clear the sale of the LT&SR to the MR was going ahead. *The Times* of Thursday, 25 January 1912 under the heading 'LONDON BILLS IN PARLIAMENT' made mention that the MR (LT&SR Purchase) Bill would be introduced in parliament in the House of Lords. Naturally, the GER opposed the Bill. According to *The Times* of Tuesday, 25 February 1912:

MIDLAND-TILBURY, AMALGAMATION, GREAT EASTERN OPPOSITION. Yesterday was the last day for the deposit of petitions against the Bill for vesting the undertaking of the London, Tilbury, and Southend Railway Company in the MR Company. A petition has been deposited on behalf of the GER praying to be heard against the Bill.

The GER was not the only railway company to oppose the Bill. According to *The Times* of Wednesday, 24 April 1912, the GNR also opposed the Bill. The GER regarded east and north-east London, east Hertfordshire, Essex, Cambridgeshire, Suffolk and Norfolk as its fiefdom. Provided a rival railway company did not provide too much opposition it would tolerate it, as in the case of the Colne Valley and Halstead Railway. Thus it was quite prepared to tolerate the LT&SR. The MR was a different thing. Firstly the MR would gain its own route to the London docks that was independent of the use of the GER. Secondly, the MR was rather more wealthy than the GER and could make any improvements to the LT&SR that the GER if it acquired the latter Railway could not. The GNR opposed the Bill on the ground that the GNR's traffic to Tilbury was competitive with the MR's traffic to Tilbury. According to the *Railway Clearing House Handbook of Stations* for 1904, the GNR's access to Tilbury Docks was over the NLR, LT&SR and the lines of the London and India Docks Company. The GNR said that its access to the Victoria Docks was also affected. Access to the latter, though, was over a branch line from London and India Docks Lines and GER stations. What the GNR got for withdrawing its opposition to the Bill was, according to H.D. Welch in *The London, Tilbury and Southend Railway* (Oakwood Press 1951), running powers over the LT&SR as far as Tilbury.

Lord Claud Hamilton in his report to the 99th half yearly meeting of the Company held on 30 January 1912 said, 'A Bill to authorise the MR Company to purchase the undertaking of the LT&SR has been deposited. This and other Bills affecting the interest of the GER Company will receive the careful consideration of the Directors'. At the following half yearly meeting held on 30 July 1912, he reported that the Bill had been passed by the House of Lords and a committee of the House of Commons. An agreement had been reached with the MR Company for the protection of the GER Company's interests.

The reason that the GER did not acquire the LT&SR was that it could not. Unlike the MR, or for that matter the L&NWR, the GER's main income came from agricultural traffic, holiday makers and season ticket holders, some of whom paid ludicrously low fares compared to other companies, whereas the other two main companies had the lucrative coal trade which made them rather wealthier than the GER and thus in a better position to take over another smaller railway company.

In the MR's Act of the acquisition of the LT&SR, it was required to electrify the direct line from London to Southend. The electrification was dependent on the quadrupling of the section of line from Stepney to Bromley-by-Bow and the rebuilding of Fenchurch Street station. The GER agreed to allow the electrification of the line into Fenchurch Street. After the take over, the

MR commissioned a report by the electrical consulting engineers Merz and McLellan who came up with a number of schemes which involved diverting LT&SR line trains away from Fenchurch Street in tunnel either from Campbell Road Junction near Bromley-by-Bow via Aldgate to the Bank station and from Cannon Street Road via Aldgate to the Bank or from Cannon Street Road via a new Underground station at Fenchurch Street to the Bank. The conclusion reached was that rather than the underground schemes the weight was in favour of enlarging Fenchurch Street station. When the report was put to the MR Board, the Chairman, Sir Guy Granet, said that he was unable to make any recommendations as he was about to commence negotiations with the GER over the enlargement of Fenchurch Street station. At the beginning of 1914, the MR made an initial drawing of the formations of possible electric trains for the London, Tilbury and Southend line. The drawing shows formations of either ten or eleven carriages which would either be locomotive hauled or multiple unit trains. These would have either been all compartment carriages, all open carriages (of which some would have lavatories) or a mixture of open carriages and compartment carriages. The drawing, which is in the Essex Record Office in Chelmsford, describes the open carriages as corridor carriages, but this is a misnomer as there is no gangway connection with other carriages and in the case of the compartment carriages there is no side corridor. As far as is known no diagrams of a side view of what the trains would have looked liked was produced – or has survived. As only the line via Upminster would have been electrified and not the section between Barking and Pitsea via Tilbury, according to Peter Kay in Volume 3 of his history of the London, Tilbury and Southend Railway, the suggestion was given to terminating trains using the Tilbury loop at Barking.

 The GER's immediate reaction to the Midland take over was to ban a new class of 4-6-4 side tank engines being built for the LT&SR, from running over the L&BR into Fenchurch Street station, allegedly as they were too heavy for the viaduct. This was regarded as an act of spite. Their designer, Robert Harben Whitelegg, the locomotive superintendent of the LT&SR, had been assured by the Great Eastern that there would be no problems. According to the late Kenneth Leech, who was the last surviving former employee of the LT&SR, whilst the locomotives were bigger than any previous locomotive built for the railway, their maximum axle load and loading per foot were lower than those of the railway's 79 class 4-4-2 side tank locomotives which been delivered in 1909 and their weight per foot run of total wheelbase and overall length were only 4 per cent and 7 per cent greater than the 79 class. Kenneth Leech was of the opinion that possibly the GER would allow a small company, such as the LT&SR, something it would not allow a large one, such as the MR. Peter Kay in Volumes 3 and 8 of his *History of the London, Tilbury and Southend Railway* clarifies this. According to him, in early 1912 the GER, after seeing a piece on the 4-6-4 side tank locomotives in the railway press, went and obtained particulars. The Company quickly concluded that they could not allow them to run into Fenchurch Street and in February 1913, the GER General Manager, Walter Hyde, served notice on the MR and included in their prohibition the former LT&SR Class 37 rebuilt 4-4-2 side tank locomotives as well on the grounds that the LT&SR had never sought permission for their use either.

At the GER's Ways and Works Committee meeting on 19 February the Company's General Manager Walter Hyde told the Committee that many other LT&SR locomotives were too heavy. Obviously, the GER could not tell the MR to withdraw the Class 37 rebuilds without a fight and did not do so. Seeing the contentious politics of the situation, the GER's Directors asked Hyde to report further which he did on 4 March only to say that the engineers now wished to prohibit six classes of GER locomotives as well, two of which the Company's Locomotive Superintendent, Alfred John Hill, would not agree to. To strengthen the L&BR viaduct to take all the locomotives in question, including the 4-6-4 side tank locomotives, would cost £122, 000. Following consultations with the GER's Solicitor, Hyde decided to ask two outside engineers, Sir John W. Barry and Mr C.L. Morgan, to prepare an independent report. Morgan submitted a report, which was considered by the GER Board on 2 January 1914. The report concluded that there was no risk of the arches failing, but the extra vibration would bring greater maintenance costs. The GER was already pressing forward with the work of renewing the arches and strengthening the bridges. The former LT&SR Class 69 0-6-2 side tank locomotives would be allowed to use the route as an exceptional load. The heavier GER locomotives should no longer be allowed on the line.

Since the GER would not allow the MR to operate the 4-6-4 side tank locomotives into Fenchurch Street Station, the MR prepared a design for a 2-6-4 side tank locomotive for the London, Tilbury and Southend section. The

GER put a stop to this being developed. In short 'If we can't have it, we're going to make it hard for you'.

The Midland Railway London, Tilbury and Southend Railway takeover Act

Under this, the GER obtained running powers for its Colchester main line trains over the T&FGR from a new loop which would have to be constructed at Forest Gate. A contentious thing in the Act was for a curve at Hornchurch to enable trains to run direct from London to Romford. The line from Barking to Upminster was to be quadrupled and the Romford to Upminster line to be doubled and electrified. Understandably, the GER was not very happy at the thought of Metropolitan District Railway electric trains at Romford.

Walter Hyde, the GER's General Manager at the time of the MR's takeover of the LT&SR, has been held to have been the scapegoat for the GER's loss. The *Great Eastern Railway Magazine* of March 1914 announced that Hyde had tendered his resignation and had appointed Henry Worth Thornton, the General Superintendent of the Long Island Railroad, as his successor. Hyde retired on 4 April that year. If Hyde really was to blame, he would have gone earlier than early 1914. *Railway and Travel Monthly* of March 1914 indicates stress as the cause of his resignation saying, 'The numerous friends of Mr Walter H. Hyde, the General Manager of the GER, will sincerely sympathise with him, that the heavy strain of the duties should have necessitated him to place his resignation in the hands of the Directors'. Hyde, during his time in office from January 1910, had to deal with several things that had an effect on the GER. Apart from the MR's takeover of the LT&SR there had been a railway strike in August 1911 and a coal strike in the early part of 1912. Something previous General Managers of the GER had not had to deal with, even if the GER was not too badly affected by them.

It is interesting to speculate what would have happened had the London, Tilbury and Southend Railway not been taken over by the MR. By 1912, not only were 4-4-0 locomotives of the two Claud Hamilton classes running to Southend, but also the new 1500 class 4-6-0s. The use of large express locomotives on what was a very short run could be deemed to be wasteful. The LB&SCR used side tank locomotives of the 4-4-2 wheel arrangement on the London to Brighton service and Brighton was 50 miles from London as opposed to just over 41 for Southend from Liverpool Street. It is known that a design for a 4-6-2 side tank locomotive was prepared by the GER. Unfortunately, the date of the diagram of this is January 1920. This does suggest that after the end of the First World War the Great Eastern Railway was thinking of building a large tank locomotive. Had the design been developed, the use of such a locomotive would be on the Southend service.

How the Great Eastern Railway would have competed with electric trains between London and Southend over the former LT&SR line is something that is open to speculation. That speculation is useless as the MR's proposals to electrify the London, Tilbury and Southend line came to nothing, almost certainly due to the outbreak of the First World War in August 1914. Similarly nor did Great Eastern Railway Colchester line trains run into St Pancras station via the Tottenham and Forest Gate Junction Railway.

Attempted Amalgamation

In the summer of 1907, Sam Fay, the General Manager of the GCR, met with Oliver Bury, the General Manager of the GNR, at the Royal Victoria Hotel in Sheffield to settle outstanding claims between the two Companies. Fay and Bury got on well with each other. The GNR had an account for £80,000 against the GCR which had a counter claim for a similar amount. According to George Dow in Volume 3 of his history of the GCR, over the wine and talking of one thing and another connected with the figures, the two men came round to the idea of an amalgamation of the two Companies as the fifty year agreement that had been made in 1858 between the GNR and what was then the MS&LR was soon to expire. Fay and Bury decided to submit their views to their respective Boards, who were understandably somewhat lukewarm at first, but finally agreed to go ahead under a special meeting held on 21 November 1907 which reached 'heads of agreement'. There were negotiations between Lord Allerton, the Chairman of the GNR, and Sir Alexander Henderson, the Chairman of the GCR. The Boards of the two railways decided that the 'heads of agreement' were in accordance with the 1858 Act. From 1 January 1908 or as soon thereafter as both Companies' shareholders and the Railway and Canal Commissioners should approve, there would be a joint committee of 13 GNR and 12 GCR directors. The first Chairman of the new Company would be Lord Allerton and Sir Alexander Henderson would be the Deputy Chairman. The Committee would control all of the line and would receive all the receipts except for the former Lancashire, Derbyshire and East Coast and Sheffield District railways which the GCR would manage and pay net receipts. What was being proposed was a working union in the same way that in 1899 the South Eastern and the London, Chatham and Dover railways had formed a working union which became known as the South Eastern and Chatham Railway. Under the proposals, the GCR's General Manager Sam Fay would become the General Manager of the Joint Committee with Richard Hill of the GNR as Solicitor and C.L. Edwards of the GNR as Accountant. Oliver Bury, the displaced General Manager of the GNR, and the displaced Solicitor and displaced Accountant of the GCR were to be adequately compensated out of their respective companies' own funds. Oliver Bury would join the GNR Board and the joint committee. The two Companies' shareholders approved the agreement at extraordinary general meetings of the Companies held on 20 December 1907.

The agreement aroused strong opposition. The *Railway Magazine* was suspicious of a working union saying that SER shareholders had suffered from the working union with the LC&DR whilst forgetting that it had done something for the latter Company's shareholders and had improved services. The *Railway Magazine* said that it was doubtful if the Railway and Canal Commissioners would approve the working union. The *Daily Telegraph* supported the agreement. *The Times* took a balanced neutral stance. The *Locomotive Magazine* felt that there would be opposition from the MR and also the GER, which would be particularly affected by the traffic from the GCR to the London Docks, which hitherto the GER had hauled from Lincoln and which in future was more likely to be diverted to the GNR route. The Board of Trade opposed the agreement, which it contended that at 999 years was far too long, besides which the monopolistic idea of amalgamation might lead to an unjust increase in rates and thus affect the commerce of the country. The MR would have been affected as it competed with the GCR for traffic to Leicester, Nottingham, Sheffield and Manchester and with the GNR for traffic to Leeds and Bradford. In addition to what the *Locomotive Magazine* said about the GER, it had competition with the GNR between London and Cambridge.

According to *The Times* of 22 February 1908:

THE GREAT NORTHERN AND GREAT CENTRAL AGREEMENT
The application by the GNR and the GCR for sanction to an agreement for the joint working of the two companies will come on for hearing before Mr Justice A.T. Lawrence, the Hon. A.E. Gathorne Hardy, and Sir James Woodhouse, in the Railway and Canal Commission Court at the Law Courts, on Wednesday morning next. Considerable opposition is being offered to the scheme, among the opponents who have lodged objections being the Great Western, Great Eastern, MR, London and North Western, North Eastern, Lancashire and Yorkshire, North Staffordshire, Hull and Barnsley, and Sheffield District railways, the Board of Trade, the Mansion-House Association, the Notts and Derby Flower Millers' Association, the Calico Printers' Association, the Hull Corporation, the Grimsby Corporation, the Lincolnshire Chamber of Agriculture, and many others. The hearing of the case is expected to occupy a considerable time.

The hearing took place on 26 to 27 February 1908.

The GER's objections were presented on 27 February. According to the *Eastern Daily Press* of 28 February 1908:

Mr. Freeman K.C., speaking for the Great Eastern Railway Company, contended that the agreement proposed was ultra vires [beyond their legal power or authority]. In the case of the line built by the Great Eastern and the Great Northern jointly through March to Lynn and Cromer and other places, the proposals of the two companies would entirely alter their position. It was true the two companies professed by Section 3 to nominally keep out of the scheme that particular railway but they could bring in and pool the profits and losses of that particular railway just as it was part of their general system. There was absolutely no power provision in the Act in respect of these proposals, and he submitted the whole thing was ultra vires.

It is not quite sure what Freeman meant when he said the line built jointly by the GE and the GN through March to Lynn and Cromer and other places. it is as if he is mixing up the GN&GE Joint Line with the M&GN Joint Railway.

The Commission gave its judgement on 2 March 1908. According to *The Times* of 3 March:

> The Railway and Canal Commissioners gave judgment yesterday in the matter of the proposed working agreement between the Great Northern and GCR Companies upon the preliminary question whether the agreement was within the statutory powers of the companies. The Commissioners, for reasons set forth at length by Mr. Justice A.T. Lawrence, held that the agreement was not within the powers conferred by the Acts of Parliament, and gave judgment to that effect. On subsequent application by counsel for the two companies, the Court of Appeal fixed Monday next for the hearing of the appeal from this decision.

The appeal hearing took some days starting on 9 March 1908. According to *The Times* of the following day:

> In the Court of Appeal, before the Master of the Rolls and Lords Justices Moulton and Buckley, the hearing was begun of the appeal of the Great Northern and GCR companies from the decision of the Railway Commissioners that the proposed working agreement between the two companies is not within their statutory powers. Arguments were proceeding when the Court adjourned.

In *The Times* of 11 March 1908 at the conclusion of the hearing on 10 March, the Master of the Rolls was reported as saying, 'For the convenience of the parties I think it right to say at once that we are all of the opinion that the preliminary objections must prevail, and we hope to give our reasons for so holding on Friday next.'

The Times of 14 March reported that, 'the Master of the Rolls and Lords Justices Moulton and Buckley read their judgments dismissing the appeal of the Great Northern and GCR Companies from the decision of the Railway Commissioners that the proposed working agreement between the two companies was invalid as being beyond their statutory powers.'

The Times of 1 April 1908 reported that the directors of the Great Northern and GCR Companies had finally decided not to promote a Bill in parliament that session to validate the agreement between the two companies which the Railway Commission had held to be ultra vires (beyond their statutory powers).

According to the *Locomotive Magazine* of April 1908 under the heading

GREAT NORTHERN AND GREAT CENTRAL JOINT BILL – Having failed to obtain the sanction of the Courts for their 'working agreement' made at the close of last year, the directors of the two companies concerned propose to promote a joint Bill in the next session of Parliament to effect to the wishes of their shareholders.

According to Dow in his history of the GCR, John Gooday, the GER's General Manager at the time, at a meeting with Sam Fay, the GCR's General Manager, protested that he had joined up with that Company's greatest competitor. Fay then asked, 'Why not come into the amalgamation also?' The offer was accepted and after the MR had been given an opportunity to participate and had declined, negotiations had begun in the autumn of 1908 for a tripartite working union to go before parliament in the ensuing session.

It is clear from *The Times* of 11 August 1908, that wind of the proposal had already got out:

SHEFFIELD DISTRICT RAILWAY COMPANY. The ordinary general meeting was held yesterday at Hamilton-House. Sir Robert A. Hadfield, who presided, said that the Company had had to incur expenditure in connexion with the Great Northern and GCR Companies' agreement which was before the Railway Commissioners last Sessions. It was most essential that they should appear in opposition to that agreement, in order to protect their interests and see, that with so many conflicting interests, they were not left out in the cold. Although the amalgamation scheme was eventually thrown out, the Company were enabled to establish a position for themselves which would very much strengthen their position with regard to any future agreement on similar lines. It was now generally known that an amalgamation was contemplated between the Great Northern, the Great Central, and the Great Eastern Railway Companies; it was no doubt a right step to take, speaking of railway interests generally, and should, he felt, have the support of their company, provided their interests were fully protected. The directors would carefully watch the scheme when it came before Parliament. The revenue showed a slight advance over that of the corresponding period of last year. The report was adopted.

Even before the Bill for the working union was presented to parliament, the three Companies had entered into a working agreement. The *Locomotive Magazine* of November 1909 reported that the result of the working agreement was beginning to be illustrated 'by the closing of various receiving offices for goods, the discharge of numbers of railway workers, the curtailment of superfluous trains and a deceleration of many others'.

The Times on 18 November 1908 reported in Questions in the House of Commons on 17 November in reply to a question by Mr Wardle, the Labour Member for Stockport, about Railway Agreements, the President of the Board of Trade, Winston Churchill, said that he understood that an agreement between the Great Northern, the Great Central and the Great Eastern Companies would be submitted for the consideration of parliament.

The Times of 23 November 1908 reported:

Application is intended to be made to Parliament in the ensuing Session by the GREAT NORTHERN, the GREAT CENTRAL, and the GREAT EASTERN RAILWAY COMPANIES for leave to bring in a Bill to provide for the management, working, and maintenance as one joint undertaking, either in perpetuity or for such period as may be specified in the intended Act, and on such terms as may be defined by it, of the three companies' undertakings 'or some part or parts thereof respectively, subject to such exceptions, limitations, and provisions' as the Act may prescribe.

Amongst other things, the Bill would contain clauses that authority would be asked for to repeal or alter the provisions of the agreement dated 12 May 1893, between the MR and the Great Northern Companies scheduled to and confirmed by the (E&MR) Act, 1893, of those companies, and to relieve the Great Northern Company from and to render inapplicable to the joint committee all or any of the obligations under that agreement or Act with respect to the management, &c., of the railways referred to in the agreement and the Act. The Bill would also contain clauses authorizing any one or more of the three companies to make a railway, to be called the Lincoln Avoiding Line, commencing in Canwick by a junction with the railway of the Great Northern and Great Eastern joint committee, and terminating in Greetwell by a junction, with the Market Ranse branch of the Great Central Railway.

The Times of 25 November 1908 reported, in the notice relating to the comprehensive working union of the Great Northern, Great Central, and Great Eastern Railways, there appeared also proposals for the construction of a 'Lincoln avoiding line'.

According to Dow, whilst many sections of the Press applauded the scheme, British governments, unlike the Continental governments, had been devoid of a coherent policy for transport since the eighteenth century, variously fostering railway amalgamation and then condemning it. And given the mood swings and that parliament had supported the previous railway working union, that of the South Eastern and London, Chatham and Dover railways, the chances were that this working union attempt would be damned. A special meeting of the three railway Chairmen with Winston Churchill in January 1909 produced some support, at a price, but was unavailing. There were 52 objections to the Bill's second reading. Although it was accorded the reading, during the debate so much hostility was expressed that Churchill said that the second reading would not be inconsistent with the House rejecting the Bill on the third reading and so the three companies withdrew the Bill.

The Times of 23 April 1909 reported that the London News Agency had been officially authorised to state that, after the fullest consideration, the Great Eastern, Great Northern, and Great Central Railway Companies had decided not to proceed further with the Bill for their amalgamation and that the companies had communicated their reasons for taking that step to the President of the Board of Trade.

The *Locomotive Magazine* of May 1909 reported:

THE G.N., G.C. AND G.E. RAILWAY 'COMBINE.' Despite the support given by the Government and the Parliamentary representatives of the railway servants, the directors of the Great Northern, Great Central, and Great Eastern Ry. Companies towards the close of last month decided not to proceed further with a Bill for a working agreement between the three companies, their reason for abandoning the Bill after the second reading had been carried being that they were not prepared to meet the conditions which the instructions to the Select Committee imposed on the enquiry. The working arrangements made between the three companies are still in force, however.

One result of the working agreement between the three Companies was reported in the *Locomotive Magazine* of October 1909 that a standard design of 10 ton wagon was to be prepared that was interchangeable in all details for the Great Central, Great Eastern and GNR Companies.

Electrification

In the period 1900 to 1922, a number of railways in England electrified some of their lines. In the case of the steam operated underground railways in London and Liverpool it was because of the foul atmosphere caused by the steam locomotives. In the case of the main line companies that electrified part of their system it was mainly because of tramway competition, or in the case of the MR's Lancaster to Morecambe and Heysham line as an experiment or in the case of the NER's Newport to Shildon electrification for the haulage of heavy mineral traffic or the case of the L&YR's Liverpool to Southport electrification as a way of increasing its revenue against a competitor – the Cheshire Lines Committee.

One type of traffic that was ideally suited to electrification was suburban traffic. It was this that led to the proposals around the beginning of the twentieth century for electric tube railways in London which were covered previously in this chapter.

The GER had the heaviest suburban traffic in Britain, if not the world, all of it operated by small tank locomotives. In the early part of the twentieth century, the carriages used were close coupled 8ft-wide four-wheelers seating five-a-side in the third and second class compartments and four-a-side in the first class compartments. To increase train capacity, the GER introduced some new carriages with 9ft-wide bodies to carry two additional passengers in each compartment. To match the new carriages, the Company's Locomotive and

Carriage Superintendent, James Holden, had the bodies of the original 8ft-wide bodied carriages cut down the centre, with extra flooring spliced in and additional end panels and roof boards inserted. The sides of the coaches were slightly inclined inwards from the cantrail downwards to allow sufficient turn under at the bottom of the footboards and various side protrusions such as grab handles, door hinges, and the roof edge were altered to come within the maximum width permitted. Later on, some of the four-wheel bodies were mounted in pairs on new bogie underframes to provide the better riding qualities of bogies on older non-bogie rolling stock.

In truth, though, this was only a short-term solution to the capacity problem. Ultimately the answer lay in electrification.

In America, the Long Island Railroad serving the cities of Brooklyn and New York had similarities to the GER in that it had a heavy suburban traffic. On the other hand, it did not have the agricultural traffic of the GER. The British railway nearest to the GER in terms of the type of traffic carried was the L&SWR, which started electrifying its suburban lines with the first line being done in 1915.

Of the English railways using electric traction, only the underground railways had anything approaching that of the American lines. The Metropolitan Railway operating steam and electric traction and carrying both passengers and goods traffic was the nearest equivalent. When Walter Hyde decided to retire with ill health with the GER considering electrifying some of its suburban lines and given that none of the existing English railway managers of railways that had suburban lines that had been electrified had the same experience or carried the same amount of traffic, it made perfect sense to go to America. It was, to quote Reg Davies writing about Lord Claud Hamilton in *Great Eastern Journal* No 137, 'most desirable that the GER had as its General Manager a man "who thoroughly understood electricity and the working of railways by that method".' According to Davies, Hamilton had visited Canada and America in 1912 and he may have heard of Thornton there. Henry Worth Thornton was born in Logansport, Indiana on 6 November 1871 and on leaving university in 1894 joined the Pennsylvania Railroad. He then held a variety of engineering and operating posts on that railroad and its subsidiaries until he left to join the GER in 1914, including in 1912 when he was made General Superintendent of the Pennsylvania Railroad's subsidiary, the Long Island Railroad.

Railway and Travel Monthly of March 1914 reported that Lord Claud Hamilton's announcement at the Annual Meeting of the GER that the Directors had appointed Thornton, an American, to be the General Manager of the Company caused more much amazement than such a remarkable appointment would create under other circumstances. The magazine quoted Lord Claud Hamilton as saying that it was most desirable that the GER should have a General Manager who thoroughly understood the principles of electricity and the working of railways by that method. The magazine continued that the appointment clearly foreshadowed Lord Claud Hamilton's desire to electrify the GER's suburban system. The expense of the electrification would be so immense that the shareholders would have to carefully count the costs and the results that were likely to accrue therefrom before sanctioning the expenditure of the money. The magazine added that the GER had already reduced fares in the hope of retaining the traffic, but the motor buses seemed to be already firmly established in the district. It was unlikely that, plus the largely increased capital charges, that sufficient additional passengers would be carried to produce better financial results than those obtaining from steam operation. Indeed, the actual result might be the carrying of many additional hundreds of thousands of workmen, which was already the bête noire of the GER, at an actual loss.

The motor bus that was the cause of the trouble was the London General Omnibus Company's famous B type bus, which first went into production in 1910. By 1913, around 2,500 of the buses were in service.

In 1911, the London General Omnibus Company was operating the following routes which provided competition to the GER:

No 8	Seven Kings – Stratford- Bank-Willesden
No 14	Wanstead-Leytonstone-Stratford-Bank-Putney
No 22	Hackney-Bank-Putney
No 25	Old Ford-Bank-Victoria Station

The Times of 14 February 1914 carried a paragraph which began:

AMERICAN MANAGER FOR A BRITISH RAILWAY SURPRISE AND REGRET. NECESSARY REFORMS ON THE GREAT EASTERN

Lord Claud Hamilton announced yesterday at the annual meeting of the GER Company that Mr. Henry W. Thornton, General Superintendent of the Long Island Railroad, which is controlled by the Pennsylvania Company, had been appointed to succeed Mr. Walter Hyde as General Manager of the GER.

The appointment will cause general surprise, not unmixed with regret, that for the first time in history the directorate of a great British railway should have found it necessary to go abroad for a general manager. This feeling does not arise from any questioning of Mr. Thornton's ability and experience, or of the efficiency of American railways; but it is thought that, in view of the fact that this country not only enjoys a railway system which, with certain exceptions, is a model to other countries, but has supplied pioneers of railway progress to all parts of the world, an Englishman might have been found capable of initiating the very necessary reforms on the Great Eastern.

The *Great Eastern Railway Magazine* of March 1914 in an article on the First Annual Meeting mentioned Thornton's appointment and information about him.

Henry Thornton was not the only American to join the GER. At the beginning of 1917 on the retirement of Horace Wilmer, the Chief Engineer, Thornton assumed the post jointly with that of General Manager. The reason for this was so that he could introduce into the Engineer's Department immediately under his wing John Miller, who was an Ulster-born engineer who had served under him on the Long Island Rail Road. In March 1919, Miller assumed the post of Chief Civil Engineer.

It is clear that the GER regarded electrification of its suburban lines as the answer and asked the British Westinghouse Company to investigate its suburban traffic. The report was produced in September 1918 and strongly favoured electrification on a third rail direct current system subject to consultation with the Railway Company's officials. Even before British Westinghouse had produced its report, it is clear from diagrams dated February 1914 and September 1915 that the GER was serious about electrification of its suburban lines. The diagrams were titled as follows: 'GER Graphical Comparison of Seats

Provided and Passengers carried on UP trains Loughton to Liverpool Street on 22.10.1912' and described as 'Graph for period 9am to 1pm with seats per minute provided by 12 electric trains per hour Copy of Electrical Engineers' drawing dated 19.2.14'; 'GER Suggested Electric Service between Ilford and Liverpool Street; Ilford and Fenchurch Street; Loughton and Liverpool Street; Loughton and Fenchurch Street; Barking and Liverpool Street; Woolwich and Liverpool Street during the Morning Rush Hours' and described as 'Diagram and graph Endorsed: referred to in Sub Committee minutes of 11.2.14'; 'Copy of Electrical Engrs Dg No 611; GER-Electrification of Suburban Lines Diagram of Main Line Steam Trains (based on 'Flying Junction' scheme) and described as 'Graph of Liverpool Street to Romford A Busy Saturday in August B Ordinary Weekday Evening in August Copy of Electrical Engrs Dg No 610'.

Had the MR been able to electrify the LT&SR main line from Fenchurch Street, whatever electrical system was used by the GER would have had to be compatible with that Company's electrical system. According to the report produced in September 1918, electrification would increase the traffic potential at Liverpool Street by at least 50 per cent. The report proposed the electrification either of all GER lines within a 30-mile radius of Liverpool Street and Fenchurch Street out to Hertford, Bishop's Stortford, Ongar and Chelmsford as well as the line to Southend or all of these lines except the sections from Broxbourne to Bishop's Stortford and Shenfield to Chelmsford. In regard to rolling stock, all the carriages would have to be bogie carriages. The electric trains would be three coach electric multiple units. The carriages would be of the non-corridor compartment sort. The report did look at corridor carriages which were used on the fast Southend services. The question of where the electrical equipment for the trains should be put was also considered, whether it should be placed under the floor (as in the motor coaches of the L&SWR electric multiple units) or in a separate compartment (as in the motor coaches of the L&NWR electric multiple units). The use of electric locomotives for the haulage of main line passenger trains and goods trains including main line goods trains and for shunting was also considered. The report even considered possible schedules. Other things included were a proposal for flyovers at Bow Junction where the lines from Fenchurch Street and Liverpool Street joined and for Chingford line trains at Clapton and quadrupling as far as either Harold Wood or Shenfield as well as power supply and power distribution. The electrical load centre would be at a point north of Stratford. A site for the generating station had already been earmarked by the GER's engineer. It was to be a part of the old property of the Thames Iron Works at Thames Wharf near Tidal Basin. According to *Railway and Travel Monthly* for October 1916, the site had been purchased not for the GER's own purposes, but to prevent any other competitive company getting hold of it. No diagrams of the formations of the proposed rolling stock/motive power were produced. Although the conclusions were favoured by Thornton, they were not in the main acted on.

Meanwhile, *Railway and Travel Monthly* for January 1919 in an article on British Express Trains and Locomotives said, 'We can hardly doubt that the electrification of the GER's huge suburban system will follow …' The magazine's hopes seem to have been born out when its March 1920 edition reported that the Board of the GER had instructed the General Manager (Thornton) in conjunction with other experts to prepare a scheme of electrification. The investigation had not proceeded far enough to predict financial results for the Railway. According to the book *Liverpool Street Station*, in December 1919 Thornton had presented to the GER's Board a report that he had created with the help of two electrical engineers, of whom one was George W. Gibbs of the Pennsylvania Railroad of America. In the minds of the report's writers, the suburban lines of the GER were ripe for electrification. Once the scheme was complete it was expected that there would be an increase in traffic of 50 per cent carried in trains that would cost 10d less a mile than steam trains to run. Even if the change to electric traction along with necessary changes to track and signalling cost, as they thought, £5.5million, the Company could expect an increase in profits of £308,000 a year. Thornton, in order to get the most from the new system, was keen to develop the outer suburban traffic rather than see the increased capacity that the electric trains would provide be taken up by cheap workmen's fares. He said that they would prefer to drive traffic originating within 6 miles of Liverpool Street to the trams and buses. One advantage that had not been mentioned in other reports was that if steam was eliminated from Liverpool Street, as there would be none of the ventilation problems that were associated with steam traction, it would be possible to build offices and hotels over the tracks and therefore the revenue obtained from those properties would increase the Company's revenue. However, the June 1920 edition of *Railway and Travel Monthly* carried an article entitled 'the Great Eastern Railway's Operating Problems' about a paper read by Thornton to the Institute of Transport called 'Some Railway Operating Problems', which made no mention of electrification and the August 1920 edition carried an article by G.A. Sekon entitled 'Successful Alternative to Electrification – The Great Eastern Railway's Remarkable Augmentation of its Western Suburban Services'. This was the famous 'Jazz Service'. What the article does not say is why the GER chose not to go down the electrification route. So, what happened? Fred V. Russell, the GER's Superintendent of Operations, came up with an alternative scheme albeit one that only covered the west side suburban service, but which at an outlay of £80,000 cost rather less than the sum of £3million for electrification. Russell's scheme involved: the rearrangement of tracks and point work at the termini in order that the need for conflicting movements was kept to a minimum; new crossovers installed so as to allow flexibility of routing and for more train movements to take place in parallel; signals resisted with judicious additions to permit closer headways; the length of peak hour trains standardised at the maximum length permissible (16 carriages) given both the physical restraints and the locomotive power available; the overall length of journey times reduced by the omission of lesser used station stops; off peak services reduced to six carriage formations with faster timings; at Liverpool Street a new circulating area created within the platform barriers to enable arriving train loads of passengers to be dispersed quickly via any exit; train identification prominently displayed to speed boarding and ensure that passengers were in no doubt that they were joining the correct train and; first class carriages displayed a prominent yellow band over the top of their compartments and second class carriages displayed a prominent blue band over the top of their compartments. The result was an evening peak hour service with trains on the Enfield, Walthamstow, Chingford and Palace Gates services departing every two minutes from Platforms 1 to 4 at Liverpool Street. After every fourth train there was a gap of four minutes. The overall result was a service of 24 trains per hour. Overall, the Railway managed to increase the number of peak hour trains during the busiest period by between one and a half and one and three quarters. The new service came into operation at the beginning of July 1920. Cecil J. Allen in *The Great Eastern Railway* says that on the first Saturday of September 1920 during the Saturday rush hour, only four Enfield and Chingford trains started late, one by one minute and three by half a minute.

As to why the Railway went for a short-term expedient and how Russell persuaded Thornton to adopt it can be found in the Company's finances. The GER's ordinary dividend stock was only paying between 2½ and 2¾ per cent from 1912 onwards, whereas the GNR was paying over 4 per cent and the L&SWR over 5 per cent during the same period. The GER was not a wealthy railway company. Despite that it is obvious, even from contemporary accounts, that Thornton and the GER were aware that the Jazz service was only a stopgap as according to *Transport and Travel Monthly* for December 1921, as the magazine had then been renamed, the GER had a scheme for the electrification of the whole of its suburban system from Liverpool Street to Enfield, Palace Gates, Chingford, Loughton, Epping and Ongar together with the suburban sections of the main lines as far as Broxbourne and Gidea Park respectively. This is compounded by a diagram prepared by Stratford Works dated 19 March 1922 showing distances between seats and size of compartments of proposed electric stock. The title of the drawing was 'Diagram Showing Distance Between Seats and Size of Compartments Proposed Electric Train Suburban Stock' and the description was 1ft to 1in sectional elevation and endorsed: 'Tracing made from a copy made by the SE&CR and the dimensions are those of the GER compartments and seats'. The SE&CR was also intending electrifying some of its lines. Further in the period 1917-20, Stratford works diagram list has plans of L&SWR electric stock. The SE&CR planned and the LSWR did use three carriage electric trains comprised of two motor coaches with a trailer coach in between. Clearly the GER's electric trains would have been of the same formation. This seems to back up what Thornton had said when he wrote to the Minister of Transport, Sir Eric Geddes, in July 1920 that 'undoubtedly we shall have to electrify sooner or later and I am still proceeding with the electrification scheme'.

Signalling

Until 1899, the caution indication of a distant signal was given by a red light, exactly the same as that of a home signal, but in that year, in order to obtain a

170   The Great Eastern Railway

distinction, the GER began to experiment with the Coligny-Welch distant lamp, which at night displayed an illuminated white fish-tail against the signal light, whether red or green. This later became standard practice on the GER.

In 1899, the GER installed the first electro-pneumatic power signalling in Great Britain in the signal box controlling Spitalfields goods yard at the exit from Bishopgate Goods Station.

Water troughs

In the days of steam, a way that a locomotive could replenish its water supply other than by a water crane was through water troughs laid between the rails and where the locomotive's tender or side tanks could pick up water without stopping. These enabled trains to make longer runs without stopping for water. These were first installed near Tivetshall in 1896 and at Halifax Junction, just south of Ipswich, in 1897.

The GER's lines had a number of swing bridges including the one at Trowse just south of Norwich, where class D56 4-4-0 No 1816 is seen on the 1pm Liverpool Street to Cromer on 17 September 1910. (Ken Nunn).

The Great Eastern Railway 1896 to 1922 171

The GER installed water troughs near Tivetshall in 1896 and at Halifax Junction, just south of Ipswich, in 1897. Class D56 4-4-0 No 1823 is seen taking water on the water troughs at Halifax Junction on the 1pm Liverpool Street to Cromer on 10 September 1910. (Ken Nunn).

The GER had mail bag apparatus at Romford, Brentwood, Ingatestone, Witham, Kelvedon and Manningtree. Class D56 4-4-0 No 1855 is seen exchanging mail bags near Brentwood on the 3.30pm Ipswich to Liverpool Street on 10 June 1908. (Ken Nunn).

Named trains

The GER had only one officially named train and one unofficially named train. The latter was the 'North Country Continental' which had begun running from Harwich to the north in 1882. In 1906 it had sections for York, Manchester, Liverpool and Birmingham. This ceased during the First World War but was revived afterwards. The other train was the 'Norfolk Coast Express' which dated back to an experimental non-stop train run from Liverpool Street to Cromer and back on 3 November 1895 made by oil-fired 2-2-2 locomotive No 1006 with a light train of 140 tons and no higher water consumption than the contents of the 3,100 gallon water tank.

In the summer of 1897 following the installation of the water troughs, the daily Cromer Express began running non-stop from Liverpool Street to North Walsham. The train assumed its title, the Norfolk Coast Express, in 1907 and in that year had, besides the main train for Cromer, a portion for Mundesley-on-Sea and Overstrand detached at North Walsham and a portion for Sheringham detached at Cromer Junction. The train only ran during July, August and September and ceased running with the outbreak of the First World War

The GER's most prestigious express trains other than the Continental expresses were the Cromer expresses. Class S69 4-6-0 No 1505 is seen on such an express near Ingrave signal box on the 1pm Liverpool Street to Cromer on 5 August 1913. (Ken Nunn).

in 1914. Following the end of the war, although the train was revived it was not named and unlike before the war did not run on Sundays according to *Bradshaw's Railway Guide* for July 1922.

Pullman Cars

As mentioned in the previous chapter, the 'North Country Continental' had had a Restaurant Car since 1891. In 1896, further Restaurant Cars were introduced on the GER on the services from Liverpool Street to Yarmouth and to Cromer. Like the train introduced in 1891, the Restaurant Car sets were vestibuled within the set and had no connection to the rest of the train. Corridor carriages started coming into use from 1906. Elsewhere, bogies started replacing four and six wheeled carriages, but these latter types of carriages still remained in use at the end of the GER's existence on 31 December 1922.

Far grander carriages, though, appeared on the GER on 11 November 1920 when the first Pullman Cars started running. The story goes back to 1874. Pullman Cars originated in America and were the brainchild of George Pullman. In 1872, James Allport, the General Manager of the MR, who at that time was concerned at the lot of third class passengers who were treated on most railways as unwelcome intruders, visited America to see Pullman Cars. Following Allport's visit to America, the Traffic Committee of the MR debated the possibility of using Pullman Cars on that Railway and Pullman himself appeared before the Company's shareholders in February 1873. Following an agreement signed on 18 February 1873, a Pullman Car train service started running between London and Bradford on 1 June 1874. The Pullman Cars used on the MR consisted of two sorts – sleeping cars and parlour or drawing room cars. The sleeping cars could be converted for day use. The parts of the cars were made at Pullman's Detroit workshops and sent over to England where they were assembled at the MR's workshops in Derby. When the kits for the Pullman Cars were being assembled, Pullman approached the GER setting out the virtues of his cars and giving details of the agreement made with the MR. The Traffic Committee of the GER received the information on 11 March 1874 and left the matter to the Company's Chairman to decide. One imagines that the territory served by the GER was not really suitable for the use of Pullman Cars, its main lines being of a rather shorter distance than the MR's main line from London. Just over four and a half years later, at the meeting of the Locomotive Committee of the GER on 19 November 1878, the General Manager, Samuel Swarbrick, was asked to report on the question of running Pullman Cars on the Railway.

In 1882, Pullman made an offer to the GER to place two drawing room cars at the Company's disposal for 12 months on terms that were acceptable to the then General Manager William Birt, who recommended to the Traffic Committee in September 1882 that they be placed into service between London and Norwich via Cambridge, suggesting the 12.03 from St Pancras to Norwich and the 11.16 from Norwich to St Pancras. His suggestion was accepted. But nothing further was heard of this.

The next that we hear about Pullman Cars is just after the First World War. At this time, the Pullman Car Company in Britain was owned by Sir Davison Dalziel. From the facts that are available we know that the GER's General Manager, Sir Henry Worth Thornton, as he now was having taken British citizenship, spoke to the Company's Board on 3 July 1919 suggesting that Pullman run their cars over the Company's system. This was agreed in principle, subject to the details being submitted to a future meeting of the Board. This was done and on 6 November 1919 the Company's Board received the results of the negotiations with the Pullman Car Company. The principal details of the agreement were minuted. The agreement was for a period of 15 years expiring on 15 April 1935. The GER's Board approved the terms and after scrutiny by the Company's Solicitor, Mr E. Moore, were signed and sealed on 6 January 1920. *Railway and Travel Monthly* for March 1920 reported that the GER's Deputy Chairman, Sir Alwyn E. Fellowes, in his speech at the Company's Annual Meeting, had said that the Company had entered into an agreement with the Pullman Car Company to provide cars for its main line services and that it was expected that they would commence running during the summer. In fact, the initial service began on 11 November 1920. There were two Pullman Cars initially put into service on the GER – the *Arcadia* and the *Corsair*. They were first class buffet cars with seating for 21 passengers and had a kitchen and were built by Clayton Wagons of Lincoln. Prior to going into service, they were exhibited at Liverpool Street station on 8 November 1920. The Pullman Cars ran on Mondays to Saturdays on services between London and Cambridge in the case of *Arcadia* and London and Southend and London and Clacton in the case of *Corsair*. On Sundays, cleaning and maintenance work was done to the

Pullman Cars. A supplementary charge was payable to ride in the Pullman Cars. In a report to the GER's Board on 2 December 1920, Thornton reported that the Pullman Cars had not been well patronised. *Transport and Travel Monthly* in December 1920 reported that first class passengers could now travel to East Coast resorts served by the GER by Pullman Car. The fact that Cambridge was clearly not on the coast apparently did not stop it being included within the definition! The *Great Eastern Railway Magazine* for December 1920 carried an article on the Pullman Cars. Over time, further services and Pullman Cars were added to the roster. Not only were more first class Cars added to the roster, but also second class and third class Cars. In total, 20 Pullman Cars were running on the GER at the end of 1921; five first class, two second class and three third class Cars were built by Clayton Wagons and five first class and five third class by the Birmingham Railway Carriage and Wagon Company. Only first class Cars were named. By March of 1922, Pullman Cars were in service to the following destinations from and to Liverpool Street: Bury St Edmunds, Cambridge, Clacton, Cromer, Harwich (Town and Parkeston Quay), Hunstanton, Lowestoft and Southend. In addition, there was also a return service between Lowestoft and Peterborough; previously, Walton and Yarmouth had also been served. There were also the Newmarket race specials which used Pullman Cars. These ran from St Pancras station and not Liverpool Street station. Because second class still existed on Continental boat trains, this explains the need for second class Pullman Cars. *Transport and Travel Monthly* for July 1922 reported that commencing that month there was a Sunday non-stop Pullman Limited express from Liverpool Street to Clacton and vice versa. The train comprised first and third class Pullmans that would cover the non-stop journey of 69¾ miles in 90 minutes. The train commenced running on 16 July. In November 1922, Thornton resigned as General Manager of the GER to take over as President of the Canadian National Railways and left his successor, Sidney Parnwell, who took up his post on 1 December, with a problem – one month before the Grouping and the GER became part of the LNER. During August 1922, Thornton had entered into an agreement with Dalziel, the Chairman of the Pullman Car Company, for the supply to the GER of six additional third class Cars. The question of ordering the six additional Pullman Cars had not been put before the GER's Directors and at the announcement of this at the Board meeting of the Company on 22 December 1922 the Chairman, Lord Claud

Hamilton, considered that it was very doubtful whether it was advisable to add to the number of Pullman Cars already on the GER. This was now ten days before the GER became part of the LNER. It is not clear if Parnwell was aware of the agreement before taking office and may only have discovered it on taking up the position. He may have discussed the matter with the Chairman, who reported it to the Board. The Board, after hearing from Parnwell, resolved that he should meet Dalziel to get the agreement cancelled. Failing that, he was authorised to make such alternative arrangements as he considered to be in the best interests of the Company. John Watling, writing about Pullman Cars on the GER in *Great Eastern Journals* 65 to 69, says that the wording of the Board's report and its decision suggests that the extra cars had not been delivered or put into service and that there was room to negotiate. Following the absorption of the GER into the LNER, Parnwell became Divisional General Manager, Southern Area of the LNER, charged with the problem of what to do with the impending arrival of the additional Pullman Cars. It is difficult to know what happened after the Grouping, but John Watling suggests that the additional

The GER started running Pullman cars in 1920. Their use on the railway does not seem to have been particularly successful. Here is class D56 4-4-0 No 1848 passing Stratford on a Clacton bound Pullman train on 24 June 1923, just after the grouping. The train was introduced in July 1922. (Ken Nunn).

Pullman Cars were delivered and were used by the LNER in a new Harrogate Pullman Car train introduced in to service on 9 July 1923 from King's Cross to Harrogate.

Apart from their use in the continental expresses, Pullman Cars were not a success. Other than in continental expresses, and a set used for excursions and a Sunday Clacton Pullman train, Pullman Cars were withdrawn from the line on 7 April 1924 and transferred to the East Coast main line out of King's Cross.

Changes to Services

The biggest change to services occurred in 1914 with the 'radical alterations' that came into force on 5 October of that year. Probably not the best month in 1914 to bring in changes that had been planned somewhat earlier. But who was to know that the First World War would not be over by Christmas of that year? The *Great Eastern Railway Magazine* for October 1914 carried a brief summary of the alterations, whilst the editions for November and December and for January 1915 carried a three-part rather more technical article by Cecil J. Allen. That for November 1914 was about the principles and preparations, that for December 1914 the Cambridge main line and that for January 1915 the Colchester main. The summary article in the *Great Eastern Railway Magazine* for October 1914 said, 'Commencing Monday, October 5th, very considerable alterations and improvements in the Company's timetables are to be made.' *Railway and Travel Monthly* for November 1914 also carried an article on the alterations. The radical alterations were a complete shakeup of the main line and branch line timetables. The person behind the shakeup was the new General Manager, Henry Thornton, although the actual work was carried out by a committee under the Electrical Engineer, H.W. Firth.

It was during the period covered by this chapter that a number of halts were opened by the GER. The first one was Hockerill Halt on the Bishop's Stortford to Braintree line which opened on 7 November 1910 for the convenience of golfers using Bishop's Stortford Golf Links. The Halt did not have the facility to issue tickets, so only passengers who already held tickets could use it. The next Halt was at Ashdon between Saffron Walden and Bartlow on the Audley End to Bartlow branch which did have the facility to issue tickets. The Halt opened on 14 August 1911. The *Chelmsford Chronicle* of Friday 18 August 1911 reported,

'A new halt situated between Saffron Walden and Bartlow and called "Ashdon Halt" has been provided on the Saffron Walden branch of the GER.' According to Christopher Ketteridge and Spike Mays in *Five Miles from Bunkum – A Village and its Crafts* (Eyre Methuen 1972), when Captain J.A. Collins went to live at Ashdon Hall he approached the GER with a proposition about providing a platform near the level crossing at Ashdon. The Company agreed on condition that intending passengers subscribe £12 to the cost. The villagers were more interested in becoming passengers than subscribers, so Collins paid the cost and promised to purchase a first-class season ticket. As soon as the halt was opened, the villagers of Ashdon started using the Halt. Other Halts opened by the GER during the period covered by this chapter were: in 1914 Thorpeness on the Aldeburgh branch on 29 July 1914; in 1922: Barons Lane Halt at Barons Lane Public Siding near Purleigh on the Woodham Ferrers to Maldon line on 10 July 1922; three halts on the Cambridge and Mildenhall branch, known as Fen Ditton, Exning Road, and Worlington Golf Links (actually 'Mildenhall Golf Links' for a short initial period) on 20 November 1922; Bannister Green and Stane Street on the Bishop's Stortford to Braintree line 18 December 1922; Yaxley on the Mellis to Eye line on 20 December 1922; Seven Hills on the Bury and Thetford line on 20 December 1922; and Mill Road on the Thaxted branch on 18 December 1922.

In 1922, when the Southend Arterial Road was being built from Gallows Corner in Romford to Southend, a halt was opened at Bridge 774 between Wickford and Rayleigh on the Southend line for the workmen of Messrs Muirhead, MacDonald, Wilson and Company who were building the road. The halt was for the sole use of the workmen and not the general public as it was provided so that the men could get to work more easily, following a request by the Ministry of Transport to take on more men. The Ministry of Transport had been created in 1919 and governed roads, railways and inland waterways. The halt closed on 1 May 1925 after the completion of the road.

During the period 1902 to 1914, practically all of the main and secondary English railways put rail motors in to service. There were two main reasons for introducing rail motors. One was to regain traffic from competing tramways and the other was to save money on already un-remunerative branch lines. Most of the rail motors were propelled by steam, but some by internal combustion engines. The NER was unique in having only internal combustion powered rail motors. The GWR had the largest fleet comprising 99 steam powered and one internal combustion powered rail motor. The GER was unique in not having any rail motors. That does not mean that it did not consider building a rail motor; in October 1903, the company had prepared the designs for no less than three steam rail motors. The line selected for the rail motors was that between Felixstowe Town station and Felixstowe Pier station, which was worked as part of the Ipswich, Westerfield, Felixstowe service and involved a reversal at Felixstowe Town station. The idea seems to have been to operate the section of line from Felixstowe Town to Felixstowe Beach as a separate service from the main service. The one thing the three designs had in common was that they had a small vertical boilered 0-2-2 side tank locomotive attached to the coach portion of the rail motor, the cab of the locomotive towering above the coach part. The three designs were: an open saloon with room for 71 third class passengers, with a partition dividing the smoking and non-smoking sections and a railed balcony at the far end supported by pillars with gates at each side with provision for doors at the inner end; a seven compartment body with provision for 84 third class passengers and: a six compartment body with provision for 72 passengers. None of the proposals had any provision for a guard or for the driver to drive the rail motor from the outer coach end in push-pull fashion . One must assume that the driver would have used the large rear windows of the cab to see out when he was driving backwards and station staff would have told the driver when to start. Although the proposed rail motor is mentioned in the Locomotive Committee minutes of 1 December 1903 nothing else is heard of the idea. In the *Great Eastern Journal* No 188, an article by John Watling mentions that in October 1903 Stratford Works prepared six drawings showing outline elevations and plans of what he describes as 'rigid framed units entitled "Arrangement of Steam Carriage for Carrying Passengers".' According to John Watling, the drawings were related to a report considered by the Traffic Committee on 1 December 1903 which 'considered the possibility of introducing a Motor Car service between Derby Road (Ipswich) and Felixstowe Town'. John Watling goes on to say that it was envisaged that two rail motor cars about 50 feet long carrying 62 third class passengers and operated by two men would operate the service. Apparently, service variations, fare structures and connections with steamers at Felixstowe Pier station were considered. In *The Tramways of East Anglia* (Light Railway Transport League 1969), R.C. Anderson says that Ipswich

Corporation Tramways, which were electrified in 1903, operated a route from Whitton via Cornhill to Derby Road station and that a spur had been laid into the station yard that was used when special excursion trains operated from that station. The only rail motors to run over GER lines during the Company's existence were three obtained by the Port of London Authority to work the Millwall Extension Railway in 1920 replacing three Manning Wardle 2-4-0 tank locomotives and ex-GER carriages. Two were from the GWR and had vertical boilered 0-4-0 tank locomotives inside the body of the rail motor as motive power. The third was from the Port Talbot Railway and had an 0-6-0 ordinary boiler tank locomotive within the body of the rail motor. Rail motors were not the most successful vehicles, generally, but not exclusively, not having the capacity to cope with extra traffic or to haul an extra carriage. A lot did not survive the First World War or just beyond. A push-pull train operated by a smallish tank locomotive was a better bet.

As mentioned earlier the GER first thought of using push-pull trains in April 1913 for a service on the Shenfield to Southend line stopping at proposed halts as well as the existing stations but that the idea was abandoned. The next attempt was made in October 1914 when a push-pull train was tried on the Mildenhall branch. The train comprised a small 2-4-2 tank locomotive and two carriages, one of which had a driving compartment at one end which was a compartment to enable the driver to drive the train remotely, the locomotive being left in the hands of a fireman who was passed for driving. The *Great Eastern Railway Magazine* for December 1914 carried an article on the train as did the *Locomotive Magazine* for the same month. Both magazines called the train an 'Auto Train'. The train was not a success and after several weeks it was transferred to the Somersham to Ramsey branch on the Great Northern and Great Eastern Joint Line where again it did not meet with success. After that it was transferred to the Churchbury loop where, commencing on 1 March 1915 and lasting until 30 June 1919, a passenger service had been introduced to serve munitions factories in the vicinity of the line. Finally, on 12 July 1920, not one but two auto trains started work on the Seven Sisters to Palace Gates branch. Whilst auto trains had advantages, they were a problem in that they were a fixed set and additional carriages could not be added to the train if the need arose, nor could a goods vehicle such as a van be added if needed as might happen on a rural branch line where some trains ran as mixed passenger and goods trains.

Another idea tried by the GER was conductor guard working. This involved the closing of ticket offices on some rural lines and the train guard issuing tickets. In order to do this, the trains on the branches in question had to have gang-wayed carriages in order for the guard to be able to walk the train. These commenced in 1922 on the following branches: Braintree-Bishop's Stortford; Woodham Ferrers-Maldon; Bury St Edmunds-Thetford; Mellis-Eye; and the Mildenhall branch. The *Great Eastern Railway Magazine* of February 1923 carried an article on halts which also mentioned conductor-guard working. John Watling in his article in *Great Eastern Journal* No 188 says that conductor guard working was introduced on the Bentley to Hadleigh, Cambridge to Mildenhall and Bury St Edmunds to Thetford lines on 8 August 1921, followed on 14 August that year by Mellis to Eye and Heacham to Wells. He also says that from 14 August 1921, in order to enable ticket staff to be dispensed at North Weald and Blake Hall on Sundays, on the through trains from London to Ongar there were two vestibule carriages at the 'northern end being served by a conductor guard for traffic north of Epping'. He goes on to say that conductor guard working was introduced on 1 December 1921 between Maldon East and Woodham Ferrers, Thetford and Swaffham and Wickham Market and Framlingham. Additionally, all Sunday trains and certain weekday trains on the Witham to Maldon East line had conductor guard working. On 2 January 1922, the Ely, Sutton and St Ives line went over to conductor guard working followed on 1 March by Somersham to Ramsey, on 3 April North Walsham (GER) to Mundesley and Cromer (the Norfolk and Suffolk Joint Line) and 21 August Bishop's Stortford to Witham. The service on the Norfolk and Suffolk Joint Line was provided by the M&GNJR.

Road Services

The first railway company to operate motor buses in the British Isles was the Lynton and Barnstaple Railway in Devonshire which from mid-May to mid-July 1903 ran a service using two buses from its Blackmoor station to Ilfracombe. Unfortunately, one of the drivers was prosecuted for speeding and in consequence the motor buses were withdrawn. The buses were soon purchased by the GWR which in mid-August started a service from Helston to the Lizard. The GWR went on to have the largest fleet of railway owned buses in the country. In early September 1903, the NER started a service from Beverley to Leven, Brandesburton, North Frodingham and Beeford. On 18 July 1904, the GER entered the fold when it started a service from Lowestoft, to Kessingland, and Southwold using three Milnes-Daimler double deck buses seating thirty-six passengers. Drivers were recruited from the Locomotive Department and conductors from the Traffic Department, mostly porters.

Further routes and buses followed, the latter being built by the GER at its Stratford Works. On 7 August 1905, a circular tour from Lowestoft to Oulton Broad started which ran in the summers of 1905 and 1906. On 14 August 1905, a service was started from Clacton to St Osyth which ran during the summers of 1905, 1906 and 1907. On 21 August 1905, a service was started from Ipswich to Shotley, which ran throughout the year. On 29 August 1905, services were started from Loddon to Beccles and Trowse station (near Norwich). On 1 September 1905, a service was started from Colchester to West Mersea. A proposed service from Colchester to Nayland never started. On 8 September, services were started from Chelmsford to Writtle, Danbury and Great Waltham. A proposed service to Stock was not started. Apparently the squire was concerned about the quality of the people it would bring to the village. The parish council and the Rector supported the idea of buses coming to the village. On 9 October 1905, the Trowse service was extended to Norwich (Victoria) station. Unfortunately, not all was well with the buses and in an effort to ease the position by early November both the Loddon services and the Colchester service were temporarily withdrawn. However, this did not solve the problem and on 20 December 1905 the remaining services at Lowestoft, Ipswich and Chelmsford were withdrawn.

John Cummings in *Railway Motor Buses and Bus Services in the British Isles* (Oxford Publishing Company 1978) reckoned that the staff of the bus overhaul section at the GER's Stratford Works must have seen little of their families over Christmas 1905 as a strict programme was laid down for overhauling the buses, which in the event ran only a few days late. The Lowestoft service restarted on 3 January 1906 and the others had all restarted by 12 March 1906. In 1906 it was proposed to run a service from Romford to Gidea Hall Estate using three buses, but the proposal was not taken up and the Company eventually subsidised a local bus operator. Cummings does not make it clear if this was George Heath of the Bull Inn, Hornchurch when in December 1910 the GER arranged for a local bus proprietor to run a service of omnibuses or brakes on weekdays between Emerson Park, Great Nelmses and Squirrels Heath and Gidea Park station in connection with the GER's trains. Gidea Park station was opened on 1 December 1910 and named Squirrels Heath and Gidea Park. It changed its name to Gidea Park and Squirrels Heath in late 1913.

Further buses followed from Thornycroft in 1906 and Maudslay in 1907.

The GER had bus garages at Chelmsford and Colchester stations and at Loddon, whilst at Ipswich it was at Crott Street by the locomotive shed. At Lowestoft there was a purpose built bus garage in Denmark Street for three buses and a corrugated one for six.

At Colchester, there was competition from the old established horse bus proprietor A.W. Berry, who in either 1899 or 1904, depending which source one believes, had started running a motor bus service between Colchester and West Mersea using vehicles that were both smaller and faster than the GER's buses. Clearly the Railway Company was hoping to drive out the competition with its bigger, but slower buses. It failed. On 27 February 1909, the GER's buses were withdrawn on the assurance that A.W. Berry would run to Colchester station.

On 1 July 1908, new services were started from Bury St Edmunds to Horningsheath and to Stanton. These proved a failure and were withdrawn on 28 February 1909 as was the Loddon to Beccles service.

Competition arose at Lowestoft in the summer of 1912 when United Automobile Services started charabanc operations. When Lowestoft Corporation granted the Company licenses to operate buses to Southwold, the GER withdrew its services, doing so after 18 January 1913.

At Chelmsford in July 1913, an agreement was reached with the National Steam Car Company, which had its works in the town, to take over the GER's buses from the town. The last GER bus ran on 19 July 1913 and the first National Steam Car Company bus on 22 July. By the outbreak of the First World War, the National Steam Car Company was operating buses from Chelmsford to Writtle, Danbury, Boreham, Stock, Great Waltham, Margaretting and Leaden Roding. The National Steam Car Company's buses were powered by liquid fuel (naphtha) steam boilers and not petrol.

Just as the GER was losing bus services, it started one from Harwich to Upper Dovercourt on 1 April 1914. The route was worked by buses hired from

Thomas Tilling of Peckham. The First World War saw a number of changes to the remaining bus services. Following the closure of Norwich (Victoria) station on 22 May 1916, the Loddon to Norwich route was diverted to Norwich (Thorpe) station, whilst the Ipswich to Shotley route was withdrawn in August 1916 when Shotley Royal Naval Station became a 'prohibited' area and did not resume until November 1919 but had been withdrawn permanently by the beginning of 1922. In 1920, the GER decided to try and restart the Loddon to Beccles service, which it did in January of that year. Unfortunately, United Automobile services were running on the same route and in August of that year applied for the licences of the GER's routes from Loddon to Norwich and to Beccles and was granted them. The Harwich to Upper Dovercourt route survived into LNER days but was withdrawn on 30 September 1923.

The Great Eastern London Motor Omnibus Company, which was registered in March 1906, had no connection with the GER and was formed to take over and extend the motor omnibus services of the Great Eastern Suburban Tramways and Omnibus Co.

Ships

In 1903 passenger ships ceased sailing to Rotterdam leaving only freight ships. From 1903 until 1927, when the abattoir at Harwich Parkeston Quay closed, the freight ships called at the Hook of Holland to pick up meat for the abattoir.

The period covered by this chapter saw a number of technological innovations, wireless communication being one. In 1908, all ships sailing to and from the Hook of Holland were fitted with wireless, whilst the following year all ships sailing to Antwerp were fitted with wireless. 1908 had also seen the first turbine powered steamer put into service by the GER, when the Turbine Steam Ship *Copenhagen* entered service. The ship had been built by John Brown and Company of Clydebank and had been launched on 22 October 1907 by Miss Ida Hamilton, the daughter of Lord Claud Hamilton. *Copenhagen* was followed into service in August 1908 by the *Munich* and in July 1910 by the *St Petersburg*.

In 1899, the GER, backed up by considerable pressure from commercial circles, secured from the General Post Office the carriage of mails to and from Holland previously held by the London, Chatham and Dover Railway.

1910 had seen the start of a summer only service from Parkeston Quay to Gothenburg in Sweden by the Swedish Thule Line.

Bradshaw's Continental Railway Guide for May 1913 has the following places served from Harwich: Antwerp, Esjberg, Hamburg, the Hoek van Holland (Hook of Holland) and in summer only, Gothenburg.

At a more local level, a ferry for foot passengers and bicycles from Harwich to Felixstowe was started in 1912 by the GER using a small launch, *Pinmill*. The service was an immediate success and a second service was started between Harwich and Shotley. In 1914 the larger ships *Epping* and *Hainault* entered service. During the First World War the services were suspended. Other local ships were three double ended paddle steamers, *Suffolk* (1895), *Essex* (1896) and *Norfolk* (1900), which plied up and down the Orwell between Ipswich, Harwich and Felixstowe.

August 1914 saw the start of the First World War. The services to Gothenburg and Hamburg ceased on 3 August 1914, the day before Britain declared war on Germany, the Hook of Holland passenger service was suspended on 6 August. On 12 August all passenger services were transferred from Parkeston to Tilbury. On 13 August the Esjberg service, now running from Tilbury, was transferred to Leith near Edinburgh. On 4 October the service from Tilbury to Antwerp was suspended, whilst the following day the service to Rotterdam was suspended only to resume on 13 October. Following the Armistice on 11 November 1918, services from Parkeston to the Hook of Holland and Rotterdam resumed on 26 November, the service to Rotterdam having been transferred to Tilbury after Parkeston Quay was closed to all civilian shipping on 8 May 1916. The resumption of services from Parkeston Quay to the Hook of Holland and Rotterdam was followed on 6 February 1919 by the service to Antwerp and on 10 October that year by the service to Esjberg. 7 April 1921 saw the start of a summer only service from Parkeston Quay to Zeebrugge in Belgium.

Hotels

Following the completion of the eastern train shed at Liverpool Street station there was an awkward piece of land left between the new part of the station and the eastern block of the station hotel. This made an ideal site for an extension to the hotel, which was a project that the Company had in mind when it commissioned the extension to the station. It was not until 1899 that the extension to the hotel was commissioned. The contract went to the furnishing company of Maple and Company. The architect awarded the contract to design the extension to the hotel was Colonel Robert W. Edis, who had designed the Boscombe Spa Hotel at Bournemouth in 1873 and the Constitutional Club in London. Work on the hotel extension was carried out very quickly with the agreement being made in March 1899 and by May 1900 furniture for the newly completed extension was being chosen. In September 1900, the Baltic Association took up a tenancy in part of the hotel, where it remained until 1903. Following the completion of the extension to the hotel, the old part of the building was closed for two months so that it could be altered and redecorated to bring it up to the standard of the new. The reopening took place in December 1901.

This was not the only hotel the GER owned. At Harwich, the Company's hotel suffered a major drop in trade and, resulting from the losses, was put up for auction on 21 February 1907 as a going concern. The hotel closed on 27 April 1908, but following opposition from local traders, the council and the general public the GER had a rethink and the hotel was refurbished and reopened on 2 April 1912. During the First World War the hotel was requisitioned by the military as a hospital and on its return to the Railway Company did not reopen until 21 April 1920, but then closed for good in September 1923. At Felixstowe, the GER acquired the Felixstowe Hotel in 1920.

National Events

For the Diamond Jubilee of Queen Victoria on 22 June 1897, the *Railway Magazine* noted that the GER was exceptionally busy with the Jubilee traffic. Special arrangements were made on a very extensive scale. They commenced on 18 June and extended to 24 June.

1900 saw the Paris International Exhibition at which the GER exhibited the first member of its new class of 4-4-0 express locomotives No 1900 *Claud Hamilton*. The *Locomotive Magazine* of August 1900 recorded 'The Great Eastern Railway is well represented by its new four-coupled express engine, fitted to burn oil fuel as well as coal, built to Mr Holden's design'. According to the same magazine for September 1900, the GER had been awarded a Grand

4-4-0 locomotive No 1900 *Claud Hamilton* in original condition, but with a high sided tender. This was the most celebrated of all GER locomotives and won a Gold Medal at the 1900 Paris International Exhibition. The photograph was taken at Stratford in September 1912. (Ken Nunn).

Prize, James Holden the Locomotive Superintendent a Gold Medal, Messrs A.J. Hill and A.M. Bell Silver Medals and Messrs F.V. Russell, T. Darby and C. Spencer Bronze Medals. The Summer Supplement of the magazine had an article on locomotives at the exhibition and included a colour painting of locomotive No 1900 *Claud Hamilton*.

For the Coronation of King Edward VII and Queen Alexandra on 9 August 1902, the GER ran excursions from Norfolk and Suffolk to London on both 8 and 9 August. At Wells, for Coronation Day, Driver Woodhouse and Fireman Houseago decorated their engine, No 1 Class 2-4-0 No 117, with garlands for the occasion. They paid for the decorations out of their own pockets. The engine was photographed that day at Norwich.

January 1911 saw the publication of the first issue of the GER's own 'house magazine' – the *Great Eastern Railway Magazine*. The magazine survived the grouping and ceased in 1926 and was replaced by the *LNER Magazine* in 1927. The first article in issue No 1 was on the Chairman of the Company – Lord Claud Hamilton. In the north of England, the NER in the February 1911 edition of the *North Eastern Railway Magazine*, which had also started in January 1911, congratulated the GER on the success attained by the first number of the *Great Eastern Railway Magazine*. *Railway and Travel Monthly* for February 1911 carried a brief article on the arrival of the *Great Eastern Railway Magazine*. The *Railway Magazine* for the same month similarly carried a brief article on the first edition of the *Great Eastern Railway Magazine* as did *The Locomotive Magazine* of that month.

1911 saw the Coronation of King George V and Queen Mary on 23 June. The *Daily Telegraph* of 23 June reported that on the suburban branches of the GER there were a number of 'heavy trains' run in the build up to the Coronation. *Railway and Travel Monthly* for September 1911 reported that thanks to an unfortunate crowd scare that had been engineered by the newspapers, the GER's early morning trains that were put on in connection with the Coronation were not used to the extent anticipated. Coronation traffic on the Railway on the whole was quite satisfactory.

From 18 to 19 August 1911 there was a national railway strike. The GER was not as seriously affected as other railways. *Railway and Travel Monthly* for September 1911 reported that as it closed for press on 18 August, Liverpool Street station seemed to be the busiest station in London in the usual way. The *Chelmsford Chronicle* of 25 August said that a large number of GER drivers and firemen had, at what I interpret to be Stratford locomotive depot, come out on strike on 18 August and that the major disruption was to the suburban service out of Liverpool Street which was curtailed by about 25 per cent. The worst disruption was to the Company's services out of Fenchurch Street, which was very considerable. The *Chronicle* said that some GER men were on continuous duty for 24 hours on Saturday 19 August and that some passengers had given those who were working tips and also substantial sums were raised by collections in the trains. On the Yarmouth express, an appeal by an enthusiastic passenger for those working the train raised enough to pay the workers 10 shillings each. To those staff who continued working during the strike, the Company granted extra pay. The reason why not all railwaymen on the GER did not come out on strike was that not all belonged to a trade union. And of those that did, not all chose to go out on strike, those at Stratford being more heavily unionised and being more loyal to the union than those elsewhere. If one looks at the management of the GER, the Chairman Lord Claud Hamilton looked on the Railway's staff in the same way that a commanding officer in the army looked on his men. Hamilton had served in the Grenadier Guards between 1862 and 1867. According to Reg Davies, writing in *Great Eastern Journal* 137, Lord Claud Hamilton combined paternalistic concern for the welfare of the Company's staff with a refusal to accept collective bargaining. He felt there was no need for a third party – the trade union – in the relationship between management and staff.

In 1912 there was a coal strike lasting 37 days. Railways, being dependent on coal as fuel for the locomotives and also for the power stations of those that used electricity, were badly affected. *Railway and Travel Monthly* for April 1912 reported that none of the GER's passenger trains were withdrawn during the period of the strike. That spoke for the large reserve of coal that the Company had and that it had a large number of engines capable of being converted to burn oil fuel.

1912 saw the Golden Jubilee of the GER on 7 August. The August edition of the *Great Eastern Railway Magazine* was a special jubilee number and carried a large number of articles on the GER including details of a special dinner held in the Hamilton Hall of the the Great Eastern Hotel at Liverpool Street on 15 July presided over by Lord Claud Hamilton and the Lord Mayor of London. The August 1912 edition of *Railway and Travel Monthly* in its section 'Apposite Aphorisms' mentioned the Jubilee of the GER and mentions amongst other things that the dinner held on 15 July was for 250 guests. In the September 1912 edition of the magazine in the same section, mention is made of the *Great Eastern Railway Magazine*'s special edition of August 1912. The *Railway Magazine* for August 1912 had an article on the Golden Jubilee of the GER including the dinner.

The Flood of 1912

1912 not only saw the Golden Jubilee of the GER, it also saw the Norfolk floods of 26 August in the district around Norwich. The floods not only affected Norfolk but also Suffolk and Huntingdonshire and started in the early hours of the morning prior to dawn with drizzle and by dawn it was raining fast. The rain turned into a deluge that lasted all day. In 12 hours, 6 inches of rain were recorded. The gross average rainfall of the 24 hours was 7.5 inches. Brundall had 8.09 inches and Norwich had 7.3 inches. Over an area of 1,039 square miles, the average was 5 inches, which was a third of a year's rainfall in a day.

The flood seriously disrupted the train services of both the GER and the M&GNJR and the disruption lasted until 2 October. According to the *Great Eastern Railway Magazine* for October 1912 the following lines were blocked: Forncett to Wymondham; Wymondham to Norwich; Wymondham to Dereham; Fakenham to Wells; County School to Wroxham; Norwich to Cromer, Cromer Junction to Sheringham; North Walsham to Overstrand, via Mundesley; Yarmouth to Norwich, via Acle; Brundall to Norwich; Brundall to Reedham; Beccles to Tivetshall; Melton to Wickham Market; Stowmarket; the Wickham Market to Framlingham Branch; the Southwold Railway; and the Somersham to Ramsey Branch.

According to the *Locomotive Magazine* of October 1912, the heavy floods on 26 August 1912 in the district around Norwich had seriously disorganised the train services of the GER and the M&GNJR. Owing to the collapse of a three-arch bridge at Flordon, the Ipswich main line was not re-opened until October 2. In the meantime, the Norwich traffic was worked via Forncett and Wymondham or, after 28 August, Cambridge. Cromer and Sheringham were isolated until 29 August and 3 September respectively. Other sections that were affected were: the Wymondham and Wells, which partially re-opened on 5 September and throughout on 10 September; the Reedham, Yarmouth and Lowestoft lines via Norwich, which re-opened from Norwich to Brundall on 30 August; Cantley to Reedham, which re-opened on 5 September; and Brundall to Cantley which re-opened on 1 October. The Waveney Valley line was soon re-opened between Tivetshall and Harleston, and between Beccles and Bungay, and on 30 September Harleston to Homersfield; the remainder was opened for through traffic on 7 October, this being the last section affected by the deluge. Other branches which were affected for a few days were the Framlingham branch and Warboys and Ramsey line.

The worst affected section was on the line between Ipswich and Norwich where the bridge over the River Tas between Forncett and Flordon was completely washed away when the water level rose nine feet. The rails were left suspended in mid-air. The Engineering Department started remedial work at once and the Traffic Department did its very best to rearrange train services in other parts of Norfolk for the passengers affected. Although the bridge piers and the metal trusses of the bridge had been built on 22 September and the final span erected on 26 September and track laid, it was 2 October before the

The Norfolk floods of 26 August 1912 caused havoc to the GER. Here is a photograph of one of the first trains into Norwich passing Lakenham Bridge. The destructive power of the floods can all too easily be seen here. (Author's collection).

bridge and the line were ready for traffic following the testing of the bridge by two Claud Hamilton class locomotives on 1 October.

The Midland and Great Northern line was seriously damaged. Two trains and engines were stranded on the line between North Walsham and Melton Constable for nearly a fortnight. All trains for Yarmouth were sent in the meantime via Sheringham and Runton Junction to North Walsham. Through working was not restored until 1 October. According to Peter Paye in *The Southwold Railway* (Lightmoor 2018), the Southwold Railway was closed only on 27 August.

The *Great Eastern Railway Magazine* reported that motor buses were used between the points of interruption where the public roads would permit.

In addition to the re-opening dates mentioned earlier, the *Great Eastern Railway Magazine* gave the following dates: Stowmarket re-opened on 27 August, as did the Framlingham and Ramsey branches; the section of line from Melton to Wickham Market was blocked for two brief periods, but traffic was worked in either direction to and from the point of obstruction.

Accidents

The GER suffered three serious accidents. The first and the worst was at Witham on 1 September 1905 when all fourteen carriages of the 9.27am

Liverpool Street to Cromer express, hauled by a Claud Hamilton Class 4-4-0 locomotive No 1851, derailed whilst travelling through the station at a speed of no less than 50 to 60 miles per hour. Ten passengers and a luggage porter were killed when several of the carriages somersaulted on to the platforms causing considerable damage to the rolling stock and the station. Seventy-one passengers were seriously injured.

The original inquiry by Lieutenant Colonel P.G. von Donop found that the derailment occurred at a trailing crossover which was being worked on by three platelayers who maintained they had just been clearing and repacking the ballast which would not have impaired the stability of the track; and the only contributing cause was the high speed of the train. However, six weeks after the original inquiry was held another witness was found. A shunter who was waiting for the express to pass before reporting to the signal box stated he saw that the 'key was out of the rail' and saw the rail jump up as the locomotive passed the crossover and the leading coach ploughed into the ballast. When the enquiry was reopened, the three platelayers stuck to their original story that they had just been clearing and repacking the ballast. When the driver and fireman of the express were recalled, they recounted that as their train approached Witham they saw that three men were working furiously on the track ahead; so furiously that the driver feared they would not move out of the way in time; and that all three had their eyes riveted to a certain point of the track. The reconvened enquiry therefore found that the platelayers had rashly loosened the rail fastening and had been unable to make good their mistake in time.

The *Daily Telegraph* of 2 September carried an article headed 'RAILWAY DISASTER ON THE GREAT EASTERN. CROMER EXPRESS WRECKED. 10 KILLED – 44 INJURED. TRAIN ON A PLATFORM. CARRIAGE IN FLAMES. TERRIBLE SCENES'. The *East Anglian Daily Times* of 2 September carried an article headed 'DISASTER TO THE CROMER EXPRESS. AWFUL CALAMITY AT WITHAM. DASH INTO STATION BUILDINGS. DERAILED CARRIAGE ABLAZE. TEN KILLED. OVER TWENTY BADLY INJURED'.

Fred Spalding, the local Chelmsford photographer, whose postcards were sold on the Essex bookstalls of the GER, took a series of photographs of the disaster and sold them as postcards. Understandably the GER did not allow those postcards to be sold on its stations.

The accident to the 9.27am Liverpool Street to Cromer express on 1 September 1905 was caused by a loose rail. The Chelmsford photographer Fred Spalding took a number of photographs of the accident and sold them as postcards as seen here. here. But not on GER stations! (Author's collection).

In 1913 there was another accident on the GER, this time at Colchester when at about 3pm on Saturday 12 July, the 1pm express train from Cromer to London, hauled by 1500 class 4-6-0 locomotive No 1506, running through Colchester station on the Up main line at high speed collided with the tender of a locomotive that was running light and at the time of the collision was moving forward slowly on the same line, the locomotive in question being Intermediate class 2-4-0 locomotive No 471. In the collision, part of the train was derailed and the driver, fireman and guard of the express train were killed. Fourteen passengers, an inspector travelling on the locomotive of the express train and the driver of the light running locomotive were injured, the latter seriously. The cause of the collision was due to an error on the part of the signalman. Locomotive No 1506 was so badly damaged that it was scrapped and never replaced, the number 1506 never again being used by the GER. The *Daily News* of Monday 14 July reported that accident under the article headed 'G.E.R. EXPRESS WRECKED. DISASTER TO CROMER TRAIN. THREE KILLED. REMARKABLE ESCAPE OF PASSENGERS'.

On 1 January 1915, less than five months after the start of the First World War there was another accident on the GER, this time at Ilford when the

8.20am passenger train consisting of eighteen four-wheeled carriages from Gidea Park to London hauled by a 2-4-2 tank locomotive was running through the connection at the west end of Ilford station leading from the Up Local line to the Up Through line when it was run into at the fouling point of the two lines by the locomotive of the 7.6am Up express from Clacton to London hauled by Claud Hamilton class locomotive No 1813 consisting of six eight-wheeled bogie carriages and one twelve-wheeled bogie carriage. At the time of the collision, the local train was travelling at about 10 to 15 miles an hour and the express train at about 20 to 50 miles an hour. Ten passengers, most of whom were travelling on the local train, were killed and over 500 passengers complained of injury. The cause of the accident was because the driver of the express train took 'insufficient care in noting the positions of his signals when approaching Ilford'. Reports on the accident also noted that it would have been much less likely if some form of Automatic Warning System had been in use and recommended its introduction.

The *Daily News* of 2 January 1915 reported the accident in an article headed: 'DISASTER ON G.E.R. 2 TRAINS WRECKED AT ILFORD. 9 DEAD, 25 INJURED. HEAVY ENGINE PLUNGES INTO A YARD'.

As far as is known, that was the only time that the loop line via Chigwell and the eastern curve at Seven Kings was used for the diversion of trains whilst the accident was being cleared up and the line repaired.

This was not the only disaster to befall the GER during the period covered by this chapter. The GER owned steamships too and one hit the headlines for all the wrong reasons on 21 February 1907. The GER's SS *Berlin* hit bad weather off the Hook of Holland, crashed into a breakwater and broke in two. Attempts to rescue survivors were hampered by the storm and 128 people died. The Dutch Prince Consort was among those hauling bodies out of the water the next day.

Nor was the *Berlin* the only casualty. In October 1908, the SS *Yarmouth*, badly overfilled with cargo that had slipped, disappeared en route from the Hook. A body with a ship's lifebelt was found the following day and the Board of Trade set up an enquiry. It found that the cargo crates on the poop and foc'sle had caused the vessel to overturn. The GER stopped this practice at once.

The Great War

The outbreak of the First World War on 4 August 1914 meant that under the Regulation of the Forces Act, brought in that day, all railways came under the control of the government.

4 August 1914 was August Bank Holiday Monday. On that day the banks were closed and remained so on 5 and 6 August. This caused a problem for visiting foreigners wanting cash. According to J.A.B. Hamilton in *Britain's Railways in World War 1* (George Allen and Unwin 1967) the GER came to the rescue of stranded Americans and announced that having for some years having enjoyed the patronage of many Americans travelling to the Continent by its routes to the Hook of Holland and Antwerp desired to offer such assistance as lay within its powers to American citizens who might be under temporary embarrassment pending the reopening of the banks on 7 August. The assistance amounted to cashing travellers' cheques up to £10.

Even before the declaration of war, there had been the suspension of the General Steam Navigation Company's service from Harwich to Hamburg and the Swedish Thule Line to Gothenburg on 3 August, the former for obvious reasons and the latter because it traversed German waters. As mentioned previously, following the outbreak of war the Hook of Holland passenger service was suspended on 6 August. On 12 August all passenger services were transferred from Parkeston to Tilbury. Prior to the temporary suspension of services from Parkeston on one of the last boats from Antwerp to Parkeston there were about 300 children. On 13 August, the Esjberg service, now running from Tilbury, was transferred to Leith near Edinburgh. On 4 October, the service from Tilbury to Antwerp was suspended, whilst the following day the service to Rotterdam was suspended only to resume on 13 October. Just prior to the suspension of services from Parkeston, there had been problems with running the ships which was made more difficult by the number of men who had been called up for naval or military purposes. Because other men were needed to dig trenches, the GER's Marine Superintendent had to call up old seamen to make up its crews. Also at Harwich, the Great Eastern Hotel was taken over as a military hospital.

The GER did not get involved as such with the movement of men and equipment for the war until the second day of the war when following the compulsory purchase of horses for the army, the Company provided twelve trains comprising 146 cattle wagons and twelve brake third six wheeled coaches to transport requisitioned horses to Colchester as well as a party of the Norfolk Yeomanry to Ipswich to guard amongst other things railway bridges west of the town. Even at this early stage, the fear of sabotage and invasion was in the government's mind. The trains to Colchester started from Southend, Aylsham, Halesworth, Fakenham, Attleborough, Swaffham, Bury St Edmunds, Peterborough, Ely, Godmanchester and Cambridge.

During the following days there were further moments of requisitioned horses on the fourth, fifth, sixth, seventh and tenth days of the war. The next movement of troops took place on the eighth day of the war when a cavalry ambulance based at Warley, near Brentwood, moved to Harrow where the high command decided to concentrate the 4th division, of which they were a part. In Harrow they encamped on the playing fields of the public school. This was because the government decided to delay sending all available troops at first to France in order to see how the situation developed. The first troops to go to France was the brigade of field artillery consisting of the headquarters, three batteries of 18 pounder field guns and their ammunition column. Two cavalry regiments based at Colchester and Norwich went to France. Further movements followed until 19 August.

At the same time as this was going on, to enable the German Ambassador and his staff to return home to Germany safely, the British government chartered the GER steamship *St Petersburg* at Government expense to convey them across the North Sea. A special train was chartered at Government expense to take the German Ambassador and his staff from Liverpool Street to Parkeston Quay. The train was hauled by a 1500 class 4-6-0, No 1526, and left London at 8.6am on 6 August. The *St Petersburg* on return carried the British Ambassador to Germany and his staff. According to the *Great Eastern Railway Magazine* for September 1914, the Ambassador's departure was a rather dignified affair. The crowd who witnessed it bared their heads and stood in solemn and dignified silence. Apart from the Company's officials, the crowd were ordinary working people.

It was reported in the September issue of the *Great Eastern Railway Magazine* that the Company had started building a nine-car ambulance train and the first war-relief committee had been formed to look after the wives and families of those men who were reservists and who had been called up. The GER ambulance train (train No 3) performed its first service from Southampton to

Cambridge in the first week in September. Many of the wounded were from the Battle of Mons.

During the war, the GER supplied nine ambulance trains: Nos 3 and 22 for home use; Nos 12, 17, 20, 28 and 36 for overseas use; and Nos 61 and 75 for service with the United States Army, following that country's entry in to the war in 1917. Train No 12 comprised seven GER and nine L&NWR carriages and was thus technically a joint ambulance train. The Hospital Trains of the GER were worked via New Cross and the Thames Tunnel. All other Hospital Trains to the northern lines from the Channel Ports had to be worked via Clapham Junction and the West London Extension Railway as the loading gauge of the Metropolitan Railway's 'widened lines' prevented the use of that route.

The GER also designed a 'Commissariat Train' which could supply bread and roast or boiled meat 24 hours a day to 2,000 men. The train was self contained and was fed with steam from the locomotive and water from the tender. It comprised a boiling and steaming van, baking and roasting van, store van, staff van, butchers' van, refrigerator and guard's van.

On 11 September the first party of Belgian refugees arrived at Liverpool Street.

Shortly after the outbreak of the First World War, on 16 August 1914 Class T26 2-4-0 No 1253 (later No 410) is seen passing Thoby signal box on the 10.55am Colchester (St Botolphs) to Plymouth troop special comprised of carriages and horse boxes. (Ken Nunn).

On 7 March 1915, the 11.30am Dover to Norwich ambulance train hauled by Class D56 4-4-0 locomotive No 1838 is seen approaching Ingrave signal box. The Red Crosses on the sides of the ambulance carriages can clearly be seen. (Ken Nunn).

Following the outbreak of the war, the GER's ships were requisitioned by the Admiralty and used as naval auxiliaries, three GCR ships having been borrowed in their place.

The first deaths of GER men serving in the armed forces now occurred. The first man to die was Police Constable Benjamin Stokes of the Company's police force who was attached to the Grenadier Guards and called up for service at the outbreak of war. He met with a fatal accident at the swimming bath, Wellington Barracks, on 27 August. The Great Eastern Railway Magazine for November carried the names of eight men who had died. Three were from HMS *Hogue* and one was from HMS *Cressy*. Both ships were sunk by a German submarine on 22 September. The other four men were in the army.

During August and September of 1914 there was a curious atmosphere, with mobilisation and recruitment drives going on at the same time that the holiday season was still in full swing with a full summer service. It seems that the holiday traffic continued into September. The *Railway Magazine* said that the GER, along with the GNR, was able to maintain a large proportion of holiday and excursion facilities. The fishing trade carried on even though fishing in the North Sea was becoming somewhat dangerous for fishing boats from mines and enemy ships, be they surface or submarines. Many of the fishermen and trawlers eventually became involved in minesweeping.

On 9 October, Antwerp fell to the German forces. The December edition of the *Great Eastern Railway Magazine* told the story of the defeat of Antwerp and the heroic work done by Mr Pain, the GER's Agent in Antwerp. On the last boat out of Antwerp:

> The British Consul and his party, the English GER staff, were on board, and all British persons who were known to be in Antwerp had been advised of our departure. We also carried a large number of the French colony. The British Chaplain had declined to come, as he had heard that a number of British wounded had been brought in, and he felt that it was his duty to stay.

The *Amsterdam* became an armed boarding steamer armed with one 4 inch gun and one 12 pounder. The *Vienna* was used as an accommodation ship for about 3½ months in 1914 followed by a brief spell early in 1915 as one of the first Q ships, using the name *Antwerp* as well as her own. For the rest of the war, the ship became an armed boarding steamer with an armament of two 12 pounder guns. The *Dresden* was requisitioned by the Admiralty about two months after the start of the war and renamed HMS *Louvain*. The following year the ship was converted into an armed boarding steamer with two 12 pounder guns and served for the greater part of the war until sunk in the Eastern Mediterranean on 22 January 1918 by enemy submarine UC 22. The *Munich* was requisitioned by the Admiralty in 1914 and converted into a hospital ship with 231 beds. In 1916 the ship was renamed St Denis. At the end of the war the ship was returned to railway control but retained its new name. The *Copenhagen* remained in North Sea service for a time carrying Belgian refugees, but was later used as a troop ship until 1 January 1916 when she was taken up as an ambulance carrier.

On 5 March 1917 the *Copenhagen* was torpedoed about eight miles east of the North Hinde light ship with the loss of six lives. The *St Petersburg* was requisitioned by the Admiralty and renamed *Archangel* in 1916; the ship was used as a cross-channel troopship. After the war, *Archangel* returned to railway ownership.

In 1917 the GER bought a ship – *Kilkenny* – a passenger and cargo ship from the City of Dublin Steam Packet Company according to *Railway and Travel Monthly* for October 1917. In 1919 the ship was renamed *Frinton*.

As mentioned previously there was the presumption that the war would not last a long time as on 5 October the 'Radical Alterations' timetable for main line and branch services came into operation. Because of the war, most of the new express trains that were introduced did not last long and were cancelled in early February 1915 and only partially restored in July 1915 at slightly less ambitious speeds. According to Railway and Travel Monthly for September 1914 the GER was fitting up at Stratford Works a corridor ambulance train. Restaurant and kitchen cars and other coaches were being altered for the purpose. The East Anglian Daily Times of 12 August said that the GER was converting its restaurant and kitchen cars into ambulances. As obviously not all restaurant and kitchen cars had been converted some were restored at the end of August. Railway and Travel Monthly for October reported that they were reinstated in the down direction on 31 August and in both directions on 1 September. According to local newspapers in the interval passengers had to make do with a pot of tea and bread and butter supplied from refreshment rooms! J. A. B. Hamilton in 'Britain's Railways in World War 1' (George Allen and Unwin 1967) says that at time of the 1915 pruning of the 'Radical Alterations' timetable the GER withdrew some of its restaurant cars and was the first company to do so. One must assume in that instance it was for the duration of the war.

In November 1914, it was believed that the Germans were about to land on the coast of Norfolk. Immediate troop movements were ordered entailing the running of 840 trains. According J. A. B. Hamilton it is not clear how many ran, but it did involve the fifty-four hour closure of the North and South-West Junction Railway and the NLR. He says that during that time, 177 troop trains ran over the route as well as a like number in the opposite direction. In Norfolk, the GER's line from Norwich to Cromer, including the connection to Sheringham and the Norfolk and Suffolk Joint line via Mundesley, was closed from 6am to 6pm on 17 November.

It was because of this fear of a German invasion that shortly after war broke out the War Office realised that armoured trains were essential coastal defences and two such trains were provided – one for East Anglia and one for the East Coast of Scotland. The first train was delivered in December 1914 and the second in May 1915. The first one was stationed in Norfolk at North Walsham and the second at St Margaret's on the North British Railway. The trains comprised an infantry van, a locomotive, tender, and a gun carriage. The infantry vans were supplied by the GWR, the trucks for the gun carriages by the Caledonian Railway, the upper part of the gun carriages by the L&NWR and the locomotives and tenders by the GNR. Two N1 class 0-6-2 tank locomotives which had condensing apparatus were purchased by the government from the GNR, Nos 1587 and 1590. Following the end of the war, the locomotives were not returned to the GNR, who had to make an offer in 1922 to the Disposals Board for them. They re-entered service in March 1923 following the formation of the LNER. Plans were prepared for what to do if the Germans had invaded Britain. The railways were to be used for the passage of troops and not for the evacuation of civilians. Unfortunately, by Christmas 1914 it was clear that the war was not going to be over by the end of that year.

During 1915 two further ambulance trains were built by the GER – Nos 17 and 20 – and were for overseas use.

According to *Railway and Travel Monthly* for March 1915, the GER was maintaining a regular service of six sailings a week between Parkeston Quay and Rotterdam for the importation of food into this country- despite the presence of German mines in the North Sea and GER locomotives and trains had penetrated a considerable distance on the MR system.

1915 brought a new menace – air raids. The first air raid had taken place on 24 December 1914, when a single bomb was dropped on Dover. During the course of the war, the air services of the German Navy and German Army mounted over fifty bombing raids on Britain. Some were by Zeppelin airships, some by Shutte Lanz airships and some by aircraft. According to Geoff Ashton writing in the *Great Eastern Journal* No 164, the first air raid over GER territory was by airships over Norfolk on the night of 19/20 January 1915. The danger of hostile aircraft had been recognised from the beginning of the war. Station staff were instructed to keep a lookout for them and report them by telegraph to the GER's headquarters in London, from where the information was then passed to the Great Eastern Military Office under the Superintendent of Operations to be passed on by him by telephone to General Headquarters, Home Forces. Soon after air raids began, the GER adopted a system of tracking the course of individual raiders using coloured headed pins on a map of the GER's system. When news was received from a station master, which was generally on the coast, that a raider was in the vicinity of his station, a white headed pin with a label recording the time of the sighting was stuck into the map over that station. As the raider proceeded onwards and other reports were received, the course taken was marked out with more white headed pins. From these timed pins it was a very simple matter to trace the course of the individual raiders which were plotted by pins with different coloured heads. When bombs were reported to have been dropped, the locality was marked with a red triangle or a black hexagon and if an airship or aeroplane was brought down this was marked with an appropriate symbol. On the conclusion of an air raid, the GER staff prepared another map that recorded the routes followed, marking the inward routes in blue and outwards in red with arrow heads recording the direction of travel.

Dennis Swindale in *Branch Line to Southminster* (Stour Valley Preservation Society 1981) said that Station Masters, Inspectors and others were instructed to report immediately to the Chief Traffic Manager the presence and the movement of any hostile aircraft using the prefix 'P.A.' and giving as far as possible the following information: the number of aircraft; whether an aeroplane or an airship; the time of the observation; the direction in which the aircraft was seemingly proceeding and; if any bombs were dropped. When an air raid was imminent, Down trains were instructed to continue to their respective booked station, but Up trains were required to pull up at the next available station in order to allow passengers to alight if they so wished and they were not permitted to proceed from the platform except to allow a following train to enter the platform to discharge its passengers.

With air raids came blackouts in which no lights were permitted to be shown. This required blinds to be drawn in carriages and stations, etc. Locomotive fireboxes were a particular hazard as the opening of these by a fireman could result in light being shown, alerting a hostile aircraft to the presence of trains.

Edwin A. Pratt in *British Railways and the Great War* (Selwyn and Blount 1921) said that in October 1914 the Railway Executive, acting on information from the Office of Works, arranged to pass on information by telephone to the railway companies in order that light could be extinguished or reduced until the danger had passed. Towards the end of the month, the Admiralty, which had control over the anti-aircraft organisation, suggested to the Railway Executive Committee that as the lighting of trains had rendered railway lines very conspicuous to British airman at night, they were likely to become a good guide for enemy aircraft heading towards London and that railway companies should be asked to place notices in the compartments of carriages asking passengers to keep the blinds drawn at night. They could in case of necessity be raised when a train was standing still in a station. The companies were advised of this, and action was taken accordingly. Pratt says that during a Zeppelin raid over Kent,

Essex and London on 27 August 1915 in which ten people were killed and forty-eight were injured, all lights in trains and stations on the Great Eastern and South Eastern and Chatham railways had been extinguished by the direction of the Railway Executive Committee between 11pm and 1.15am. As these measures were not considered adequate by the authorities, the latter suggested that on any future occasion all traffic on the lines of the said companies leading from the coast to London should be stopped while the raids were taking place. This was not very popular as it would have impacted on the running of trains on other lines beyond what was then regarded as the danger zone, so it was agreed to resume the previous arrangements.

Railway and Travel Monthly for June 1915 mentions how a Zeppelin unsuccessfully tried to bomb a GER train near Bury St Edmunds. According to the *Magazine*, as the train steamed along in what was described as a mad neck and neck race between it and the Zeppelin, the Zeppelin dropped five bombs at it which missed it, falling wide of the mark. The train steamed in to Bury St Edmunds unscathed. The *Magazine* said that it took its hat off to the driver of the train and hoped that he signalled his escape by a loud derisive crow on the whistle.

Whilst the display of notices in carriages about closing the blinds and intimating that heavy penalties would be incurred for noncompliance had a limited effect, the reduction of lighting in stations, goods yards, etc had the unfortunate effect of seriously hampering goods and passenger traffic in the London area. Given that there was a prospect of more government traffic, the Admiralty was asked to relax the regulations, provided that on the approach of hostile aircraft lights were lowered or extinguished. The Admiralty agreed to this. However, in 1916 it was decided that trains should no longer be stopped when an order to 'Take Air Raid Action' was sent out. In future, trains were required to slow down so that it would not be necessary to keep the firebox door of engines open and that where this was necessary it should be done for as short a time as possible. When possible, stoking should be done when the engine was under cover. It was felt that whilst a train running at reduced speed might be visible to airmen, the small amount of risk that it would afford as a guide to airmen would be less than if the entire train service was stopped. Another problem was that not all carriages had blinds in the window. Third class carriages tended not to have them and guards vans, lavatories and corridors did not. Another problem was that passengers actually raised the blinds to look at the raiders when a raid was taking place. It was decided that when a raid was threatened, all lights in the train would be extinguished. To prevent light from open fireboxes of locomotives being seen by enemy aircraft, the GER provided its locomotives with thick canvas curtains fixed to the top of the cab.

To try to stop the raiders, Britain established home defence airfields and used anti-aircraft guns. For example, in Essex, home defence airfields were established at Fairlop (called Hainault Field), Suttons Farm at Hornchurch, Rochford, Goldhanger and Stow Maries.

As a result of air raids twelve GER workers were killed and twenty-six injured. Twelve carriages were damaged or destroyed in air raids, but no goods waggons.

According to Pratt the following places (amongst others) were bombed in 1915: Liverpool Street Station, Bishopsgate Goods Station, Leman Street Station, Lowestoft, Southend and Parkeston.

In terms of air raids, Pratt mentions the following examples for 1916: Lowestoft, Stowmarket, Harwich, Fairlop and Bury St Edmunds.

Sometimes some of the raiding aircraft were shot down. This happened to the Zeppelins L32 and L33 on the night of 23 to 24 September 1916. Of the two, the L33, having had its gas bag 'pinged' by anti-aircraft gun fire and leaking gas, was brought down intact by its commander at Little Wigborough and the crew taken prisoner by the local police. The L32 on the other hand was brought down in flames at Great Burstead by incendiary bullets fired by Second Lieutenant Frederick Sowrey flying a Royal Aircraft Factory. BE2c aircraft from Sutton's Farm, Hornchurch. All crew members of the L32 were killed. People wanted to see the crash site and the nearest station was Billericay. Six special trains were put on from London to enable people to visit the crash site and Billericay station ran out tickets to enable people to return home. It was almost certainly the station's busiest day in GER days since the opening of the line from Shenfield to Wickford on 1 January 1889.

There were more air raids. To give some examples; Bishopsgate Goods Station, Stratford, Felixstowe, Southend and Rayleigh were bombed in 1917 as was Liverpool Street Station. The raid on Southend on 12 August caused a bit of a stink as it occurred in broad daylight and no warning was given of it. Guard Charles Humphreys who was on his way to the station to work a train was killed. At Stratford in a raid on 30 September a driver who was seriously injured died of his wounds the next morning. At Liverpool Street station, the daylight raid on 13 June 1917 was, according to Pratt, 'a most unfortunate experience'. Three bombs were dropped at the country end of the station at about 11.45am wrecking several carriages of the 12 noon train for Hunstanton which was standing at Platform No 9 loading up for departure and also two carriages in the dock between Platforms Nos 8 and 9 in use at the time by a Medical Board for the physical examination of GER recruits. Of the three bombs, one failed to detonate, one hit Platform 9 and the third hit the aforementioned passenger train. In the carnage, sixteen people were killed of whom ten were GER staff and thirty-six were injured of whom twenty-three were GER staff. According to Cecil J. Allen, a former employee of the GER, in his autobiography *Two Million Miles of Train Travel* (Ian Allan 1965), the raid occurred on a Saturday morning (it was actually a Wednesday) and suddenly telephone messages began to come into the General Manager's office at Liverpool Street that German aeroplanes had crossed the coast and then in rapid succession they heard that they were passing Shenfield, Romford, Ilford and Stratford and that it was then time to make a hasty retreat. Allen dashed down the stairs of the hotel bridge and along No 9 platform to the CLR subway and had just got to the bottom when there followed the roar of the bombs exploding at the outer end of the station. According to him the bombs fell on the 11.50am train to Hunstanton. The Rev Andrew Clark, the Rector of Great Leighs in Essex, recorded in his diary hearing an unusual drumming noise in the east and south-east at about 10.45am and was later told that there had been an air raid on London that had upset Liverpool Street station. He said that his daughter had heard it at 11.15am. The *Daily News* of 14 June carried a headline '536 KILLED AND INJURED IN THE RAID' and an article headed 'TRAIN STRUCK BY BOMB. RUINS CATCH FIRE IN STATION. Another article under the heading 'YESTERDAY'S AIR RAID' and 'TRAIN HIT, PASSENGERS KILLED' said that seven people were killed and seventeen injured when the train was bombed. The name of the station was not mentioned. *The Times* of the same day carried an article headed 'AIR RAID ON LONDON. 97 KILLED; 439 INJURED. MIDDAY ATTACK BY 15 AEROPLANES. BOMBS ON SCHOOL AND TRAIN'. Apart from not mentioning which station was bombed, the article says that bombs hit an incoming train! Siegfried Sassoon in *Memoirs of an Infantry Officer* (1930), which is the second volume of his fictionalised autobiography, mentions the bombing of Liverpool Street station:

Anyhow on a glaring hot morning I started to catch a train to Cambridge … At Liverpool Street there had occurred, what under normal conditions, would be described as an appalling catastrophe. Bombs had been dropped on the station and one of them had hit the front carriage of the noon express to Cambridge. Horrified travellers were hurrying away. The hands of the clock indicated 11.50; but railway time had been interrupted; for once in its career, the imperative clock was a passive spectator. While I stood wondering what to do, a luggage trolley was trundled past me; on it lay an elderly man, shabbily dressed and apparently dead. The sight of blood caused me to feel quite queer. This sort of danger seemed to demand a sort of courage dissimilar to front-line fortitude. In a trench one was acclimatized to being exterminated and there was a sense of organised retaliation. But here one was helpless; an invisible enemy sent destruction spinning down from a fine weather sky; poor old men bought a railway ticket and were trundled away again dead on a barrow; wounded women lay about in the station groaning. And one's train didn't start … Nobody could say for certain when it would start, a phlegmatic porter told me; so I migrated to St Pancras and made the journey to Cambridge in a train which halted good-naturedly at every station.

Beyond the fact that Sassoon had got St Pancras and King's Cross mixed up as the GER had ceased using St Pancras on 15 January 1917, it is reasonable to assume that he was an eyewitness to what he described in the novel. According to the *Cambridge Daily News* of 14 June, the air raid caused train services to be suspended for several hours. One of those caught up in the delay was the Chief Scout Sir Robert Baden-Powell who was visiting Cambridge that day. He had intended taking the 12 o'clock train from Liverpool Street, but did not arrive in Cambridge until after 4 o'clock.

And then there was the Silvertown Explosion. According to Rodger Green writing in *Great Eastern Railway Journal* No 106, on 19 January 1917 there was a huge explosion at the Brunner Mond Factory at 6.45pm in the melt pot room when 53 tons of TNT exploded. Every building within 400 yards of the plant was demolished and a number of factories were reduced to rubble. Across the North Woolwich Road, the fire station was wrecked and most of the houses in Fort Street and Mill Road were demolished, with considerable damage done to buildings in nearby roads and fires raged in flour mills in the Victoria Docks. The explosion was felt as far away as Cambridge and Silvertown was left isolated with the first help arriving at 7.30pm. Seventy-three people died, 426 were treated in hospital of whom ninety-six were seriously injured and at least another 600 were treated in the streets by doctors and first aiders. Stratford No 1 branch of the National Union of Railwaymen sent a vote of condolence. Lord Claud Hamilton, representing the GER, sent his condolences. Four GER employees were injured by falling debris and one who was amongst the dead was George William Galloway, an engine driver on the line, who with his fireman, who escaped injury, were shunting in the siding at the time. James Kidd, a grain porter on the line, suffered an injury to his left leg from which he later died. The cause of the explosion was never established.

Following the outbreak of the war, because so many railwaymen answered the call and joined the forces, the conveyance of troops and war supplies were threatened. Paradoxically, it was just at this time that many women who were employed in domestic service and manufacturing jobs were losing their jobs. By the start of April 1915, 47,000 women had registered for war work. Some of these were employed in the manufacture of ammunitions and in that month an agreement was reached between the National Union of Railwaymen and the Railway Executive Committee. Under this it was agreed that, firstly, women's war work would not be regarded as setting a precedent regarding their employment in peacetime, secondly that railwaymen serving in the forces were guaranteed reinstatement on their return from the forces; and thirdly that women substituting for men would receive no less than the minimum male rate of pay. Following the bar against women being appointed to male railway positions being lifted, the railway companies were inundated with applications. On the GER for example, the Chief Mechanical Engineer's department took on 130 women and girls in place of male staff to do railway work, apart from 400 employed on the making of munitions. They were employed as clerks, brass polishers, painters' assistants, machinists, core makers and general labourers. Other jobs included ticket collectors, cleaners, goods checkers, and porters. It is easier to say in what work women were not employed. Because of the length of training it took, women were not employed as firemen or drivers. Because of the dangers involved, women were not employed as shunters. The first mention in the *Great Eastern Railway Magazine* of women being employed in men's jobs was in the July 1915 edition when women ticket collectors were noted as working at Liverpool Street station. *Railway and Travel Monthly* for May 1916 mentions women employed as parcel porters, also at Liverpool Street.

On four occasions between December 1914 and May 1915, the GER ship *Colchester*, which had a speed of 14½ knots, was to use her speed to escape from enemy submarines. On 28 March *Brussels*, under the command of Captain Charles Fryatt, tried to ram the German submarine U33, which had ordered her to stop about eight miles off the Maas light ship. In June she used her speed of 16½ knots to evade submarines on three occasions. On 20 July she was missed by a torpedo when about 20 miles east of the South Inner Gabbard buoy. On 2 March 1915 the GCR ship *Wrexham*, on loan to the GER and under the command of Captain Fryatt, when ordered to stop by an enemy submarine, thanks to the great efforts of its engineers escaped after a chase of 30 miles.

Beginning in 1915, the Lea Valley became a centre of war industries. The activity was sited mainly around Angel Road, Edmonton, at the Royal Gunpowder and Royal Small Arms Factories at Waltham Abbey and Enfield Lock and at Ponders End Shell Works. The production requirements were such that the factories could not subsist on local 'walking' labour and whilst most of the workforce came by tram or the existing train services from the London end of the Lea Valley, the GER was called on to re-open the Churchbury Loop for passengers. This it did on 1 March 1915, using the auto train that had previously been tried on the Mildenhall and Ramsey branches. On 12 June 1916, a halt was opened at Caterhatch Lane between Churchbury and Turkey Street. The service on the loop ran only on weekdays. The service lasted until 30 June 1919. This was not the only service provided for munition workers as there was also one from Ilford to North Woolwich which used the eastern curve at Stratford and so enabled the trains to by-pass Stratford station. This service, which started in 1916, was used by munitions workers in the munitions factories on the North Woolwich line and lasted until early 1921. Most of these workers were women.

Margaretting Halt was between Ingatestone and Chelmsford. This halt, which was not shown in the public timetable, first appeared in the working timetable in May 1918 and lasted until the end of October 1921. Latterly it was used only for workers at the Hoffman's ball bearing company in Chelmsford.

From 1915 to 1919 the Lower Edmonton to Cheshunt passenger service which had been withdrawn in 1909 was reinstated for munitions workers and was worked by a push-pull train which is seen here entering Theobalds Grove station on 20 March 1915. (Ken Nunn).

The GER at its Stratford works carried out munitions works. Pratt says that the Company carried out the re-forming of 3.5 million cartridge cases; the brazing of 1.5 million cartridge cases; the forging of 18,800 4.7-in. shells; the breaking of 150,000 tons of steel bars into shell billets; the machining and completion, except filling, of 37,000 6-in. Howitzer shells, and the manufacture of £55,000 worth of gun and rifle details. The company also built ten gun carriages and sixteen limbers for 6-in. long-range guns; they built, for the use of our Armies overseas, 440 road-transport wagons, and 225 covered goods wagons having a capacity double that of the standard GER wagon, and they provided two workshop repair trains, each consisting of five vehicles, for Egypt; five complete ambulance trains for British troops on the Continent; two similar trains for use in Great Britain and two for the American Army. Among other items were the building of 950 and the converting of 388 miners' trucks, and the making of 30 water-tank carts and 1,750 ambulance stretchers. In addition to all this, the company provided for service in France, after first subjecting them to a thorough repair, 43 of their standard goods locomotives (class Y14). They also sent overseas twenty 20-ton loco coal wagons, one 20-ton steam breakdown crane, twenty of their suburban brake vans (these being altered and equipped to serve as brake vans for goods trains in use in France), and 30,000 sleepers (22,000 new and 8,000 second hand). Two Belgian State Railway 0-6-0 steam locomotives of Class 32 were repaired at the GER's Stratford Works. These were not the only other railway's locomotives that were repaired at Stratford. According to the *Locomotive* for September 1916, four Caledonian Railway goods engines were repaired at Stratford and painted grey instead of the blue of their home railway. Their numbers were 561, 713, 736 and 755. The same magazine for October that year reported that the Caledonian Railway had sent 0-6-0 No 321 (0-6-0) and 0-4-4Ts Nos 244, 426 and 786 to Stratford for repair. The *Locomotive Magazine* got things wrong in this instance; locomotives Nos 244, 426 and 786 were 0-6-0 side tanks. *The Great Eastern Railway Magazine* for May 1919 said that only four Caledonian Railway locomotives had been repaired at Stratford. I can find no evidence to confirm a report in the *Locomotive Magazine* of April 1915 that 'To cope with the congested coal traffic a number of LB&SC goods engines were recently lent to the GER for about a week, and worked between March and Stratford. Several MR engines were also borrowed for similar duty.'

42 Class Y14 0-6-0s saw service with the Railway Operating Department of the Royal Engineers in France and Belgium during the First World War. Here No 534 is seen on such a duty with a van near Mordicourt South signal box on 9 October 1918. (Ken Nunn).

The April 1915 edition of the *Locomotive Magazine* reported:

For the last four years all new passenger carriages for the Great Eastern Ry. have been mounted on bogies, and it has now been decided to convert about 500 of the older four-wheeled suburban stock into bogie carriages. The four-wheeled carriage bodies measure 27-ft. over headstocks, so that two bodies can be placed on a bogie underframe 54-ft. long, thus reducing the dead weight but not altering the seating accommodation. The panels and moulding at one end of both bodies are removed and the roof boards trimmed off flush. The bodies are then placed on the underframe and the framework is butted and bolted together. A moulding covers the side joint, clearly visible in the illustration, and the roof joint is filled in and covered with canvas, bedded in stiff paint. The bodies are fastened to the steel underframe by body bolts, and stop blocks at each end. Should it be necessary to remove the body, it has of course to be divided and lifted in two sections. We illustrate the first converted train of eight bogie vehicles recently completed at Stratford Carriage Shops, under the supervision of Mr. A.J. Hill, chief mechanical engineer.

The year saw a reduction in train speeds on the GER. *Railway and Travel Monthly* for October 1915 reported 'The Great Eastern Railway's reconstructed timetables, which were the cause of some rejoicing a year ago, lasted only nine months, and in July we found the trains had been made slower all round, and, over one section at least, slower than they have been for many years'.

There were other changes. The GER replaced the beautiful royal blue livery of its locomotives with a rather dull battleship grey. Both the *Railway Magazine* and *Railway and Travel Monthly* first mention this in 1916.

Commencing on 13 December 1915, the GER with the GNR and GCR instituted limited common user arrangements for goods rolling stock. Other companies later inaugurated similar arrangements.

In 1915, the GER opened, close to Liverpool Street Station, a soldiers' and sailors' hostel for the convenience of men arriving in London from different parts of the country who had to wait for early morning trains to proceed on their journey. The hostel had accommodation for about 50 men.

During the war, the ELR saw use by military trains in addition to its normal traffic. The railway was fairly heavily used in the early stages of the war and in particular for traffic to Newhaven and Littlehampton. Later the West London railways were found to be more convenient. Nevertheless, the ELR continued to be used by hospital trains at a rate of about one a day. At least on one occasion during an air raid on London, a hospital train remained in the shelter of the Thames tunnel until the danger had passed. David Gould in *The South Eastern and Chatham Railway in the 1914-18 War* (Oakwood Press 1981) records that in 1917 a Red Cross train was seen near St Johns on that railway with two GER 2-4-2 M15 class tank locomotives, Nos 216 and 217, at the head and he surmises that they had taken over the train at Hither Green and were working it to Liverpool Street via the ELR.

The other cross-London route that was used to reach the GER was via the NLR to Victoria Park. It was on this route that in November 1914 ordinary traffic was suspended for fifty-four hours.

By 1916, in order to conserve coal supplies, unnecessary travel was being discouraged. 1916 proved to be an eventful year. Amongst other things, three more ambulance trains were constructed, two for overseas use and one for home use. There was also the Egg and Poultry Train. According to *Railway and Travel Monthly* for September 1916 the purpose of this innovation by the GER was to increase food production. The Company, having consulted various organisations involved with food production, undertook to supply at a peppercorn rent sites for egg collecting depots in the station yards, to consider the question of freight in relation to quantities of eggs sent by rail and to make experimental trials in certain districts, with a motor egg collecting van. The Company also proposed, as soon as the necessary arrangements could be completed, to run a train through certain districts with an egg demonstration van equipped to give practical demonstrations and lectures on the question of eggs and of poultry keeping, under the superintendence of Mr Edward Brown, FLS, and qualified assistants. According to the magazine for November 1916, the purpose of the train was to show East Anglia how best to raise poultry and eggs for the table. The train visited various places in Essex, Suffolk, Norfolk and Cambridgeshire and gave visitors the chance to learn from experts about different breeds of poultry and how to hatch, rear, feed and house the chicken; and what to look for when grading eggs – with tips on how to test the age and quality of an egg without breaking the shell. The train catered for all levels of interest and there were leaflets to take home supplied by the Board of Agriculture.

This was not the GER's only involvement in agriculture. According to *Railway and Travel Monthly* for November 1916, the Company had purchased Dodnash Priory Farm in Bentley in Suffolk to be able to supply its hotels at Liverpool Street and Hunstanton. The company already had a piece of land at Chigwell where it was growing fruit to supply its hotels.

The GER's Egg and Poultry Train was later borrowed by the NER and, according to the *North Eastern Railway Magazine* for April 1917, on 15 March 1917 commenced a tour of that Company's principal stations in Yorkshire.

The year saw a number of closures of stations. The company announced that from 1 May, the following stations would be closed; Bethnal Green, Cambridge Heath, Coborn Road, Globe Road, Leman Street, Bishopsgate (Low Level), London Fields, Shadwell, Barkingside, Chigwell Lane, Earsham, Geldeston, Mardock, Stanhoe, West Mill, Buckenham, Maldon West (Passengers only) and Bradfield and Trowse (Passengers only). However, the closures were postponed until 22 May when the list was changed to the following: Barkingside, Cambridge Heath, Chigwell Lane, Coborn Road, Earsham, Geldeston, Globe Road, Leman Street, London Fields, Bishopsgate (Low Level) and Shadwell. Maldon West and Trowse were closed for passengers only as was Norwich (Victoria). Bradfield, Buckenham, Stanhoe, West Mill and Mardock were kept open. The reason for the closures was staff shortage during the war; but the GER, in deciding which stations could be closed, took into consideration other travel facilities available for passengers who had been using those stations now to be shut up. Of these, Barkingside, Cambridge Heath, Chigwell Lane, Coborn Road, Earsham, Geldeston, Leman Street, London Fields, Shadwell, Maldon West and Trowse were reopened after the war.

In 1917 the Snape branch was closed for a short period. As a result of German U-boat action in the North Sea resulting in food shortages, barley was required for food stuffs and malting ceased. This meant that there was no traffic to and from the maltings at Snape. The line re-opened after a few months carrying wheat and hay as well as some barley. The other service to close was the passenger service from Liverpool Street to Barking which ceased on 1 May 1918. Apart from goods trains there were also boat trains to and from Tilbury, but that latter ceased in June 1924. 15 January 1917 saw the GER ceasing to use

St Pancras station other than for Royal specials and Newmarket race specials apart from a brief usage in 1922 and 1923 by a train to and from Hunstanton. Royal specials and Newmarket race specials continued to use St Pancras until June 1924 when they transferred to King's Cross. In 1917 the GER's through trains from London to York were also taken off and briefly reappeared between 1919 and April 1921. A Sundays only service from Liverpool Street was running in 1922. A service that ceased after the outbreak of the war never to return was the GER train that ran from Newmarket to Harpenden on the GNR branch from Hatfield to Dunstable for the Harpenden races. Harpenden Racecourse ceased operating after 1914. The trains from Newmarket were the only GER trains for many years to use the GER owned Shepreth-Cambridge section of the Hitchin to Cambridge line.

There were also some new connections put in. These were on the Tottenham and Hampstead Junction Joint Railway and were at Crouch Hill where the track on the previously unused track-bed leading to the Great Northern was laid and brought into use on 15 May 1916 but closed in 1920 and the track lifted in 1922. 1916 also saw the physical provision of a link with the NLR at Gospel Oak station.

During the war a number of new works were undertaken for war traffic. Pratt shows two examples – an extension of the Up platform at Chelmsford and a temporary loading dock at Thurston.

There were more reductions in train services. *Railway and Travel Monthly* for September 1916 hints at this, saying that many of the trains shown in the working timetable had the word 'suspended' in the times column, the summer service being somewhat similar to the winter service.

In 1916, the War Office adopted the district around Barnham, Suffolk, as a trial ground for 'tanks'. Obviously, these had to be kept secret. The GER comes into the story when a siding connection between their lines and the trial ground was laid down, supplemented by the construction of a special dock where the new traffic was to be dealt with. These preparations completed, the unwieldy monsters, as they then appeared, began to arrive in specially-constructed vehicles, their transport over the railways being attended by exceptional precautions and regulations as to speed limits on certain sections of line. A number of special trains loaded with 'Tanks' which had undergone their trial were made up at Barnham for the various ports of embarkation.

8 March 1916 saw Parkeston Quay closed to all civilian shipping. The embargo was lifted on 13 January 1917 before being resumed again 3 October 1918, but being lifted on 26 November 1918.

1916 was not a good year for the GER's shipping services. The most notorious incident occurred on 23 June when SS *Brussels* under the command of Captain Charles Fryatt was inward bound from the Hook of Holland for Tilbury when lights were seen from the beach and a flare was fired. The ship was taken under escort to Zeebrugge in German occupied Belgium and Captain Fryatt and his crew were sent to the civilian internment camp at Ruhleben, near Berlin.

On 16 July the Dutch newspaper *De Telegraaf* reported that Fryatt had been charged with sinking a German submarine, which was a complete fabrication. On 27 July, Fryatt was tried at a court martial in Bruges Town Hall and found guilty of being a franc-tireur and was sentenced to death and at 7pm that same day, Fryatt was executed by firing squad at Bruges within the harbour grounds. Herbert Asquith, the prime minister, issued a statement in the House of Commons on 31 July and Lord Claud Hamilton, the Chairman of the Great Eastern Railway, denounced the execution as 'sheer, brutal murder'. The Mayor of Harwich opened a fund to erect a permanent memorial to Fryatt. A similar fund was opened in the Netherlands.

The GER awarded Fryatt's widow a pension of £250 per annum whilst the government granted her an extra £100 per annum pension on top of her entitlement. Fryatt's insurers, the Provident Clerk's Association, paid the £300 that Mrs Fryatt was entitled to immediately, dispensing with the usual formalities. The Royal Merchant Seaman's Orphanage offered to educate two of Fryatt's seven children.

Brussels was taken over by the Kaiserliche Marine and renamed *Brugge*, and served as a depot ship at Zeebrugge. The ship's port of registry was nominally Berlin. On 23 April 1918, the Zeebrugge Raid took place, and the ship was torpedoed several times by the British but did not sink. The *Brugge* was scuttled by the Germans on 28 October 1918 when they evacuated Zeebrugge.

Although Fryatt's execution had been deemed lawful, his body was exhumed in 1919 and returned to the United Kingdom for burial, where he was given a state funeral. His coffin was landed at Dover and transported by the South Eastern and Chatham Railway. On 8 July 1919, his funeral service was held at St Paul's Cathedral. Hundreds of merchant seamen and widows of merchant seamen and fishermen attended. Representing the government were many members of the Admiralty, the Board of Trade, the Cabinet and the War Office.

The band of the GER, augmented by drummers from the Royal Marines, played at the funeral, where a blessing was given by the Bishop of London. The route of the coffin to Liverpool Street station was lined with people, from where the GER conveyed his coffin to Dovercourt. The train from Liverpool Street to Dovercourt was hauled by Claud Hamilton class locomotive No 1849. The coach of the train conveying Fryatt's coffin to Dovercourt was hung with purple and lined with white. The engine was decorated with purple and black hangings, and on its front a laurel wreath encircled a white field on which appeared the letter F in purple. Fryatt's widow was presented with the insignia of the Belgian Order of Leopold that had been posthumously awarded to Fryatt. Fryatt was also posthumously awarded the Belgian Maritime War Cross.

Nurse Edith Cavell was executed by the Germans for treason on 12 October 1915. After the war, her body was brought back to England where the SE&CR conveyed her to London on 14 May 1919 where she received a state funeral in St Paul's Cathedral on 15 May. Later that day, the Great Eastern Railway carried her body to Norwich, where she was finally reburied on 19 May.

Brussels was not the only Great Eastern Railway ship captured by the Germans. On 21 September 1916 SS *Colchester* was operating to neutral Holland when it was captured by the Germans. Captain Bennett and his crew of 29 were interned at Ruhleben. *Colchester* was damaged in an attack on Zeebrugge on 17 February 1917. She was grounded at Kiel in 1918 and was scrapped in 1919.

1917 saw a further reduction in trains. *Railway and Travel Monthly* for February 1917 said that the timetable put into force on 15 January 1917 had 278 fewer trains than that in force in December 1916. It also mentions that restaurant cars services were considerably reduced in that timetable.

1917 saw the building of another ambulance train. This one was for overseas service. First class saloon carriage No 51 was converted for use as part of an emergency train for the War Office.

According to Volume 6 of the *British Locomotive Catalogue* (Kestrel Books 2012), 0-4-0 saddle tank locomotive No 229 was sold to the Admiralty in February 1917. According to the *Locomotive* for December 1921, 0-4-0 saddle tank locomotive No 0228 was hired by the government from the GER to work on the Royal Arsenal Railways at Woolwich Arsenal. This does not seem to be have been the only GER locomotive hired by the government as the *Locomotive* for

February 1919 reported that two 2-4-2 tank locomotives of the Company, Nos 1302 and 1308, were at the National Shipyard at Chepstow. At Richborough in Kent a new port was established in 1916 and in February 1918 a train ferry was started from there along with Southampton to Dunkirk, Calais and Cherbourg. The *Locomotive Magazine* of February 1919 reported that several of the GER's 1190 class 0-6-0 had been stationed at Richborough, whilst the edition of March 1919 said that eight of the Company's tank locomotives were stationed there. From later information it is clear that this was an error as the GER had no 1190 class. The *Great Eastern Railway Magazine* of March 1919 reported that 'Stratford has supplied Richborough with some eighteen engines: 0-6-0 tanks, S18 class 0-4-4 tanks, S44 class; and 0-6-0 tanks, R24–class.' This was slightly in error as the magazine meant 0-6-0 side tanks of classes T18 and R24 and 0-4-4 side tanks of class S44. There was never a class S18 nor was there a Stratford Works Order S18. From Volume 6 of the *British Locomotive Catalogue* we know the numbers of the members of Class S44 that worked at Richborough. It is clear that the 1190 class referred to by the *Locomotive Magazine* was the 1100 or S44 class.

The GER's General Manager Henry Thornton served during the war and in April 1917 was appointed Deputy Director of Inland Waterways and Docks. In April 1918, he was appointed Deputy Inspector General of Transportation on the continent with the rank of Brigadier General. In 1919, he became a British subject and was made a Knight Commander of the Order of the British Empire.

1918 saw two more ambulance trains built, which were for the United States Army. Orders were issued in September for the bodies for another three ambulance trains, but the underframes for only two, which seems a bit odd. Equally, in the latter part of the year 1918 four brake third carriages were taken out of traffic and equipped with an unspecified number of stretcher brackets for military traffic. Because the war had ended it is implied that they were used at home for conveying injured soldiers arriving from France.

1918 saw a reduction in services. *Railway and Travel Monthly* for May 1918 mentioned decelerations in train services that month. According to Cecil J. Allen, writing in the July edition of the *Great Eastern Railway Magazine*, whilst several of the leading railway companies were making their second or third of such revisions, on the GER the alterations which came into force on 1 May were the first really drastic reductions and decelerations of services that had taken place since the war commenced. Various Cambridge line expresses were withdrawn, and more of the London trains now stopped at all the stations between Cambridge and Bishop's Stortford to allow for removal of the locals. After the rush hour there was now only a train every two hours on the Enfield, Palace Gates and Chingford branches, whilst 'Sunday becomes literally a 'day of rest' on main, branch and suburban lines alike, the passenger services having been pared to the utmost limit possible'; on the main lines, Allen says that 'for example, only one express train is run, that being the 8.18pm from Ipswich, due in London at 10.9pm. Unlike the Great Northern, the North Eastern and the London and North Western railways amongst other companies, but like the MR, the Great Central and the L&SWR, apart from a short time at the start of the war, the GER provided restaurant cars from the beginning to the end of the war. At the end only four trains had them – 10am Liverpool Street to Cromer and 5.30pm back and 11.50am Liverpool Street to Hunstanton and 4.45pm back'.

As from 1 February 1918 the GER which, as mentioned earlier, since the late 1870s had sold seawater for domestic use discontinued doing so.

There was a strike, which lasted from 20 to 27 September 1918. It started off in South Wales and spread to the GER. The cause was, as usual, pay. The *Chelmsford Chronicle* of Friday 27 September 1918 reported under the heading 'THE RAILWAY STRIKE'. According to the *Chronicle,* only a few GER men came out on strike. Early on Wednesday (25 September) traffic was somewhat disorganised on the main lines, but by the evening practically normal services were running. All suburban routes were more or less seriously affected, and 100 churns of milk which should have been distributed to Walthamstow were still at Liverpool Street at Noon. Following a decision on 25 September by the South Wales railwaymen to resume work, the GER men resumed work on the next day. next day. I must admit the account in the Chronicle appears confusing as to how many men came out on strike!

The armistice ending fighting came on 11 November 1918. Technically this was not the end of the war as there was then the peace treaty to be signed which did not take place until 29 June 1919 – however, to all intents and purposes, the war was over by November 1918 and things began to return to normal.

According to *Railway and Travel Monthly* for December 1918, as well as forty-three GER locomotives working overseas, thirty-six of the Company's locomotives were in regular use on the lines of other British railway companies.

During the war a total of 9,734 members of GER staff had joined the forces of whom 1,220 lost their lives.

Peace

After the war the GER decided, like all the cities, towns, villages and organisations that had lost people in the war, to erect a war memorial to those who died. The Great Eastern Railway War Memorial plaque, which cost £3,316, contained the names of the 1,220 members of staff who lost their lives and was created by Farmer & Brindley. It listed the dead in 11 columns, with carved marble pilasters to either side, surmounted by a segmental pediment housing the arms of the Great Eastern Railway. An inscription at the top read: 'To the glory of God and in grateful memory of the Great Eastern Railway staff who in response to the call of their King and Country, sacrificed their lives during the Great War'. The memorial was located in Liverpool Street station's booking hall. It was unveiled on 22 June 1922 by Field Marshal Sir Henry Wilson and dedicated by the Bishop of Norwich.

Even before the peace treaty had been signed, the first signs of a gradual return to pre-war services began with the introduction of a new timetable on 13 January 1919. Indeed, according to the *Great Eastern Railway Magazine* for February 1919, from which this information is taken, some improvements had been made to the suburban services in November and December 1918, soon after the armistice. According to *Railway and Travel Monthly* for March 1919, four sets of restaurant cars were now working on the GER. Parkeston Quay saw the resumption of civilian shipping on 26 November 1918 when services to the Hook of Holland and Rotterdam resumed, followed on 6 February 1919 by the service to Antwerp. The ship that inaugurated the resumed service to Antwerp was the GCR ship *Marylebone* on loan to the GER. 10 October that year saw the resumption of the service to Esjberg. 7 April 1921 saw the start of a summer only service from Parkeston Quay to Zeebrugge in Belgium. *Railway and Travel Monthly* for July 1919 reported that the number of additional trains to and from East Coast resorts and the numerous existing trains speeded up from 1 July showed that the GER was amongst those railways anxious to revert to a pre-war train service.

Whilst it was hoped that after the end of the war that things would return to what they were before the war, they did not. Between the end of the war and the absorption of the GER into the LNER was a turbulent time. In 1919 and in 1921 the Railway was affected by two strikes. The first was in 1919 from midnight of 26/27 September to 5 October and was over the government's decision to reduce rates of pay which had been negotiated during the war. The government agreed to maintain the rates for another year and after subsequent negotiations the result was the standardisation of wages across the railway companies and the introduction of an eight hour day. According to *Railway and Travel Monthly* for November 1919, about 90 per cent of the operating staff of the GER went on strike; about 2,000 volunteers took their places. Schools for enginemen and signalmen were opened at Liverpool Street station, although the strike did not last long enough for the full benefit of the work of the volunteers to be felt. Attention was concentrated on the suburban lines and quite a good service was provided during the whole of the strike. To facilitate working, signalling and interlocking arrangements were altered, and traffic over certain lines was restricted to one service. While this method worked admirably during the strike, it prevented normal working being resumed until the Wednesday (8th) after the strike, whereas other railways were operating a full service by the Tuesday (7th). To give a flavour of the services operated during the strike, here is what *The Times* of 1 October said:

GREAT EASTERN SUBURBAN LINE.

Between Liverpool-Street, Walthamstow, Chingford, and Enfield Town about half-hourly from 6am to 6pm. Between Liverpool-Street and Ilford about every half hour from 6.30am to 6pm, running through to Romford and Gidea Park at intervals. Between Liverpool-Street and Loughton about every half hour from 6.30am to 5.45pm, running through to Epping and Ongar at intervals. CAMBRIDGE LINE. Liverpool-Street to Cambridge 9am and 3pm, calling at Stratford, Tottenham, and all stations beyond. Cambridge to Liverpool-Street, 9am and 2.30pm calling at all stations to Tottenham, also at Stratford. COLCHESTER LINE. 9.55am 'Liverpool-Street to Norwich, calling at Harold Wood and stations beyond, with connexions to Southend, Southminster, Clacton, and Beceles. 2.0pm, 5.0pm, Liverpool Street, to Southend, calling at Harold Wood and all stations beyond. 3.0pm Liverpool-Street 'to' Ipswich. Calling at Harold Wood and all stations beyond with connexion to Clacton. 4.0pm Liverpool-Street to Southend and Southminster, calling at Harold Wood and all stations beyond. 8.10pm, 12.10pm Southend to Liverpool Street, calling at all stations to Brentwood. 9.30am-Southend to Liverpool-Street, calling at all stations to Brentwood, with connexion from Southminster at 8.45am, 9.0am Ipswich to Liverpool Street, calling at all stations to Brentwood, with connexion from Clacton at 8am, 10.0am Norwich to Ipswich and Liverpool-Street calling at all stations to Ingatestone, leaving Ipswich at 3pm with connexion from Clacton at 2pm. 2.20pm Southend to Liverpool-Street, calling at all stations to Brentwood, with connexion from Southminster at 1.50pm,3.30pm Beccles to Ipswich, calling at all stations.

Miners' Strike

Between 31 March and 28 June 1921 there was a national coal strike which resulted in a reduction in train services and railways were severely affected financially.

On Sunday 24 April, the GER closed its system on Sundays save for one morning train in each direction on the Cambridge and Ipswich main lines. From Thursday 28 April it published a new 'strike' timetable which was said to reduce passenger mileage by 140,000 weekly, to which was added another list of cancellations on 11 May, the result of which was to leave only two 'Up' fast arrivals from the Cambridge line on weekdays (11.32am and 6.10pm into Liverpool Street), two fast services to and from the Ipswich main line, eight daily trains (one of them fast) to Cambridge, and two or three services a day on branch lines. Over Whitsun 1921, the GER closed its suburban lines entirely from the Saturday 14 May until the Tuesday morning 17 May. Prior to that, to augment its train services, greatly restricted by the shortage of coal, in the short space of three weeks the GER converted fifty engines from coal to oil burning.

The adoption of oil fuel and the importation of Belgian and American coal improved the situation so that the GER augmented its service considerably on 30 May. The end of the coal strike did not mean the full resumption of services immediately. The GER issued another temporary timetable on 1 July and postponed the introduction of the full summer service until 18 July.

In order to replace its own locomotives which had been borrowed by the government for war service and were in need of overhaul, the GER borrowed

44 GCR type 2-8-0s which had been built for the Railway Operating Division of the Army. In total, 521 of these locomotives were built between 1917 and 1920; by mid-1920, 40 of the locomotives were working for the GER. The reason that more were built after the war ended was to keep industry busy during the run down from munitions work. The locomotives were allocated to work on the Great Northern and Great Eastern Joint Line, but owing to loading gauge restrictions they could not work elsewhere on the GER and whenever they were repaired at Stratford Works they had to be towed 'dead' with their outer chimney removed. All had been returned by 1 January 1922. The GER unsuccessfully tried to buy twenty or thirty SE&CR N type 2-6-0s from the government which were under construction for the same reason as the GCR type 2-8-0s. Because delivery could not be promised by 30 September 1920, the request was declined.

1919 had seen the first internal combustion engine locomotive to work on the GER when a Simplex 0-4-0 petrol tractor was purchased.

In 1919 the colour of the GER's carriages was changed from teak to maroon. Locomotives stayed battleship grey.

The GER had a flourishing Athletic Association, whose ground for many years was adjoining the Railway at Romford, but in 1921 this had to be vacated owing to the requirements of widening work. A new and bigger ground called Thornton Field was brought into use on the Down side of the Railway between Bow Junction and Stratford. Unfortunately, whoever decided on the site had failed to take into account that not far away were a soap works and a bone manure works. The atmosphere when the wind was in the wrong direction was not the most conducive for athletic activity and so the site was turned over to carriage sidings and the Athletic Association found accommodation elsewhere.

The Grouping begins

Following the end of the war there was a discussion what to do with the railways. The idea of nationalising the railways came up. Both Italy and Switzerland had nationalised their railways before 1910. In New Zealand and South Africa, the railways were nationalised. What emerged instead was something of a compromise. Under the Railways Act 1921 most of the railway companies of England, Scotland and Wales were amalgamated into four large companies – the Great Western Railway now comprised the GWR and most of the Welsh railways including the Cambrian Railways and Midland and South Western Junction Railway and a few other minor railways. The London, Midland and Scottish Railway now comprised the L&NWR, including the L&YR which the former absorbed in 1922, the MR, the Caledonian Railway, the Glasgow and South Western Railway, the Highland Railway, the Furness Railway, the North Staffordshire Railway and some other minor railways. The Southern Railway now comprised the L&SWR, the LB&SCR and the working partners of the SE&CR – the SER and the London, Chatham and Dover Railway and a few other minor railways. The LNER now comprised the NER including the Hull and Barnsley Railway, which the former absorbed in 1922, the North British Railway, the GER, the GNR, the GCR, the Great North of Scotland Railway and a few other minor railways. This proposal was different from the original proposal which had envisaged six large companies. Under these the Western would have comprised all companies that became part of the Great Western Group and the Southern would have comprised all the companies that became part of the Southern Group. The North Western Group would have comprised all the English companies that became part of the London, Midland and Scottish Group. The Eastern Group would have comprised the Great Eastern, Great Northern and Great Central railways. The North Eastern group would have comprised the North Eastern and Hull and Barnsley railways. A London group would have comprised the local London railways, that is Metropolitan, Metropolitan District and the various tube railways. The Scottish Group would have comprised all the railways in Scotland. Both the London and North Western and Midland railways had some lines in Ireland including in the case of the latter a joint line with the GNR of Ireland.

The LNER commenced operations on 1 January 1923. In addition to the aforementioned companies, the L&BR, which was still in existence, was also absorbed on the same day. The Colne Valley and Halstead Railway also became part of the new company on 1 July 1923 (according to the *Locomotive Magazine* of July 1923 and confirmed by contemporary newspaper accounts of February and July 1923) as did the MSLR on 1 July 1924. This was because this company had been in the hands of a receiver since October 1906. The Southwold Railway was not included in the LNER and remained independent. It has been commented on that what parliament refused in 1909 – the proposed working union of the Great Eastern, Great Northern and Great Central railways – it forced in 1921.

The M&GNJR became joint property of the London, Midland and Scottish and London and North Eastern railways. The ELR remained independent and the former LT&SR as part of the Midland Railway became part of the London, Midland and Scottish Railway.

Meanwhile the GER's General Manager Sir Henry Thornton had left the Company on 1 December 1922 to take up the post of President of the newly formed Canadian National Railways. It is said that the choice for the post of General Manager of the LNER was between Thornton and the NER's General Manager Ralph Wedgwood and that Thornton's departure left the way clear for the latter. Thornton was succeeded as General Manager of the GER by the Assistant General Manger Sidney Parnwell. On the formation of the LNER, Parnwell was appointed Divisional General Manager of the Southern Area of the LNER – the former GER, GNR and GCR systems. Parnwell was replaced on 28 June 1924 by Alexander Wilson, Divisional General Manager, North Eastern Area of the LNER. It has been said that Parnwell was not up to the job. In his defence, I would argue that he had only one month to settle in as General Manager of the GER before he was given responsibility for three constituent railways of the LNER. It is a pity that Thornton had landed him with what proved to be a poisoned chalice and that Parnwell could not have been given early retirement and someone with more experience from one of the other pre-grouping companies employed. After all, Thornton's appointment as General Manager of the GER in 1914 was unprecedented. The Southern Area of the LNER had a total route mileage of 3,095 miles which was greater than the total route mileage of the smallest of the four groups – the Southern Railway whose total route mileage was 2,115½ miles and whose General Manager, Sir Herbert Walker, had been a General Manager of one of the constituent companies (the L&SWR) since January 1912, rather longer than poor Parnwell's tenure as General Manager of the GER. Thornton's fellow American John Miller did not follow him to Canada.

The last Annual General Meeting of the GER took place on 20 February 1923. Lord Claud Hamilton conducted his last meeting. The *Great Eastern Railway Magazine* of March 1923 carried a report.

Under the LNER, teak replaced maroon as the livery of the GER's carriages and apple green the livery of the locomotives. Stratford works built its last locomotive in 1924 when it turned out class L77 0-6-2 tank locomotive No 999E.

E being the suffix for former GER locomotives prior to their numbers being increased by 7,000.

The *Great Eastern Railway Magazine* of July 1923 noted, 'One of the first fruits of grouping, by the way, is that Great Northern 2-6-0 (Class H2) express goods engines of the "1640" Class are working between Spitalfields, March and Doncaster for which some of the locomotives were stationed at Stratford and Whitemoor.' The *Locomotive Magazine* of August 1923 reported that some of the former GCR (Class 8F) 4-6-0s Nos 1100-4 were working over the Great Northern and Great Eastern Joint Line from March on fruit, fish and vegetable trains. These locomotives, because they were not built to the GER loading gauge, would not have been able to work any further south over former GER lines.

Because the GER had paid rather better wages than the other constituent companies of the LNER, its staff suffered a pay freeze until the others wages caught up with them.

There was a strike by the members of the drivers and firemen's union, the Associated Society of Locomotive Engineers and Firemen, from 21 to 29 January 1924. It would be true to say that train services on the GER lines during the strike were somewhat patchy.

Just after the Grouping came the inauguration of the Harwich to Zeebrugge train ferry for goods vehicles. The origins of this go back to GER days. In March 1923 a new company was formed – the Great Eastern Train Ferry Company – to operate a train ferry service between Harwich and Zeebrugge. Three ferries were purchased along with, initially, two and later three First World War termini from Southampton, Richborough and Dunkirk. At 11,00 am on 24 April 1924, a special train arrived at Harwich with Prince George (later Duke of Kent) on board to officially open the new service. After setting the bridge equipment in motion, he was given a guided tour of Train Ferry No 2 before she set sail to Zeebrugge. Train Ferry No 3 joined the service the following day sailing daily except Sundays; the third ferry entered service on 17 July 1924.

With the absorption of the Colne Valley and Halstead Railway and the MSLR into the LNER, the cessation of locomotive building at Stratford and Parnwell's departure, 1924 could be held to be when the GER finally ceased to exist.

Appendix

Locomotives, Rolling Stock, Ships and Motor Buses 1862 to 1924

Locomotives

Tank locomotives – which have their water tanks and coal bunkers on the locomotive as opposed to locomotives having separate tenders – are described as saddle for those having their water tank in a saddle over the boiler, well tank for those having their water tank under the coal bunker and side tank for those having their water tanks in tanks on the side of the boiler.

Robert Sinclair was both the last Locomotive Superintendent of the ECR and the first Locomotive Superintendent of the GER. He was in office from 1856 to 1866. For the sake of continuity, I will mention all those locomotives that were built to his design both prior to and after the formation of the GER.

All of the locomotives built in Sinclair's time for the ECR retained these numbers when the GER was formed in 1862.

During Sinclair's time, six outside cylindered 2-4-0s, Nos 301 to 6, were built by P. Rothwell and Company in 1858. These were Class Z. They were withdrawn in 1873-5.

Between 1859 and 1866 a total of 110 outside cylindered 2-4-0s, Nos 307 to 416, were built by the following builders:

Nos 307 to 326 by Neilson and Company
Nos 327 to 341 by Robert Stephenson and Company
Nos 342 to 356 by R. and W. Hawthorn and Company
Nos 357 to 381 by Kitson and Company
Nos 382 to 406 by the Vulcan Foundry Company
Nos 407 to 416 by Schneider and Company.

These locomotives were Class Y. No 327 was exhibited at the International Exhibition in London in 1862. Some of these locomotives were the first locomotives on the GER to be fitted with cabs for the enginemen. Originally, locomotives were not fitted with cabs and the enginemen were exposed to the elements from both the front and rear, but also from above. Later a weatherboard or spectacle plate was provided at the front as a windscreen for the enginemen. On some tank locomotives this was also provided at the front of the rear coal bunker. Later cabs of varying sorts were fitted on the locomotives.

Ten of the Y Class were rebuilt to Class U13 in 1882. Amongst other things, this involved increasing the diameter of their driving wheels from 6ft 1in to 6ft 3in. These were Nos 307, 321, 328, 341, 344, 356, 376, 379, 382 and 384.

Twenty were rebuilt as 4-4-0s in 1876 to 1878. These were Nos 308, 311-2, 314, 317, 320, 324-5, 327, 329, 342, 349, 360, 366, 370, 381, 385, 406, 412 and 416.

All of the Y Class locomotives were withdrawn between 1883 and 1894. A lot of the locomotives of Class Y were renumbered into the duplicate list in 1888 and 1890. The duplicate numbers were 0307-9, 0311-2, 0314-7, 0319-21, 0324-5, 0327-32, 0335-6, 0339-41, 0344-5, and 0349. 0351-2, 0355-62, 0365-6, 0370, 0372-3, 0375-80, 0382, 0384-6, 0389, 0393, 0396-7, 0405-9, 0411-6.

In 1862, Stratford Works built five 2-4-0 well tanks, Nos 120 to 124 of Class X. The boilers of these locomotives were built by Slaughter Grunning and Company. They were all withdrawn between 1880 and 1884, but number 122 was used as a stationary boiler until 1907. No 121 was possibly renumbered 121A, whilst No 122 was renumbered 1220 in 1884.

In 1864-5, Neilson and Company built twenty 2-4-2 well tanks, Nos 140 to 159 of Class V. They were known as 'The Scotchmen'. All were withdrawn between 1883 and 1888. In 1880 Nos 140-9 were renumbered 1400, 1410, 1420, 1430, 1440, 1450, 1460, 1470, 1480 and 1490.

Between 1862 and 1867, thirty-one outside cylindered 2-2-2s of Class W were built as follows:

Nos 284-8 by William Fairburn and Sons
Nos 51-60 by Slaughter Grunning and Company
Nos 289-90 by Kitson and Company
Nos 87-90 and 299-300 by Schneider and Company.

No 284 was painted cream for the wedding of the Prince of Wales and Princess Alexandra of Denmark in 1863 and hauled the Royal Wedding Train from London to Wolferton after their marriage in Westminster Abbey on 10 March.

No 87 was exhibited at the Paris Exhibition in 1867.

No 54 was scrapped after being involved in the Thorpe accident of 10 September 1874.

The W class had a reputation of performing satisfactory work and of being much steadier riding than many contemporary outside cylindered locomotives. In the late 1860s Patrick Stirling, the Locomotive Superintendent of the GNR, was in the process of contemplating designing a large express locomotive. N. Groves in *Great Northern Locomotive History Volume 2 – 1867-95 – The Stirling Era* (RCTS) says that Stirling seems to have originally contemplated building an outside cylindered 2-2-2. In 1868, Stirling approached Samuel Waite Johnson, who had succeeded Robert Sinclair as the Locomotive Superintendent of the GER in 1866, and asked to borrow a W class locomotive for the purpose of testing the merits of an outside cylindered locomotive having large driving wheels within a short wheelbase on the GNR main line. From the end of August 1868, trials lasting some weeks were conducted in comparison with GNR 2-2-2s of Stirling and Sturrock designs, having similar driving wheel dimensions to the W class, between Peterborough and London in charge of GNR driver Lloyd. The W Class locomotive in question was No 293. The result of the trials led Stirling to produce his 8ft driving wheeled outside cylindered 4-2-2s of Class A1 built from 1870 to 1895. Two of the W class, Nos 51 and 291, were rebuilt as 4-2-2s in 1873. Other than No 54 – scrapped in 1874 – the rest were withdrawn between 1883 and 1894. These locomotives underwent a certain amount of renumbering. In 1878, Nos 87-90 were renumbered 301-4 and in 1880 Nos 51-3 and 55-60 were renumbered 275-83. In 1886, the renumbering took place and the new numbers were: 0275-8, 0280-6, 0288-92, 0295-7, 0299-301.

During the period 1862 to 1866 the following locomotives came in to GER ownership from other railways:

From the Waveney Valley Railway in 1863 a 2-2-2 outside cylindered well tank built by Sharp, Stewart and Company in 1861. The locomotive was rebuilt as a 2-4-0 side tank in 1864. This was withdrawn in 1881. Its GER number was 30.

From the L&BR twelve locomotives in 1866 eleven locomotives. Six 2-2-2 outside cylindered well tanks built by Jones and Potts in 1848 whose L&BR numbers and names were: 1 *Stepney*, 2 *Shadwell*, 3 *Blackwall*, 4 *London*, 5 *Bow* and 6 *Thames*. They were withdrawn between 1873 and 1882. Another 2-2-2 well tank of different dimensions was built by Jones and Potts in 1850 – 7 *Victoria*. This was withdrawn in 1880. Two 2-2-2 well tanks built by George England and Company in 1852 – 8 *Samson* and 9 *Hercules*. They were withdrawn in 1881 and 1870. Two 2-4-0 side tanks built by the same Company in 1860 – 10 and 11. They were withdrawn in 1882. Two 2-2-2 side tanks built by George England and Company in 1849 and 1850 named Dwarf and Pigmy Giant and were exchanged in 1852 for *Samson* and *Hercules*. Their GER numbers were: for Nos 1-3; 91-3 and later 910, 920 and 930, for Nos 4-6; 95-7, but No 96 was later renumbered 960; for No 7 – 98 – later 980; for Nos 8 and 9 – 99 and 100, but No 99 was later renumbered 990; for Nos 10 and 11 – 101 and 102 – later 1010 and 1020.

Samuel Waite Johnson was Locomotive Superintendent of the GER from 1866 to 1873 when he resigned to take up the same post on the MR. Prior to joining the GER he had been Locomotive Superintendent of the Edinburgh and Glasgow Railway which became part of the North British Railway in 1865.

Johnson's first class was the No 125 class of 2-4-0s built by Neilson and Company in 1867 and originally intended for the North British Railway. The Class comprised five locomotives, Nos 125-9. They were withdrawn between 1884 and 1886. No 129 was renumbered 1290 in 1885.

In 1867 came the first of Johnson's No 1 Class or L7 Class locomotives. Forty of these locomotives were built between 1867 and 1872:

Nos 1-3, 26, 28-9, 31-6, 42-50, 100, 104-7, 160-1, 173 and 176 by Sharp, Stewart
Nos 5-6, 10, 110, 112-5 and 118-9 at Stratford Works.

They were known as 'Little Sharpies'. A number of these locomotives were lent to the LT&SR – Nos 31, 100, 104-6. No 106 was the only known GER locomotive to have been photographed on the LT&SR during the time when the former's locomotives worked the latter. It was photographed at Southend

A world away from the express services and the busy suburban services were the branch lines where No 1 Class 2-4-0 No 0104 is seen on the 10.01am Wells to Norwich near Wymondham on 6 April 1910. (Ken Nunn).

on 24 September 1879. These locomotives were some of the most successful built for or by the GER. They were withdrawn between 1901 and 1914. These locomotives had some renumberings: No 10 was renumbered 4 in 1878; No 28 was renumbered 30 in 1898; No 100 was renumbered 103 in 1878; No 119 was renumbered 27 in 1884 and No 103, together with Nos 104, 105, 107, 160 and 161, were renumbered 0103, 0104, 0105, 0107, 0160 and 0161 in 1905.

In 1868-9 Stratford Works built three 2-4-0s, Nos 116, 109 and 111 in that order. Baxter thinks that they were possible renewals of former Eastern Union and East Anglia railways locomotives. They were withdrawn between 1881 and 1884.

In 1870 two 2-2-2s were built at Stratford Works – Nos 73-4. Baxter thinks that they may have used parts from scrapped locomotives. They were withdrawn in 1877 and 1879 respectively. In 1876 they were renumbered 730 and 740.

In 1872 an outside cylinder 0-4-0 saddle tank, No 200, was obtained from Manning Wardle. It was originally named *The Chairman* and in 1894 became works shunter letter A. This locomotive, although withdrawn in 1922, was not scrapped until 1923 and could be held to have survived into LNER days.

In 1867, Hudswell Clarke and Company supplied an 0-6-0 saddle tank, No 201, and in the same year another 0-6-0 saddle tank but having outside cylinders, No 202. They were withdrawn in 1888 and 1886 respectively.

In 1868 Ruston, Proctor and Company supplied five 0-6-0 side tanks, Nos 204-8. In 1891 and 1893 Nos 205, 204 and 206 were rebuilt as crane tanks and in 1894 Nos 204-6 became works shunters B, C and D. Nos 207 and 208 were withdrawn in 1889 and 1892, but the other three locomotives were in service on 1 January 1923 and became part of the LNER.

In 1871-5, Stratford Works built fifteen 0-4-2 side tank locomotives, Nos 11-9 and 81-6. These locomotives were originally only provided with front weather boards and were only later provided with cabs. These locomotives were Class T7. They were withdrawn between 1891 and 1894.

In 1872-75, thirty 0-4-4 side tanks, Nos 134-9, 162-70 and 186-99, were built as follows:

Nos 134-9 and 162-70 by Neilson and Company
Nos 186-99 by Avonside Works.

The GER found a use for crane tank locomotives at Stratford Works. No D was originally built in 1868 by Ruston and Proctor of Lincoln as an ordinary side tank locomotive, No 206, but was converted to a crane tank locomotive in 1893 and renumbered D. (Ken Nunn).

These locomotives were originally only provided with front weather boards and were only later provided with cabs. No 189 was the first GER locomotive to be painted royal blue in 1882, whilst No 193 was fitted with James Holden's patent oil burning system in 1887. They were withdrawn between 1901 and 1912. No 134 was renumbered 201 in 1897 and almost immediately renumbered 0201. No 170 was renumbered 133 in 1878, 200 in 1897 and 0200 in 1899. Other than Nos 137, 185, 186 and 187, all these locomotives were placed on the duplicate list and had their numbers prefixed by a zero.

In 1867-79, sixty 0-6-0s, Nos 417-76, were built as follows:

Nos 417-36 by Neilson and Company
Nos 437-76 by the Worcester Engine Company.

In 1871-3 they were followed by 50 0-6-0s, Nos 477-526, built as follows:

Nos 477-96 by Beyer, Peacock and Company
Nos 497-501 by Robert Stephenson and Company
Nos 502-6 by Dübs and Company
Nos 507-11 by Nasmyth Wilson and Company
Nos 512-26 by the Yorkshire Engine Company.

Locomotives Nos 417-76 were withdrawn between 1888 and 1899 and Nos 477-526 between 1897 and 1904. The following locomotives were given a 0 prefix to their numbers in 1891: 419, 322-3, 426, 430, 432, 437, 439-40, 442, 447-50, 459-60, 464-5, 468-71, 473. The following locomotives were given a 0 prefix to their numbers between 1898 and 1902: 471, 513, 516, 518 and 520 and 521.

In 1874, Stratford Works built two 4-4-0s, Nos 301 and 302, which were the first inside cylindered 4-4-0s to be built for an English railway. They were Class C8. In 1888 they were renumbered 305 and 306. They were withdrawn in 1898 and 1897 respectively.

Between 1874 and 1903 eight outside cylindered 0-4-0 saddle tanks, Nos 209-10 and 226-31, were built as follows:

Nos 209-10 and 228-9 by Neilson and Company in 1874-6. These locomotives did not originally have cabs or even a weatherboard or spectacle plate, which they were later fitted with.

Nos 226-7 and, in 1903, Nos 230-1 by Stratford Works in 1897. These latter locomotives were built with cabs from the start. No 231 was fitted with side skirts and cowcatchers for working the quayside lines at Colchester. Nos 226 and 227 were withdrawn in 1911 followed by 210 in 1914 and 229 in 1917. The latter being sold out of service to the Admiralty in 1918. Nos 226-8 were renumbered 0226-8, in 1907 in the case of the first two and 1914 in the case of No 228. Nos 0228, 229, 230 and 231 survived to be taken over by the LNER on 1 January 1923.

From 27 May to 22 November 1872 six Metropolitan Railway outside cylindered 4-4-0 side tank locomotives, Nos 9, 10, 14, 15, 27 and 33 built by Beyer, Peacock in 1864-8, were loaned to the GER. Whilst on loan, these locomotives retained their Metropolitan Railway numbers. The reason for loan of the locomotives was a shortage of locomotives on the GER with the opening of the Hackney Downs group of lines pending the delivery of that Company's locomotives.

The GER found a use for a number of 0-4-0 tank locomotives of either the saddle tank or side tank variety as well as the tram locomotive variety. Here is saddle tank locomotive No 227 which was built in 1897 and scrapped in 1912. (Harold Hopwood).

Samuel Johnson was succeeded in 1873 by William Adams who was previously the Locomotive Superintendent of the NLR and who left the GER in 1878 to take up the same position on the L&SWR.

85 0-4-4 side tanks of Class 61 were built between 1875 and 1878:

Nos 61-80, 170-84 and 211-25. Nos 61-75 and 211-20 by Neilson and Company
Nos 76-80 and 221-5 by Robert Stephenson and Company
Nos 170-84 by Kitson and Company.

They were withdrawn between 1906 and 1913. Nos 71, 171, 174, 176, 178, 180, 181, 184, 211, 213, 215, 216, 220, 222, 224 and 225 in 1907 and 1908 were given a 0 prefix to their numbers.

Twenty outside cylindered 4-4-0s, Nos 255-74, were built between 1876 and 1877. Nos 255-64 were built by R. and W. Hawthorne and Nos 265-74 by Dübs and Company. Originally for passenger work, they were not a success in this role and were soon relegated to fast goods work. They were known as 'Ironclads'. They were withdrawn between 1894 and 1897 and were given a 0 prefix to their numbers in 1896.

Ten 0-4-2 side tanks of Class K9 were built at Stratford in 1877-78, numbered 7-10 and 20-5. They were withdrawn between 1903 and 1907. No 10 was renumbered 26 in 1898.

Fifteen outside cylindered 2-6-0s, Nos 527-41, were built by Neilson and Company in 1878-9. They were the first 2-6-0s in Britain and No 527 was named *Mogul* from 1878 to 1885. They were not a success and were the GER's only 2-6-0s. They were withdrawn between 1885 and 1887.

An 0-4-0 tram locomotive, No 230, was built by Kitson and Company in 1878. This was converted to use as a stationary boiler in 1889.

Adams is thought to have designed the LT&SR's first independent locomotives – the No 1 Class outside cylindered 4-4-2 side tanks introduced in to traffic in 1880 and originally built by Sharp, Stewart and Company.

An outside cylindered 0-6-0 saddle tank named *Resolute* built by Hudswell Clarke and Rodgers in 1876 was built for the Wivenhoe and Brightlingsea Railway during a period of dispute between it and the GER. It was taken into GER stock in 1879 following the resolution of the dispute. This was converted to a stationary boiler in 1888 and was scrapped in 1890. Its GER Number was 203.

William Adams was succeeded in 1878 by Massey Bromley, who is recorded as having a Master of Arts degree from Brasenose College, Oxford and who was Locomotive Superintendent of the GER from 1878 to 1881 when he resigned. He was killed in the Penistone accident on the MS&LR on 16 July 1884.

Bromley is best remembered for his twenty outside cylindered 4-2-2s built 1879-82. They were numbered 245-54 and 600-9. Nos 245-54 were built by Dübs and Company and 600-9 by Kitson and Company. They were withdrawn between 1890 and 1893.

Stratford Works built 50 0-4-4 side tanks of Class E10 between 1878 and 1883. They were numbered 51-60, 87-102, 231-44 and 572-91. They were withdrawn between 1903 and 1912. The following locomotives were given a 0 prefix to their numbers in 1903-7: 51-60, 87-9, 92-3, 95-7, 99-102, 231, 240, 243-4, 576, 578-9, 581-2, 585-7, 589-91.

R. and W. Hawthorn built ten 0-4-4 side tanks in 1880. They were later rebuilt in 1890-96 as 0-4-2 side tanks. They were withdrawn between 1903 and 1905. All were given a 0 prefix to their numbers in 1903.

The GER operated both 2-4-2 and 0-4-4 side tanks. One of the latter Class E10 No 060 is seen near Chantry signal box on the 3.42pm Fridays only Chelmsford to Braintree on 28 May 1909. Class E10 was designed by Massey Bromley and was in service between 1878 and 1912. (Ken Nunn).

Stratford Works built ten 0-6-0 side tanks of Class M12, Nos 542-51, in 1881. They were withdrawn between 1896 and 1902. Nos 545-6 and 549-50 were given a 0 prefix to their numbers in 1898.

Kitson and Company built ten 0-6-0s, Nos 552-61, in 1882. They were unusual in having a very high running plate. They were withdrawn between 1904 and 1906.

The following locomotives were acquired by the GER from the Thetford and Watton Railway in 1880. The numbers given are their Thetford and Watton Railway numbers:

Two outside cylindered 2-4-0 side tanks, Nos 1 and 2, built by Manning Wardle and Company in 1870. They were scrapped in 1887 and 1888.

One outside cylindered 0-6-0 saddle tank, No 3, built in 1850 by Stothert and Slaughter for the Monmouthshire Railway and Canal Company and purchased from Budd and Holt in 1874. This was scrapped in 1884.

Two 2-4-0 side tanks, Nos 4 and 5, built by Sharp Stewart, and Company in 1875. The same Company supplied two 0-4-2s, Nos 6 and 7, in 1876. Nos 4 and 5 were scrapped in 1887, whilst Nos 6 and 7 were scrapped in 1891 and 1890. Their GER numbers were for Nos 1 and 2 - 802 and 803 later 0802 and 0803, for No 3 – 801, for Nos 4 and 5 – 804 and 805 – later 0804 and 0805. For Nos 6 and 7 – 806 and 807 – later 0806 and 0807.

Three outside cylindered 2-4-0 tanks built by the Yorkshire Engine Company in 1877 for the Felixstowe Railway and Pier Company, later Felixstowe Railway and Dock Company and numbered by that Company 1-3 were acquired by the GER in 1879. They were all scrapped in 1888. Their GER numbers were 808-10 – later 0808-10.

Massey Bromley was succeeded by Thomas Worsdell, who in 1885 left the GER to take up a similar post on the NER.

Under Worsdell, in 1882-83, Stratford Works built 20 2-4-0 locomotives, Nos 562-71 and 640-9 as express passenger locomotives. These were Class G14. In 1884-85, the same works built eleven 4-4-0s, Nos 230 and 700-9. These latter locomotives were built as compounds – steam from the cylinders was used twice, once at high pressure and once at low pressure before being exhausted in to the atmosphere. In 1892, James Holden rebuilt them all as simple expansion locomotives. They were Class G16. Class G14 were scrapped between 1895 and 1901 and Class G16 between 1902 and 1904. The following members of Class G14 were given a 0 prefix to their numbers in 1898-0: 562, 568, 640, 642 and 643. All the members of Class G16 were given a 0 prefix to their numbers. Other than No 230, this took place in 1892, but in the case of No 230 in 1903.

Between 1883 and 1897, Stratford Works built ten 0-4-0 inside cylinder tram locomotives, Nos 125-34. They were used on the Wisbech and Upwell Tramway and on the Yarmouth Union Tramway from Vauxhall station to the fish wharf. They were class G15. Nos 127, 128, 130 and 131 were withdrawn between 1907 and 1914, but the remainder survived to be taken over by the LNER on 1 January 1923. Nos 125, 126 and 129 were renumbered 0125, 0126 and 0129 in 1921.

Between 1884 and 1886, Stratford Works built 30 2-4-2 side tanks of Class M15, Nos 650-79. These locomotives were fitted with Joy valve gear which earned them the nickname 'Gobblers'. Except for one which was built with Stephenson valve gear (No 674), all were rebuilt with the latter valve gear in 1895-8. James Holden and Stephen Dewar Holden built a further 130 locomotives of the same class between 1886 and 1909, all fitted with Stephenson valve gear. These were, in numerical sequence, but not building order, Nos 71-80, 91-111, 140-9, 170-89, 211-25, 232-44, 572-91 and 781-800. No 800 was numbered 790 from 1886 to 1892. Some of these locomotives were fitted with condensing apparatus. All were built at Stratford Works. Of the 160 locomotives, 42 were withdrawn between 1913 and the end of 1922.

Under Worsdell, sixty-nine 0-6-0s of Class Y14 were built between 1883 and 1886. These were in numerical order Nos 37-41, 119-24, 592-99, 610-39 and 680-99. No 41 was renumbered 600 in 1912. Nos 610-39 and 680-99 were built at Stratford Works, whilst Nos 37-41, 119-24, 592-99 were built by Sharp, Stewart and Company. James Holden, Stephen Dewar Holden and Alfred Hill built a further 220 locomotives between 1886 and 1913. They were in numerical sequence Nos 507-41, 552-51, 640-9, 800 (renumbered 609 in 1892) and, 801-945. All were built at Stratford Works. The building of No 930 on 10-11 December 1891 established a world record when it was built in 9 hours and 47 minutes. Nos 507-8, 510, 513, 517-8, 522, 531-4, 616, 695, 817-8, 826,

841, 847-8, 856-7, 869, 872, 876, 887, 892-4, 904, 911, 916, 918, 920-1 and 940 saw service in France and Belgium in 1917-19 with the Railway Operating Division of the Royal Engineers. Totalling 289 locomotives, Class Y14 was the largest class of locomotives on the GER and the largest class of locomotives to be inherited by the LNER from any of its constituent companies. They were sufficiently light but sufficiently powerful to be able to travel almost anywhere and handle all types of trains. Seventeen of these locomotives were withdrawn between 1920 and the end of 1922.

James Holden, who succeeded Thomas Worsdell in 1885, is best remembered for his Claud Hamilton Class 4-4-0s and the 'Decapod' 0-10-0 well tank. Holden came to the GER from the GWR. He is also remembered for his use of oil fuel in locomotives. James Holden retired in 1907 and was succeeded by his son Stephen Dewar Holden. The responsibility for many of the Holdens' design lay with Fred V. Russell who was the Chief Draughtsman at Stratford Works until promoted to Superintendent of Operation in 1915.

Between 1886 and 1897, Stratford Works built 110 2-4-0 locomotives of class T19. When built these locomotives had cut away cabs – that is the cabs had roofs, but were partially open at the side. They also all had round topped fire-boxes; these locomotives were numbered 700-69, 781-90 and 1010-39. Nos 781-90 were renumbered Nos 770-9 in 1904. Some of these locomotives were built for oil fuel. Oil was carried in cylindrical tanks on the tender. No 760 was named *Petrolea* for a time.

In 1902-04 the following twenty locomotives were rebuilt with Belpaire fire-boxes and single windowed cabs: 702, 724-5, 743, 750, 760, 762-3, 769, 781-2, 784, 786, and 788 (original numbers – later numbers 770-1, 774, 776, 778, 1010-1, 1014, 1017, 1022 and 1034). Because of their ungainly appearance these locomotives were nicknamed 'Humpty Dumpties'.

In 1904-08, the following sixty locomotives were similarly rebuilt, but with a leading four-wheeled bogie making them 4-4-0s: 700, 704-8, 710, 712-3, 715, 717-9, 728-35, 737-9, 741-2, 744-5, 747-8, 751, 756, 765-7, 783, 786, 788, 790 (original numbers – later numbers 772, 775, 777, 779), 1012-3, 1015-6, 1018, 1020-1, 1023, 1025-33, 1035-7, 1039). All of the Class that were never rebuilt in any form were withdrawn between 1908 and 1913, whilst of those rebuilt as 2-4-0s with Belpaire fireboxes and side windowed cabs, all were withdrawn between 1913 and 1920. Of those rebuilt as 4-4-0s, two were withdrawn in

The T19 class 2-4-0s were the main express locomotives from the mid-1880s until the coming of the Claud Hamiltons in 1900. They shared the duties with 2-2-2s and later 4-2-2s. On 13 September 1910, No 759 is seen departing King's Lynn on the 11.20am to Hunstanton. (Ken Nunn).

1922, but the remaining fifty-eight were taken over by the LNER on 1 January 1923.

In 1888, a 2-2-2, number 740, later 789 (in 1888 and 780 in 1892), was built at Stratford Works. This was the first member of Class D27. This was followed by a further twenty locomotives in 1891-93 – Nos 770-9 and 1000-9. These have been described as 2-2-2 versions of Class T19. All were withdrawn between 1901 and 1907. Nos 770-9 were renumbered 0770-9 in 1904.

In 1891 to 1902, 100 2-4-0s of Class T26 were built at Stratford Works. They were a small wheeled version of Class T19 and were known as 'Intermediates' and were very useful locomotives to the GER. Their numbers were 417-506 and 1250-9, which latter in 1920 were renumbered 407-16. All were still in service at the end of 1922.

In 1898, ten 4-2-2s of class P43 were built at Stratford Works. They were numbered 10-19 and were all built for burning oil fuel, having round topped tenders. All were withdrawn between 1907 and 1910.

Between 1900 and 1902, forty-one 4-4-0s of Class S46 were built at Stratford Works. They were numbered from 1860-1900 and had side-windowed cabs

The T26 Class 2-4-0s or 'Intermediate' Class were a very useful and very successful class. One hundred locomotives were built between 1891 and 1902. No 1256, later 413, built in 1902, is seen approaching Shenfield on the 3.27pm Southend to Liverpool Street on 5 April 1913. (Ken Nunn).

and round topped fire-boxes. The first locomotive built was No 1900 which was named *Claud Hamilton* after the Company's chairman, Lord John Claud Hamilton. According to the *Locomotive Magazine* of April 1900:

> St Patrick's Day 1900 will be memorable at Stratford as witnessing the completion of the magnificent four-coupled bogie express locomotive which has been designed by Mr Jas Holden to meet the demands of the heavy and increasing main line passenger traffic on the G.E.R. and will represent the company at the forthcoming Paris exhibition.

The locomotive was exhibited at the Paris International Exhibition that year and won a gold medal. All of these locomotives were originally built to run on oil fuel. The class and its two variants became known as 'the Claud Hamiltons'. Between 1903 and 1911 a further seventy locomotives, but with Belpaire fireboxes, were built at Stratford Works. These were Class D56. These were numbered 1790-1859. By the time of the Grouping in 1923, a number of Class S46 locomotives had been rebuilt as Class D56 locomotives. Until all the class S46 locomotives had been rebuilt with Belpaire fireboxes these could be held to

A view taken at Stratford Works showing a part of the exterior. Here we see Class D56 4-4-0 No 1840 on the weighbridge after overhaul on 8 March 1913. This locomotive had originally been built by the Company at the works in 1906. (Ken Nunn).

be called 'Belpaire Clauds'. Locomotive No 1851 was involved in the Witham accident of 1 September 1905 and locomotive No 1813 in the Ilford accident of 1 January 1915, whilst locomotive No 1849 hauled Captain Fryatt's funeral train from Liverpool Street to Dovercourt on 8 July 1919. No 1805 was rebuilt in 1923 with a larger diameter superheated boiler and became the prototype for the ten members of Class H88 which were built to Alfred Hill's design at Stratford Works in 1923. As the latter came out in LNER days they were numbered 1780E-89E, E signifying a locomotive of the former GER. They were known as 'Super Clauds.' At the end of 1922, 101 locomotives were in service with a further ten on order.

Goods engines

In 1887, a two cylinder inside cylinder compound 0-6-0, No 127, was built at Stratford Works. In 1891 it was renumbered 935 and in 1895 it was rebuilt as a simple expansion engine of class N31. Class N31 proper consisted of eighty 0-6-0 locomotives built by Stratford Works between 1892 and 1898 plus the rebuilt locomotive making eighty-one locomotives in total. Their numbers were

Here is a typical general goods train. Here we see Class N31 0-6-0 No 995 departing from March Yard on the 1.40pm March to Cambridge train on 27 July 1912. Class N31 was not a particularly successful class of locomotives compared to the similar class Y14. (Ken Nunn).

542-71, 602-8 and 949-99. They have been described as an 0-6-0 version of Class T19, but because of the arrangement of the steam chests compared to the Y14 class they were not a success. Sixty-four of these locomotives were withdrawn between 1908 and the end of 1922 leaving eighteen to be inherited by the LNER. Nos 543 and 645 were renumbered 0643 and 0545 in 1913, whilst No 564 was renumbered 0564 in 1912.

Between 1900 and 1903, sixty 0-6-0 locomotives of Class F48 were built by Stratford Works. They were numbered 1150-1209. All except No 1189, built in 1902, had round topped fireboxes. No 1189 had a raised Belpaire firebox. Between 1905 and 1911, thirty 0-6-0 locomotives of Class G58 were built by Stratford Works, Nos 1210-39. These were a Belpaire fire boxed version of Class F48 from which, by the time of the Grouping, some of that Class had been rebuilt as Class G58. All ninety locomotives of the two classes were in service at the end of 1922.

The 'Decapod' Locomotive, No 20, was the only member of Class A55 and was built in 1902 by Stratford Works for the sole purpose of proving that a steam locomotive had the same acceleration capabilities as an electric train. It was a three cylinder 0-10-0 well tank. There were two outside cylinders and

The GER's largest goods locomotives were 0-6-0s. Coal trains over the Company's line came either via the Joint Line or from the GNR at Peterborough. Class G58 No 1224 on a Peterborough to Aldersbrook train near Ingrave signal box on 26 May 1915. (Ken Nunn).

one inside cylinder. In 1906, parts were used in the building of a two cylinder outside cylindered 0-8-0. This was also classed A55 and was the GER's only 0-8-0. This locomotive was withdrawn in 1913.

Between 1892 and 1902, Stratford Works built 50 2-4-2 side tanks of Class C32 numbered 1040-9 and 1060-99. They were a tank locomotive version of the T26 2-4-0s.

Between 1898 and 1901, Stratford Works built forty 0-4-4 side tanks of Class S44. They were numbered 1100-49. Nos 1111, 1113, 1117, 1119, 1128 and 1132 worked at Richborough train ferry port in Kent between 1918 and 1919. All these locomotives were in service at the end of 1922.

Holden 0-6-0 side tanks

Between 1886 and 1888, fifty-two 0-6-0 side tanks of Class T18 were built at Stratford Works. They were numbered 275-326. Although mainly intended for shunting duties, the last ten had for a time the Westinghouse air brake fitted so that they could be used on passenger trains. These locomotives were sometimes called 'Jubilee tanks'. Some members of the class worked at Richborough train ferry port in Kent between 1918 and 1919. All these locomotives were in service at the end of 1922.

Class R24 consisted of 140 locomotives built at Stratford Works between 1890 and 1901. They were numbered 160-9, 189-208 (189 was renumbered 305 in 1909), 255-74, 327-396, 397-416. Some of these locomotives were fitted with the Westinghouse air brake for use on passenger trains. All of the class had the nickname 'Buckjumpers'. The class history is somewhat complicated as there were various rebuildings involving increasing the boiler pressure and the size of the water tanks. Those that were rebuilt were classified Class R24R. Some members of the class worked at Richborough train ferry port in Kent between 1918 and 1919. All these locomotives were in service at the end of 1922.

Class S56 consisted of twenty 0-6-0 side tanks built at Stratford Works in 1904. They were an improved version of Class R24 and were numbered 51-60 and 81-90. They were passenger engines. All these locomotives were in service at the end of 1922.

Class E22 consisted of twenty 0-6-0 side tanks numbered 150-9 and 245-54. All were built at Stratford Works between 1889 and 1893. All were fitted with the Westinghouse air brake for working passenger trains. Some of these locomotives had for a time the coupling rods removed between the first and second pair of coupled wheels and became 2-4-0s. All these locomotives were in service at the end of 1922.

Between 1903 and 1921, twelve outside cylindered 0-6-0 tram locomotives of Class C53 were built at Stratford Works. They were numbered 125-31, 135-6 and 137-9. All these locomotives were in service at the end of 1922.

In 1907 James Holden retired and was succeeded by his son Stephen Dewar Holden who reigned from 1907 to 1912 when he resigned.

The younger Holden is best remembered for his S69 class 4-6-0s, Nos 1500-1570. Seventy-one locomotives of this Class were built between 1911 and 1920. They were in many ways a six coupled version of the Class D56 4-4-0s and although not called so they could be held to be 'Six Coupled Clauds'. The Class was not unexpected as the *Locomotive Magazine* of January 1911 reported that 'Orders [were] given to the Stratford Works to build five passenger engines of the 4-6-0 type intended to work the Norfolk Coast

Express to Cromer next summer, and be the first six-coupled bogie engines built by the G.E.R.'

Nos 1500-40 and 1561-70 were built at Stratford Works between 1911 and 1917 and 1920 respectively. Nos 1541-60 were built by William Beardmore and Company in 1920-21. No 1506 was scrapped after the accident at Colchester on 12 July 1913. A member of this class, No 1526, hauled the special train taking the German Ambassador and his staff to Parkeston Quay bound for Germany on 6 August 1914 following the outbreak of the First World War. No 1534 was the first GER locomotive to be painted in LNER colours of apple green in February 1923. Arguably these locomotives were the best large express locomotives inherited from any of its constituent companies by the LNER on 1 January 1923. At the end of 1922 there were seventy locomotives in service.

In 1909-11, twelve 2-4-2 lightweight side tanks of Class Y65 were built at Stratford Works and were numbered 1300-11. The *Locomotive Magazine* for February 1919 reported that two 2-4-2 tank locomotives of the Company,

Here is a photograph taken inside Stratford Works showing an S69 4-6-0, No 1509, under construction on 12 April 1913. The S69 class 4-6-0 were the GER's only big locomotives and could be used on both passenger and goods services. (Ken Nunn).

At the end of 1922, the GER had a total of 232 2-4-2 side tank locomotives in service, the largest number on any of the British railway companies. Class G69 No 70 is seen approaching Squirrels Heath on the 11.36am ex-Liverpool Street on 2 November 1912. (Ken Nunn).

Nos 1302 and 1308, were at the National Shipyard at Chepstow. All these locomotives were in service at the end of 1922.

In 1911-12, twenty 2-4-2 side tanks of Class G69 were built at Stratford Works. They were a side-windowed version of Class M15 and were called 'Glass House Gobblers'. Their numbers were 1-10 and 61-70. All these locomotives were in service at the end of 1922.

The following class of 0-6-0s could be held to be being designed under the younger Holden's stewardship even though they came out under that of his successor Alfred Hill who was Locomotive Superintendent from 1912 to 1915 (when the role was re-designated Chief Mechanical Engineer) and remained in that role until his retirement at the end of 1922 on the formation of the LNER. Class E72 consisted of ten locomotives built at Stratford Works in 1912-13. They were numbered 1240-9. They were followed by 25 0-6-0s of Class T77 built at Stratford Works in 1916-20. The difference between the two classes was that Class E72 had Schmidt superheaters and tail rods making them look like 2-6-0s without the leading two wheeled pony truck, whilst Class T77 had Robinson superheaters and no tail rods. They were numbered 1140-9, 1250-4 and 1260-9. All these locomotives were in service at the end of 1922.

Class D81 consisted of twenty-five 0-6-0s built at Stratford Works between 1920 and 1922, although the last three locomotives did not enter service until January 1923 making twenty-two locomotives in service at the end of 1922 with three waiting to enter service. They were numbered 1270-94 and were at the time of building the most powerful 0-6-0s in the country.

Class C72 consisted of 30 0-6-0 side tanks built at Stratford Works between 1912 and 1923. These locomotives had side windowed cabs and were numbered in sequence, but not date order of building, 21-50. Nos 31-40, which were built in 1923, came out as 31E-40E. 20 locomotives were in service at the end of 1922.

Class B74 consisted of five outside cylindered 0-4-0 side tanks numbered 210 and 226-9. They were built at Stratford Works between 1913 and 1921. All these locomotives were in service at the end of 1922.

Class L77 consisted of 22 0-6-2 side tanks built at Stratford Works between 1915 and 1924. They were numbered as built 1000-11 and 990E-99E. Nos 1000-1 were built in 1915, Nos 1002-11 in 1921 and Nos 990E-99E in 1923-4. Locomotive No 999E, built in 1924, was the last locomotive to be built at Stratford Works. Twelve locomotives were in service at the end of 1922.

The GER was one of the last pre-grouping companies to build any 0-6-2 side tanks. Only twelve were built by the Company prior to the Grouping, two in 1915 and ten in 1921, a further ten following in 1923-4. Newly built No 1002 is seen at Stratford Works on 24 July 1921. (Ken Nunn).

There were a couple of other miscellaneous locomotives. *Peggy* was a four wheeled petrol locomotive built by Motor Rail and Tram Company in 1919. The same Company built a 2ft 11¾in gauge four wheeled locomotive for internal works use in 1920. These two locomotives were both in service at the end of 1922.

The following forty-four outside cylindered 2-8-0s built for the War Office in 1916-8 were borrowed by the GER from the latter part of 1919 to the latter part of 1921 but not all at the same time. All had been returned by 1 January 1922. They were of the Robinson GCR Class 8K which had first been built in 1911. Their Railway Operating Department (of the Royal Engineers) numbers were 1602-3, 10, 4, 9, 22, 6, 30, 63, 76-7, 83-4, 6, 1713, 1833, 9, 61, 9, 73, 6, 9, 81, 93-4, 1906-7, 11, 3-4, 20-1, 4-5, 31, 9, 42, 53-4, 62, 74 and 93. Due to loading gauge restrictions, they could only be used on the Great Northern and Great Eastern Joint Line and when it was necessary to repair them at Stratford Works they had to be towed 'dead' with their outer chimney removed.

There was one other form of motive power and that was horses. Their main use was for shunting or hauling a single wagon on a short branch line saving the need for a locomotive, but they were in the early days used to haul a single passenger carriage on a lightly used branch line.

Carriages

Apart from a six wheeled Royal saloon built for the Prince of Wales in 1864, some six wheeled family saloons built in 1875-6, all carriages built for the GER and its constituent companies until 1879 were four wheelers when the first six wheelers appeared. These were first and second class composites with a central luggage compartment. Third class passengers were deemed only worthy of four wheelers. Third class passengers had to wait until 1884. Four wheeled carriages continued to be built for many years.

One problem the GER faced around the turn of the twentieth century was capacity in suburban carriages. At that time, they could only seat five a side in each compartment. James Holden, who had been on the Great Western Railway when in the 1870s broad gauge carriages were being built that were capable of being narrowed from 7ft ¼in to 4ft 8½in when the final end of the broad gauge came, which was in May 1892, decided in the bodies of the suburban carriages on the Great Eastern railway to reverse the process. The carriages whose bodies were to be widened were cut down the centre and the extra section spliced in. The coach sides were slightly inclined inwards from the cantrail downwards to allow sufficient turn under at the bottom of the footboards. Various side protrusions such as the grab handles, door hinges and roof edge were altered to come within the maximum permitted width. The result was an increase in the seating capacity of each compartment from ten to twelve.

As time progressed, so did facilities. The earliest carriages had oil lamps and no lavatories and no steam heating. The first gas lit carriages appeared in 1878. Apart from a Civil Engineer's saloon fitted with electric light in 1889, this form of lighting did not appear in ordinary carriages until 1900. Whilst oil lit carriages had all disappeared from the GER at the end of 1922, there were quite a few gas lit carriages in existence. The first carriage with a toilet had appeared in 1882. Apart from a few saloon carriages fitted with heating stoves in the 1880s, from 1862 until the mid to late Edwardian period, the foot warmer was the only form of carriage heating. And that was on main line trains: suburban trains had to wait until 1921 and even then at the end of 1922 there were still some suburban trains without steam heating. The first restaurant car sets had appeared in 1891 on the North Country Continental, but the next did not appear until 1899. The first corridor trains started to appear from 1906 onwards. Prior to that date, restaurant car sets had been gang-wayed only with the sets. One must not forget that some carriages were composites having more than one class and that some had a guard's compartment attached, whilst there were also full passenger brake carriages.

From the mid-1880s, six wheelers became the norm for main line stock until 1897 when the first bogie carriages appeared. The first bogie carriages were in fact some bogie tram cars on the Wisbech and Upwell Tramway built in 1884. Apart from one train of bogie stock built in 1900, all suburban stock consisted of four wheelers until 1911. To increase the number of suburban bogie carriages from about 1915, some of the four wheelers were mounted in pairs on bogie frames.

There were some oddities, principally the tram cars built in 1871-2 for the Millwall Extension Railway and the tram cars on the Wisbech and Upwell Tramway.

Wagons

John Watling wrote two articles on GER wagons in *Great Eastern Railway Journals* Nos 84 and 86. What would be true to say is that there were wagons for all sorts of traffic from coal and general goods to cattle and horse boxes, although horse boxes tended to come under passenger vehicles, wagons for oil and for gas for lighting carriages and ballast wagons. There were even refrigerator vans. There were of course guard's vans. All wagons used by the GER and its constituent companies were four wheelers.

One must not also forget the numerous private owner wagons used on the GER. According to John Watling writing in *Great Eastern Journal* No 53, 85 per cent were designed to carry coal, but the remaining 15 per cent were designed to carry a variety of goods including petrol, oil, tar, acids, cement, salt, mustard and beer. There were even privately owned horse boxes.

The locomotives and rolling stock of the Colne Valley and Halstead Railway and the MSLR were acquired by the LNER in 1923 and 1924 respectively. From the former came five locomotives. They were all side tanks. One was an 0-4-2 built by Neilson and Co in 1877 which was similar to the GER T7 Class. This locomotive was Colne Valley and Halsted Railway No 1. There were three 2-4-2s built by Hawthorn Leslie and Co. Two, Nos 2 and 3, in 1887 and one, No 4, in 1894. They were named respectively *Halstead*, *Colne* and *Heddingham*. There was an 0-6-2 built by Hudswell Clarke and Co in 1908. This was No 5. At the time of acquisition by the LNER, the Colne Valley and Halstead Railway had some six wheeled carriages and three eight wheeled bogie carriages built originally as part of a six carriage experimental electric train by the Metropolitan District and Metropolitan railways in 1899. The Colne Valley and Halstead Railway's carriages were the Metropolitan District Railway's part of the train. There were various goods wagons. From the MSLR came three 0-6-0 side tanks, Nos 1, 2 and 3 built by Hudswell Clarke and Co in 1904, 1905 and 1909 respectively. MSLR carriages were all four wheelers. There were various goods vehicles.

Ships

The GER commenced its services to the continent in October 1863 with a once weekly service from Harwich to Rotterdam followed the next year by a similar service to Antwerp. To commence operation, the Railway Company borrowed three paddle steamers – *Blenheim, Norfolk* and *Prince of Wales*. Ambrose Greenway in *A Century of North Sea Passenger Ships* says that the GER's first passenger ships were the twin funnelled paddle steamers *Avalon* and *Zealous*, built in 1864 and 1865 respectively by J. and W. Dudgeon of Poplar (later the Thames Ironworks Company). According to Allen, Simpson and Company delivered two paddle steamers, *Harwich* and *Rotterdam*, which were, according to *Parkeston – A Century of Service*, employed on the cattle trade to Rotterdam. *Zealous* was converted in 1873 to carry cargo as well as passengers and lasted until 1887. According to Jerzy Swieszkowski in *Great Eastern Journal* No 12, *Avalon* ran aground at the Hook of Holland on 8 June 1864 and was sold back to the builders. *Harwich* and *Rotterdam* were converted to screw steamers in 1884 and 1887 and were disposed of in 1907 and 1908. *Harwich*, on its conversion to screw propulsion, was renamed *Peterborough*.

In 1865, J. and W. Dudgeon delivered a second paddle steamer named *Avalon* and another paddle steamer named *Ravensbury*. On 8 March 1870, *Ravensbury* sprang a leak and was abandoned by its crew at the river entrance to Rotterdam. The second *Avalon* was sold to Earle's of Hull in 1888 in part payment for the screw steamer *Colchester*.

In 1865 another paddle steamer – *Pacific*, built by C. Lungley of Deptford in 1864 – was obtained. The ship was sold for scrap in 1887.

1866 saw the entry into service on the Harwich to Antwerp route of the *Great Yarmouth* as a freight vessel. The ship was the first screw propelled ship in the Great Eastern Railway's fleet and was built by the Thames Graving Dock Company in London. The ship remained in service until 1873 when it was sold to Thomas Gage Beatley and later ended up in the ownership of Mr Joseph Reay of Newcastle.

In 1871, J. and W. Dudgeon built for the GER the paddle steam *Richard Young*. In 1890 the ship was converted to a twin screw propelled ship by Earle's Shipbuilding Company and renamed *Brandon*. The ship was sold to Dutch shipbreakers in 1905.

In 1875 John Elder and Company of Govan launched the paddle steamer *Claud Hamilton*, which entered service the same year. It remained in service until 1897 when it was sold to the City of London Corporation. The following year the same Company built the paddle steamer *Princess of Wales*. This ship remained in service until 1896 when it was sold for scrap.

In 1880, T. and W. Smith of North Shields built the paddle steamer *Lady Tyler*. This ship was sold in 1893 to the shipbuilders Messrs Earle's of Hull: possibly in part payment for a new ship.

In 1880 the Barrow Shipbuilding Company built the paddle steamer *Adelaide*. The ship was the last paddle steamer built for the GER and in 1896 it was sold to T.W. Ward who passed it to J. Bannatyne and Sons the following year for breaking up.

1883 saw the GER's first screw propelled passenger ships –*Norwich* and *Ipswich*. The two ships were built by Earle's Shipbuilding and Engineering Company of Hull. They were the last two ships for the GER to be built of iron; subsequent ships were built of steel. They were the first ships in the GER's fleet to have electric light – in the first class saloon and staterooms, the ladies' cabin and engine room. Previous ships were wholly lit by oil. According to Rik Alewijnse in *Great Eastern Journal* No 148 they were both sold out of service in 1905.

Following the success of the *Norwich* and *Ipswich*, further ships followed from Earles. They were *Cambridge*, which was launched in 1886 and remained in service until 1912, and *Colchester*, launched in 1886 and which remained in service at the outbreak of the First World War. *Cambridge* had the misfortune on 12 December 1911 to collide with the destroyer H M S *Salmon* killing two of the latter's crew. The *Cambridge* picked up the remainder. *Colchester*, having on four occasions between December 1914 and May 1915, had to use its superior speed to outrun and escape from enemy submarines, and had the misfortune on 22 September 1916 to be captured by enemy torpedo boats off the Dutch coast and its crew interned. The *Colchester* was then taken over by the German navy and converted in to a minelayer at Bruges. It was returned to Britain after the end of the war but was only fit for scrap. Both *Cambridge* and *Colchester* had accommodation lit by electric light and heated by steam. Previously, heating was provided by iron stoves.

In 1893 there followed the *Chelmsford*, which was the first ship in the GER's fleet to have triple expansion engines. *Chelmsford's* time with the GER was short; in 1910 it was sold to the Great Western Railway and renamed *Bretonne*. In 1894, there followed *Amsterdam*, *Berlin* and *Vienna*. *Berlin* had the misfortune on 21 February 1907 to be swept across the northern mole at the entrance to the New

Waterway at the Hook of Holland during a fierce north-westerly gale. Of those on board only ten passengers and five crew members were saved. The remaining 128 on board were lost. *Amsterdam* and *Vienna* were in service at the end of the GER in 1922. During the First World War, *Amsterdam* became an armed boarding steamer equipped with one 4 inch gun and one 12 pounder. *Vienna* was used as an accommodation ship for about 3½ months in 1914, followed by a brief spell in 1915 as one of the first Q ships, using the name *Antwerp* as well as its own. In 1920, *Vienna* was renamed *Roulers*. *Dresden* was launched in 1896 and handed over to the GER in 1897. About two months after the start of the First World War, *Dresden* was requisitioned by the Admiralty and renamed HMS *Louvain*. She was sunk in the Mediterranean on 20 January 1918 by the submarine UC 22.

The next ship built for the GER was *Brussels*. As Earle's had only recently been saved from bankruptcy by Thomas Wilson and in consequence had a full order book, the Company was forced to look elsewhere and so the order went to Gourlay Brothers. *Brussels* was launched on 26 March 1902 and was the last triple expansion passenger steamer built for the GER. During the First World War, *Brussels* was not requisitioned by the government and maintained an irregular service between Tilbury and the Hook of Holland. As mentioned Brussels was captured by the Germans on 23 June 1916.

The next three passenger ships built for the GER were *Copenhagen* which was launched in October 1907 and entered service in the spring of 1908, *Munich*, which was launched in August 1908, and *St Petersburg* which was launched in April 1910 and entered service in July of that year. All three ships were built by John Brown and Company of Clydebank and were fitted with steam turbines. Of the three, *Copenhagen* was built as a replacement for the lost *Berlin* and at the beginning of the First World War remained in North Sea service for a time carrying Belgian refugees, but was later used as a troop ship until 1 January 1916 when it was taken over by the Government as an ambulance carrier. On 5 March 1917 the *Copenhagen* was torpedoed about eight miles east of the North Hinde light ship with the loss of six lives. The *St Petersburg* was requisitioned by the Admiralty during the First World War and renamed *Archangel* in 1916. The ship was used as a cross-channel troopship. After the war, *Archangel* returned to railway ownership. *Munich* was requisitioned by the Admiralty in 1914 and converted as a hospital ship and renamed *St Denis* in 1916. At the end of the war the ship returned to railway control but retained its new name.

The GER, as well as operating trains, also operated ships and here is a photograph of the SS *Munich* launched in August 1908. The ship was built by John Brown and Company of Clydebank, Glasgow and was fitted with steam turbines. (Author's collection).

Stockholm was the GER ship that never entered GER service. Laid down by John Brown and Company in early 1917, it was bought by the Admiralty whilst still under construction as an aircraft carrier. It was launched on 9 June 1917 as *Stockholm* but renamed HMS *Pegasus* on 28 August 1917.

Kilkenny was a triple expansion steamer built in 1903 for the City of Dublin Steam Packet Company by the Clyde Shipbuilding and Engineering Company and purchased by the GER in 1917. The ship was renamed *Frinton* in 1919.

St George was built by Cammell Laird at Birkenhead in 1906 for the GWR or rather the Fishguard and Rosslare Railways and Harbour Company and was sold to Canadian interests in 1913. She was purchased from the Canadian Pacific

Railway in 1919 by the GER. The ship was a turbine steamer. The last three passenger ships built for the GER's North Sea services were *Antwerp*, which was built by John Brown and Company, and *Bruges*, built by the same company and both of which entered service in 1920. They were followed into service in 1922 by *Malines* which was built by Armstrong Whitworth and Company of Newcastle upon Tyne. They again were turbine steamers.

The GER also owned a number of purely cargo ships. These were *Cromer* built in 1902, *Yarmouth* built in 1903, *Clacton* built in 1904 and *Newmarket* built in 1907. *Cromer* was built by Gourlay Brothers of Dundee, as was *Yarmouth*, whilst *Clacton* and *Newmarket* were built by Earle's.

In addition to these ships, the GER owned paddle steamers which plied up and down the River Orwell between Ipswich, Harwich and Felixstowe. Originally it was just Ipswich and Harwich, but later included Felixstowe. They were the paddle steamer *Cardinal Wolsey* of the EUR and its GER replacement, the paddle steamer *Ipswich* built by James Ash of Cubitt Town on the River Thames in 1864. There was also the paddle steamer *Stour* also built by James Ash at Cubitt Town on the River Thames. The ship was withdrawn in 1878 and replaced by a slightly larger new building with the same name. The second paddle steamer *Stour* was built by Thames Ironworks and Shipbuilding Company in 1878. The ship was sold in 1900 for River Thames river service. In 1873 Lewis and Stockwell of London built the paddle steamer *Orwell*. In 1890, the ship was sold for scrapping. They were followed by, in 1882, the paddle steamer *Norfolk*, which was built on the River Thames. In 1897 it was sold to the Eastham Ferry Pleasure Gardens and Hotel Company in 1897 and renamed *Onyx*. The replacement ships were the *Suffolk* built in 1895 by Earle's and used as a picket ship at Harwich in the First World War and which ship re-opened its pre-war services in 1919. The *Essex* was built in 1896 by Earle's and sold in 1913. The *Norfolk* was built in 1900 by Gourlay Brothers.

There were also three small ships – *Pin Mill* (1914), *Epping* and *Hainault* (1914) ran a ferry for foot passengers and bicycles from Harwich to Felixstowe, which was started in 1912 by the GER.

Two paddle steamers were used as ferrries between North and South Woolwich. These were *Middlesex*, built in 1879 for the Woolwich Ferry and used until 1908, and *Woolwich* built in 1890 and sold in 1908 to David Wilson and Sons for the service between North and South Queensferry on the Forth.

Motor Buses

The GER operated a total of thirty motor buses. These were as follows:

Three 20 horse power Milnes-Daimler 36 seater open top double deck buses commencing service on 18 July 1904 – fleet numbers 1-3 and registration numbers BJ203-5.

Twelve 30 horse power Stratford Works built 36 seater open top double deck buses which were licensed as follows: Fleet numbers 4-6, registration numbers BJ318-20 on 4 August 1905. Fleet number 7, registration number F1499 licensed on 12 August 1905. Fleet numbers 8 and 9, registration numbers BJ329 and BJ330 licensed on 19 August 1905. Fleet numbers 10 and 11, registration numbers CL200 and CL201 licensed on 28 August 1905. Fleet number 12, registration number F1610, licensed on 30 August 1905. Fleet 13-5, registration numbers F1612, 14 and 13, licensed on 7 September 1905.

Three 24 horse power 36 seater open top double deck buses fleet number (16 and 17) and 18, registration numbers F1874 and BJ415-6 licensed on an unknown date in July 1906 for the first bus and 13 July 1906 for the other two. Number 18 could also have its body changed to make it a 23 seater charabanc.

Three Maudslay 30 horse power 36 seater open top double deck buses, fleet numbers (19), 20, and (21), registration numbers F2440-2 licensed 4 May 1907.

Two Tillings TTA 1 34 seater open top double deck buses of whom the registration number of one was LF9851, whilst that of the other one is not known and which entered service on 1 April 1914.

One Tillings TS 3 32 single deck rear entrance bus which entered service in November 1914. This bus replaced the other two Tillings buses and like them was returned to Tillings, but at an unknown date.

Six Thornycroft J 28 single deck rear entrance buses registration numbers CL3216-8 and DX2173-5. The first three entered service in August 1919 whilst the last three were licensed on 19 October 1919. They were numbered 14-9. The first three buses were sold to United Automobile Service in 1920, whilst the last three were sold to Thames Valley Traction in 1923.

There may have been other buses whose details are not known. The withdrawal dates for the pre-First World War buses were as follows: No 3 – 1909, Nos 1 and 2 – 1914, 4, 7-11, 13 and 15 – 1913, 6, 12 and 14 – 1914, 16-21 dates unknown,

Liveries

The earliest locomotives of the GER were painted in green with black and vermilion lining, although some were painted in a yellow ochre colour and they acquired the nickname of 'canaries'. These were W Class 2-2-2 No 60, rebuilt W Class 4-2-2s Nos 51 and 291 and some T7 Class 0-4-2 side tanks. The locomotive which hauled the train conveying the Prince and Princess of Wales to Sandringham on their wedding day in 1863 (W Class 2-2-2 No 284) was painted cream and also garlanded.

William Adams during his tenure as Locomotive Superintendent introduced a black livery which lasted until 1882. The GER's famous blue livery was introduced on all locomotives in 1882.

Johnson 0-4-4 side tank No 134 was the first GER locomotive to be painted royal blue when it hauled the Great Western Railway's royal train carrying Queen Victoria to Chingford on 6 May 1882 to declare Epping Forest open to the public. The finish consisted of a French grey undercoat, four coats of ultramarine blue, and several coats of blue. Lining was black with vermilion edging. Wheel tyres and axle ends were black with vermilion edges. The frames were black, although the 'Claud Hamiltons' and a few other express types used blue above the footplate. Cab roofs appeared white in official photographs, but were probably grey in regular use.

From 1890, goods locomotives were painted in unlined black, although some shunting engines also received vermilion lining. From the latter part of 1915 the GER changed to a French grey colour for all locomotives. There is some limited evidence of some locomotives being painted blue after that date; C. Langley Aldrich in *The Locomotives of the GER 1862-1962* recalled that Class G4 0-4-4 side tank No 1121 was repainted blue albeit without lining or lettering in 1919. Tram locomotives were painted the same colour as carriages; varnished teak finish prior to 1919, but from that year crimson lake. Their buffer beams were not painted vermilion as on other locomotives, but blue or grey according to the period.

Coaches were finished in a simple varnished teak finish with without any lining. The solebars were painted teak with the metalwork painted brown. The footboards were probably varnished wood. Below the solebars were entirely black, although the wooden centres on the Mansell wheels were varnished. From 1919, a crimson lake livery was introduced. The solebars and Mansell wooden centres were painted crimson, but bogie vehicles were painted with black underframes. The coach roofs were white or various shades of grey, throughout the GER's existence. Grey dominated after 1918. Wagons were painted grey.

At the time of the LNER takeover of the Colne Valley and Halstead Railway, the livery of the Company's locomotives was black and the passenger carriages a colour known as 'drab'. That of goods rolling stock is not known. The locomotives of the Mid Suffolk Railway at the time of the acquisition were painted brown as were the carriages.

The GER's ships were distinguished by having yellow funnels with black tops.

The Milnes Daimler buses were originally painted brown but were later painted red with white window pillars and top deck in line with the GER's built buses. This latter livery was used on all buses owned by the GER.

Bibliography and Sources

Firstly, I wish to thank the members of the GER Society for their help in answering my questions. Without their help I could not have written this book.

I also wish to thank Keith Ronaldson for proofreading the manuscript of this book.

Additionally, I wish to thank John Scott-Morgan for his help with the book.

A Century of Service – Parkeston 1983
Aldrich, C. Langley, *Locomotives of the GER 1862-1962*, Privately published, 1962
Allen, Cecil J., *The Great Eastern Railway*, Ian Allan, 1967
Allen, Cecil J., *Two Million Miles of Train Travel*, Ian Allan, 1965
Anderson, R.C., *The Tramways of East Anglia*, LRTA, 1969
Appendix to the Working Timetable for the Great Eastern Railway for January 1906
Badsley Ellis, Anthony, *London's Lost Tubes*, Capital Transport 2005
Boyles, John and Russell, Ronald, *The Canals of Eastern England*, David and Charles 1977
Bradley, D.L., *The Locomotive History of the South Eastern and Chatham Railway*, RCTS 1980
Bradshaw's Continental Railway Guide July 1913
Bradshaw's Handbook for Tourists in Great Britain and Ireland 1866
Bradshaw's Railway Guide especially February 1863, August 1887, December 1895, April 1910 and July 1922
British Locomotive Catalogue 1825-1923 Volume 6 GER, North British Railway, Great North of Scotland Railway, Midland and Great Northern Joint Railway, Remaining Companies of the LNER Group (Falcon Books)
British Newspaper Archive
Brown, F.A.S., *Great Northern Locomotive Engineers Vol 1 1846-1881*, Allen and Unwin 1966
Brown, F.A.S., *Great Northern Locomotive Engineers Vol 2 From Stirling to Gresley 1882-1922*, OPC 1974

Clark, Rev Andrew, *Echoes of the Great War: diaries*, Oxford 1988
Clark, Ronald H., *A Short History of the Midland and Great Northern Joint Railway*, Goose 1967
Connor, J.E., *All Stations to Poplar*, Connor and Butler 1980
Connor, J.E., *Stepney's Own Railway*, Connor and Butler 1987
Connor, J.E., *The Tottenham Joint Lines*, Connor and Butler 1993
Cook's Continental Timetable March 1873
Cummings, John, *Railway Motor Buses and Bus Services in the British Isles 1902-1933*, OPC 1978-80
Cupit, J. and Taylor, W., *The Lancashire, Derbyshire and East Coast Railway*, Oakwood Press 1984
Directors' reports to shareholders of the Eastern Counties, Great Eastern and London and North Eastern railways.
Hilton H F, *The Eastern Union Railway 1846-1862*, LNER 1946
Dow, George, *The First Railway in Norfolk*, LNER 1947
Dow, George, *The Great Central Railway Vols 1, 2 and 3*, 1959-1965
Gadsden, E.J.E., Whetmath, C.F.D. and Stafford-Baker, J., *The Wisbech and Upwell Tramway*, Branch Line Handbooks 1966
Gibbs, T.A., *The Metropolitan Electric Tramways – A Short History*, LRTA 1962
Glover, John, *Essex and the Industrial Revolution*, ERO 1972
Gordon, D.I., *The Regional History of the Railways of Great Britain – Volume 5 - Eastern Counties*, David and Charles 1968
Goudie, Frank, *Metropolitan Steam Locomotives*, Capital Transport 1990
Gray, Adrian, *South Eastern and Chatham Railways*, Middleton 1998
Great Eastern Journal
Great Eastern Railway Magazine
Greenaway, Ambrose, *A Century of North Sea Passenger Services*, Ian Allan 1986
Hamilton, J.A.B., *Britain's Railways in World War 1*, George Allen and Unwin 1967
Jackson, Alan A. and Croome, Desmond, *Rails Through the Clay*, Capital Transport 1993
Jackson, Alan A., *London's Local Railways*, David and Charles 1978
Jackson, Alan A., *London's Metropolitan Railway*, David and Charles 1986
Jackson, Alan A., *London's Termini*, David and Charles 1969
Kay, Peter, *The LT&SR – a History of the Company and Line. Volumes 1, 2 and 3*, Privately published
Ketteridge, Christopher and Mays, Spike, *Five Miles from Bunkham*, Eyre Meuthen 1972
Kitchenside, G.M., *Veteran and Vintage Railway Carriages 1839-1939*, Ian Allan

Klapper, Charles, *London's Lost Railways*, RKP 1976
Lake, G.H., *The Railways of Tottenham* 1945
Lee, Charles E., *The East London Line*, London Transport 1976
Lee, David, Taylor, Alan, Shorland-Ball, Rob, *The Southwold Railway 1879-1929*, Pen and Sword 2019
Liverpool Street Station, Academy Editions 1978
Local Transport History Library
North Eastern Railway Magazine
Paye, Peter, *The Mid Suffolk Light Railway*, Wild Swan 1986
Paye, Peter, *The Southwold Railway*, 2018
Peacock, T.B., *The Mistley Thorpe and Walton Railway*, 1946
Phillips, Charles, *The Great Eastern Railway in South Essex*, Pen and Sword 2019
Public Timetable of the Great Eastern Railway for 1882
Railway and Travel Monthly, later Travel and Transport Monthly
Railway Magazine
Riley, R.C., *Great Eastern Album*, Ian Allan, 1968
Robbins, Michael, *The North London Railway*, Oakwood 1983
Rodinglea, *The Tramways of East London*, LRTA, 1967
Rolt, L.T.C., *Red for Danger*, Pan 1966
Rowledge, J.W.P., *Heavy Goods Engines of the War Department Volume 1 ROD 2-8-0*, Springmead 1977
Sassoon, Siegfried, *The Memoirs of An Infantry Officer*, 1930
Swindale, Dennis, *Branch Line to Southminster*, EARM 1981
Swindale, Dennis, *Branch Lines to Maldon*, EARM 1977
Taylor, Alan R. and Tonks, Eric S., *The Southwold Railway*, Ian Allan 1965
The Locomotive
The Regional History of the Railways of Great Britain – Volume 3 – Greater London – H.P. White, Phoenix 1963
The Times Archive
Welch, H.D., *The London, Tilbury and Southend Railway*, Oakwood 1951
Whitehead R.A. and Simpson, F.D., *The Colne Valley and Halstead Railway*, Oakwood Press, 1988
Wingate, H. Brett and Gilham, John C., *Great British Tramway Networks*, LRTA 1962
Working Timetables for the Great Eastern Railway for 1863 and 1913
Wrottesley, A.J., *The GNR Vols, 1, 2 and 3*, Batsford 1979-1981
Wrottesley, A.J., *The Midland and Great Northern Joint Railway*, David and Charles, 1970
Harvard Lesley C, Country Chronicles: History of the Village of Stock, Ian Henry 1992

Index

Accidents 51-2, 191-4
Adams William 83, 234-5, 257
Air Raids 201-6
Alexandra Palace 73-4
Ambulance Trains 196-8, 201, 209, 212, 216-7
Armoured Trains 200-1
Antwerp 16-7, 184-5, 195, 199, 219, 250-1

Belgian National Railways Locomotives 210
Benwick 112-3
Bethnal Green 12, 58, 62, 66, 71, 79, 81-2, 213
Billericay 84, 86-7, 204
Bishopsgate/Shoreditch stations GER, Met Rly & ELR 14, 59-60, 64, 66-8, 112, 128-204, 213
Bishop's Stortford 24, 166
Bishop's Stortford, Dunmow and Braintree Railway 25-9
Blackwall 54-5, 57, 136
Blakeney 53, 99, 101
Braintree 29
Braking Systems 106-7
Brassey Thomas contracto 27-8
Broad Street station NLR 54, 59, 65
Bromley Massey 235
Broxbourne 166, 169

Bruff Peter 33-4
SS Brussels 208, 215, 253
Bury St Edmunds 36-7, 183, 203-4
Bury St Edmunds and Thetford Railway 40
Buses motor GER 182-4, 256-8
Buses and Bus Companies other than Great Eastern Railway 101, 138, 143, 164, 167, 181-4

Caledonian Railway Locomotives 210
Cambridge 38, 46
Canals 52, 55-6
Canning Town 75
Canvey Island 118-9
Carriage Lighting 104-5
Carriages 18-9, 49, 104-7, 162-3, 173-7, 248-9
Cavell Edith 216
Central London Railway 129-30
Chelmsford 103, 166, 182-3, 214
Cheshunt 59, 74, 111, 127, 209
Chingford 58, 61-2, 65-7, 69, 134, 136, 142, 168-9, 218, 220, 257
Churchbury/Southbury Loop 59, 74, 111, 127, 208
Clacton/Clacton-on-Sea Railway 34-5, 182
Claud Hamilton Locomotive 187-8, 239-40
Closures 36, 127, 129, 213

Coborn Road 81
Colchester 30-1, 33, 36-9, 110, 182-3, 193
SS Colchester 208, 216, 252
Colne Valley and Halstead Railway 36-9, 223, 250, 258
Conductor guard working 181
Cranborne Lord 14
Cromer 52-3, 99, 101, 120-2

Decapod Locomotive 134-6, 242-3
Dereham 53
Doncaster 18, 91-2, 94-7
Dunmow 23-5, 27-8

Earthquake – Essex 1884 110
East London Railway 59, 63-4, 68-71, 127-9, 212, 224
East Norfolk Railway 52-4
Egg and Poultry Train 212-3
Electrification 127-9, 151-2, 163-9
Ely, Haddenham and Sutton Railway/Ely and St Ives Railway 47-8
Enfield 12, 58, 60, 62, 66-7, 74, 81, 134, 168-9, 218, 220
Epping/Epping Railways 22-5, 169, 220
Esjberg 17, 185, 195, 219
Exhibitions - London 1862 and Paris 1867 and 1900 186-7, 227-8, 240
Eye/ Mellis and Eye Railway 39-40

Fairlop Loop 113-4
Fakenham 99
Farm 213
Felixstowe 41, 113, 179, 185-6, 204, 255
Felixstowe Railway 41, 236

Fenchurch Street 54, 56, 58-9, 76, 82-3, 88-90, 136, 151-4, 166, 188
Floods – Norfolk and Suffolk 1912 189-91
Fordham 46
Forncett 54
Fryatt Captain Charles 208, 215-6

Gallions 59, 75-6
Great Central Railway including Manchester, Sheffield and Lincolnshire Railway 91-3, 96-7, 122-3, 125-6, 155-62, 198, 208, 211, 219, 221-5, 248
Great Eastern Railway Magazine 187-9
Great Northern Railway 20-2, 46, 55, 73-4, 90-103, 123-4, 126, 150-1, 155-62, 198-201, 211, 214, 223-5
Great Northern and Great Eastern Joint Committee/Line 94-7, 222, 225, 248
Great War/First World War 184-6, 195-9, 223, 238, 243-4, 252-5

Haddiscoe 120
Hackney/ Hackney Downs 12, 62, 65-6, 81-2
Hamburg 16-7, 185, 194
Hamilton Lord John Claud 14, 94, 112, 128, 135-6, 138, 147, 151, 163-5, 175-6, 184, 187-9, 207, 215, 224, 240
Harwich 15-8, 172, 183-6, 195, 204, 213, 225, 250-1, 255
Halts 142, 148, 177-8, 181, 208
Haverhill 36-7
Heacham 50
Hertford 22, 166
High Beech 12, 61-2, 65-7

Hill Alfred John 153, 187, 211, 237, 241, 246
Hitchin 46, 214
Hither Green 126, 212
Holden James 104, 109, 134-5, 162-3, 186-7, 232, 237-8, 240, 243-4, 248
Holden Stephen Dewar 237-8, 243-4
Hook of Holland 17-8, 184-5, 194-5, 215, 219
Horses 57, 248
Hotels 17-8, 51, 76-8, 185-6, 195, 213
Huntingdon 47
Hunstanton 50-1, 213
Hunstanton and West West Norfolk railway 51
Hyde Walter 144, 153-4, 163

Ilford 82, 108, 113-4, 127, 166, 193-4, 208, 220
Ingatestone 85-6
Invasion scare 1914 196, 200
Ipswich 41, 46, 179-80, 182-5

Jazz Service 168-9
Johnson Samuel Waite 228-9
Jubilee Golden Great Eastern Railway 1912 189

Kings Lynn 51, 98-100, 120-1

Lancashire and Yorkshire Railway 91-2
Lancashire, Derbyshire and East Coast Railway 122-6
Laundry 111
Light Railways other than Mid Suffolk Light Railway 98-99, 114-8

Liverpool Street 12, 58-74, 76-82, 89, 108, 127-30, 133, 165-9, 185-6, 204-6, 213, 219
Locomotives 104-6,134-6, 152-4, 186-7, 216-7, 221-2, 224-48, 250, 257-8
Locomotive Loans and Sales 209, 216-7, 221-2, 233, 237-8, 243-6, 248
London and Blackwall Railway 55
London and North Eastern railway 176-7, 184, 223-5, 245
London and North Western Railway 36, 54, 60
London, Brighton and South Coast Railway 63-4, 70-3, 128-9, 210
London, Midland and Scottish Railway 223-4
London, Tilbury and Southend Railway including London, Tilbury and Southend Railway Section of Midland Railway 73, 82-90, 142-5
Long Melford 26-7
Loughton 22-3, 166, 169, 220
Lower Edmonton 12-3, 48-9, 62-3, 67, 74, 127, 208-9
Lowestoft 109, 120-2, 140, 182-3, 204
Lyn and Hunstanton Railway 50-1

Maldon 87-8
Metropolitan Railway 61-2, 67-72, 127-9
Metropolitan District Railway 67, 71-2, 127-9, 143-4, 148, 154
Mildenhall 45-6
Mid Suffolk Light Railway 137-42, 250, 258
Midland Railway excluding London, Tilbury and Southend Railway 47, 58, 122-6, 156, 173-4, 201, 210, 224

Midland and Great Northern Joint Railway including constituents 98-103, 119-22, 160, 191
Millwall/Millwall Extension Railway 55-7, 136, 180
Mistley, Thorpe and Walton Railway 31-4
Motor Buses GER 182-4, 256-7
Mundesley 101, 120-2, 172, 200

New Cross 63-4, 70, 72-3, 128-9, 197
Newmarket 50, 213-4
Norfolk and Suffolk Joint Committee 119-22, 181, 200
North Eastern Railway 91, 93, 187-8, 213
North Greenwich 56-7, 136
North London Railway 12, 54, 59, 61-2, 80, 130, 212, 214
North Walsham 52-3, 99-101, 119-21, 127, 172, 200
North Woolwich 88, 166, 208
Northern and Eastern Railway 112
Norwich 51-2, 99, 182, 184, 216, 220-1

Oil Fuel 104-5, 189, 221
Ongar 22-4, 28, 166, 169

Parkeston Quay 17-8, 184-5, 195-6, 201, 204, 215, 219
Palace Gates 59, 74, 134, 168-9, 218
Parnwell Sidney 175-6, 224-5
Petrol Engine Locomotives 222, 248
Pullman Cars 173-7

Radical Alterations 177, 200
Rail Motors and Auto Trains/Push Pull Trains 149, 178-80, 208-9

Ramsey Railway 97-8
Somersham and Ramsey Railway 97-8
Railway Operating Division of War Department 210, 222, 238, 248
Re-openings 208
Restaurant Cars 18-9, 173, 200, 216, 218-9, 249
Richborough Train Ferry Port 217, 243-4
Romford 127, 142, 154, 166, 182
Rotterdam 16-7, 184-5, 195, 201, 219, 250-1
Royal and Special Trains 14, 73, 196, 225, 228
Russell Fred V 168-9, 187, 238

Saffron Walden Railway 38
St Pancras 58, 90, 206, 214
Sassoon Siegfried 205-6
Sea Water 110
Ships 15-7, 184-5, 194-6, 198-200, 208, 215-6, 219, 250-5, 258
Shipping Companies 17, 185, 195, 198, 200
Signals and Signaling 107-9
Silvertown Explosion 206-7
Sinclair Robert 23, 226-9
Slip Coaches 103
Snape 213
Snow including Great Frost of 1881 110
South Eastern / South Eastern and Chatham Railway 63, 71-3, 128-9, 212, 222
Southend 82-90, 144-49, 166, 204, 220-1
Southminster 87-8
Southwold Railway 42-4, 137, 140-1
Stoke Ferry 54
Stratford 65, 75, 81, 108, 188, 204, 208

Stratford Works 104-6, 135, 182, 209-11, 222, 224, 241, 245
Strikes 188-9, 218-21, 225

Tendring Hundred Railway 29-35
Thaxted 115-6
Thetford and Watton Railway 40, 236
Third Class Paasengers 18-9, 104, 248
Thorpe St Andrew 51-2
Thornton Henry 148, 154, 163-5, 167-9, 174-5, 177, 217, 224
Tilbury 73, 83-4, 86, 185, 195, 213, 215, 253
Tollesbury 115
Tottenham and Forest Gate Railway 89-90
Tottenham and Hampstead Railway 57-8, 90, 214
Train Ferries 217, 225
Tramways 31, 41-2, 48-50, 99, 127, 136-7, 140, 179-80
Travelling Post Offices/Sorting Tenders/Mail Bag Apparatus 103, 171
Tube Railways actual and proposed 129-36

Wagons 250, 258

Walthamstow 58, 61-3, 65-8, 81, 168, 220
Walton on the Naze 31-3
Ware, Hadham and Buntigford Railway 19-22
Water Troughs 170-1
Watton and Swaffham Railway 40
Waveney Valley Railway 39, 228
Wells Next the Sea 187
West Norfolk Junction Railway 50-1
Wickford 86-7
Wisbech and Upwell Tramway 48-50
Wissington Light Railway 118
Witham 191-3
Wivenhoe and Brightlingsea Railway 30-3, 35, 234-5
Women Staff 207-8
Working Conditions 109
SS Wrexham 208

Yarmouth 52, 98-100, 120-2
SS Yarmouth 194
York 19, 97-8, 172, 214

Zeebrugge 185, 215-6, 219, 225